KU-098-326

A HISTORY OF
WORK IN BRITAIN,
1880–1950

Arthur J. McIvor

palgrave

©Arthur J. McIvor 2001

All rights reserved. No reproduction, copy or transmission of
this publication may be made without written permission.

No paragraph of this publication may be reproduced, copied or
transmitted save with written permission or in accordance with
the provisions of the Copyright, Designs and Patents Act 1988,
or under the terms of any licence permitting limited copying
issued by the Copyright Licensing Agency, 90 Tottenham Court
Road, London W1P L0P.

Any person who does any unauthorised act in relation to this
publication may be liable to criminal prosecution and civil
claims for damages.

The author has asserted his right to be identified
as the author of this work in accordance with the
Copyright, Designs and Patents Act 1988.

First published 2001 by
PALGRAVE
Houndmills, Basingstoke, Hampshire RG21 6XS and
175 Fifth Avenue, New York, N.Y. 10010
Companies and representatives throughout the world

PALGRAVE is the new global academic imprint of St. Martin's press LLC
Scholarly and Reference Division and Palgrave Publishers Ltd (formerly
Macmillan Press Ltd).

ISBN 0–333–59616–1 hardback
ISBN 0–333–59617–X paperback

This book is printed on paper suitable for recycling and
made from fully managed and sustained forest sources.

A catalogue record for this book is available
from the British Library.

Library of Congress Cataloging-in-Publication Data
McIvor, Arthur.
A history of work in Britain, 1880–1950 / Arthur J. McIvor.
p. cm. — (Social history in perspective)
Includes bibliographical references and index.
ISBN 0–333–59616–1
1. Labor—Great Britain—History.   2. Industrial sociology—Great Britain—
History.   3. Labor movement—Great Britain—History.   4. Industrial
management—Great Britain—History.   5. Industrial safety—Great Brit-
ain—History.   6. Women—Employment—Great Britain—History.
I. Title. II. Series.
HD8390.M365 2000
331′.0941—dc21   00–031114

10 9 8 7 6 5 4 3 2 1
10 09 08 07 06 05 04 03 02 01

Printed and bound in Great Britain by
Creative Print & Design (Wales), Ebbw Vale

For Kieran and Tom

Metropolitan Borough of Stockport Libraries		
000379671	cu	
Askews	331.0942	
	MAC	
	9E	

CONTENTS

List of tables and figure   ix
Acknowledgements   xi

Introduction   1

1 The Historiography and Theorising of Work   5

2 The Changing Labour Force   26

3 The *Experience* of Work: Deskilling, Intensification
   and Alienation?   43
   Skill and the Organisation of Work in
   Late Victorian Britain   44
   Technology, Organisational Change and Deskilling   52
   The Intensification of Work   66
   Conclusions   75

4 Exercising Control: Employers and the Management
   of Labour   79
   Exerting the Right to Manage in
   Late Victorian Britain   80
   Management Structures and Employers' Strategies,
   1880–1914   85
   Towards Rationalisation, Taylorism and *Real*
   Subordination of Labour, 1914–50   93
   Conclusions   109

5 Work Conditions, Occupation and Health   111
   Occupational Health and Safety before World
   War One   113
   The Impact of Economic Recession and War,
   1914–50   130
   Conclusions   145

6   Regulating Work: the Role of the State   148
    The State and the Workplace, *c*. 1880   151
    Work, Industrial Relations and the Labour Market,
    c. 1880–1914   154
    Countervailing Tendencies: the Wars and the
    Depression   158
    Conclusions   170

7   Women, Gender Relations and Inequalities at Work   174
    Gender Relations at Work in Late Victorian Britain   175
    Unpaid Work: Home and Family   181
    Paid Employment   184
    Conclusions   198

8   Trade Unions, Work and Politics   200
    The Incubation, Development and Limits of
    Trade Unionism   201
    Democratising Work? The Role and Functions of
    Trade Unions   213
    Work, Class and Politics   231
    Conclusions   236

9   Conclusion: Labour Transformed?   241

Bibliography   251
Index   265

LIST OF TABLES AND FIGURE

2.1 Economically active population by major industrial
    groups, c. 1880   30
2.2 Economically active population by major industrial
    groups, c. 1950   31
2.3 Employed workforce in Britain by industry, 1881   34
2.4 Employed workforce in Britain by industry, 1951   35
2.5 Manual and non-manual workers in Britain, 1911–51   36
2.6 Non-manual employees by industry group, 1951   36
2.7 Age profiles of occupied women, 1901, 1931, 1951   36
2.8 The industrial workforce during World War One   37
2.9 Female employment by marital status, 1911–51   38
2.10 Women employed by region, England and
    Wales, 1931   39
2.11 Occupied population by class, 1911 and 1951   40
2.12 Occupied population by class and gender, 1951   41
3.1 Workers classified by skill in member firms of the
    Engineering Employers' Federation, 1914–33   55
4.1 Employers' associations in Britain, 1914   90
5.1 Nominal weekly working hours in Britain, early 1890s   114
5.2 Persons killed in industrial accidents, UK, 1880–1914   117
5.3 Comparative mortality of males, 25–65 years of age,
    selected occupations, 1880–2   118
5.4 Work injuries and fatalities: selected trades, UK,
    1910–14   120
5.5 Lead poisoning cases reported in factories and
    workshops in Glasgow, 1900–14   122
5.6 Comparative mortality from lung and respiratory
    disease, males in selected occupations, 1880–2   125
5.7 Persons killed in industrial accidents, UK, 1915–49   132
5.8 Reported cases of industrial diseases
    (deaths and injuries), 1901–39   142

8.1   Trade union membership and density, by gender,
      UK, 1892–1950   201
8.2   Manual and non-manual trade union membership,
      GB, 1900–51   202
8.3   Trade union density by industry, 1892, 1939 and 1950 202
8.4   Working days lost through industrial disputes
      in Britain, 1893–1951   203
8.5   Membership of the ten largest unions, 1910 and 1951   206
8.6   Strike settlement by labour replacement, 1891–1919   218
9.1   Average wages by occupational class, expressed as
      a percentage of the mean for all occupational classes
      (male and female), 1913–14 and 1955–6   245

Figure

8.1   Trade union density and strike activity by
      region, 1892   204

ACKNOWLEDGEMENTS

The research for this book was undertaken over many years whilst I taught in the History Department at the University of Strathclyde. I am very grateful to the University for financial assistance over the years to air papers on my research at conferences and seminars and for granting a period of study leave in 1999 to complete the writing of the text. I would also like to thank the British Academy and Wellcome Trust who have also provided grants in support of aspects of my research on the social history of work. My gratitude also extends to my colleagues in the history department who have provided cover for me whilst on leave as well as an encouraging and critical environment in which to work. I have particularly benefited from discussion and the support of my colleague in social and oral history, Callum Brown, and in labour history Hamish Fraser, who kindly read and commented on the typescript. I also owe a great debt to cohorts of undergraduates and postgraduates at Strathclyde who have discussed and debated the many contentious issues that are grappled with in this book. Here I would like to particularly thank my special subject honours students and my doctoral students who explored new aspects of the social history of work in their theses – Billy Kenefick, Sandy Renfrew, Neil Rafeek, Ronnie Johnston and Annemarie Hughes. Of course, I am entirely responsible for the errors, weaknesses and misjudgements in the text.

Whilst working on this I have been guilty, on far too many occasions, of neglecting my family. I dedicate this book to my two sons, Kieran and Tom, whom I love more dearly than I can ever express. Last but by no means least, I would like to acknowledge my thanks to my partner, Margot, who provided much-needed support, lifted me when I was down, listened patiently to my half-baked ideas and childish excitement as the work proceeded, and read and commented on the typescript. Without her inspiration and gentle cajoling this book would probably never have seen the light of day.

INTRODUCTION

The Victorian period was probably the time when work was most important in British people's lives. Whilst the Victorian work ethic has undoubtedly been exaggerated, nevertheless workers spent most of their time from late childhood to their deathbeds in paid or unpaid toil in home, factory, farm or workshop, and employment provided the primary means on which to subsist. In this sense it is reasonable to conceptualise people's existence in this era as work-centred. Standards of living, housing and material possessions depended to a great extent upon the rewards of labour. Thus the health and well-being of individuals and families were intimately linked to employment, both through the wages earned and, more directly, via the dangers and hazards (fatigue; traumatic injury; occupational disease) that characterised almost all jobs in the late nineteenth century. The meaning and significance of work extended beyond this, however. Work brought its own psychological rewards: providing an identity and, especially for craft workers, pride, passion and purpose. Conversely, the loss of work could lead directly to demoralisation and despair, epitomised in the dole queues of the 1930s. Moreover, occupation dictated, to a large extent, a person's standing within a highly stratified and status-conscious community, as Richard Roberts noted in his sensitive evaluation of the working-class neighbourhood of Salford in the first quarter of the twentieth century.

Looking inward, the workplace provided an arena in which friendships were forged and social relationships developed, as well as a focus for the germination of collective activity and solidarity, manifest in workplace 'restrictive practices', the emergence of trade unions and strike action. The attempts of British employers and managers to obtain and sustain control over their labour was rarely complete and was invariably subject to challenge and conflict. The organisation of work was chiselled out of this interaction

1

between capital and labour over what one perceptive American observer of British industrial relations termed the 'frontier of control' (Goodrich, 1920). Looking outward, and given that work was such a pervasive influence upon people's lives, it should come as no surprise that the experience of work also had broader political connotations. Hence, developing such concepts as intensification, regularisation, deskilling and degradation, some historians have argued that the changing nature and restructuring of work over time helped to radicalise workers, to create a more homogeneous working class and to push workers into a heightened political consciousness, notably exhibited in more militant trade unions and in labour and socialist politics. In an influential thesis in the 1950s, David Lockwood (1958, p. 205) argued:

> Without doubt in modern industrial society the most important social conditions shaping the psychology of the individual are those arising out of the organisation of production, administration and distribution. In other words the 'work situation'. For every employee is precipitated, by virtue of a given division of labour, into unavoidable relationships with other employees, supervisors, managers or customers. The work situation involves the separation and concentration of individuals, affords possibilities of identification with and alienation from others, and conditions feelings of isolation, antagonism and solidarity.

This book engages with such issues, examining the social history of work in a mature capitalist economy during the later phases of industrialisation in Britain, incorporating what has been termed 'the second industrial revolution' over the period 1880–1950. The aim is to define the main characteristics of the work experience and analyse the continuities and major changes that occurred over these years. It will be argued that labour was transformed over this period in a number of significant ways, though the pace of change was uneven. The way that the labour process in manufacturing was restructured, for example, is arguably much more significant over 1880–1950 than any change in clerical work or in the sexual division of labour, where patterns of gender apartheid persisted, passing over from traditional female-dominated jobs into the new industries, clerical and shop work. Nonetheless, whilst vestiges remained, the paternalist relationship captured in the notion of 'master and servant', the common vocabulary of the mid-Victorian period, had been irrevocably superseded by 1950. By the mid-twentieth century, work took place in a mixed economy, in much larger enterprises, with well-entrenched collective organisation and collective bargaining amongst both workers and employers and with much heightened state intervention and regulation in crucial areas. In turn, much of the mid-twentieth century world of work has subsequently disappeared, as patterns of employment have been rapidly transformed in the post-industrial economy in the second half of the twentieth century and government has withdrawn from much of its responsibility to shelter and protect the weakest members of society from the vicious vagaries of the competitive market place. This transmogrification underlines the importance of understanding historical change in the workplace so that we can contextualise and better comprehend the uncertainties of work in contemporary Britain as we enter the new millennium.

Research upon the social history of the British workplace has proliferated over the recent past, to the extent that this is now an area of considerable debate and controversy. Recent work exploiting untapped seams of documentary and other evidence (such as oral testimony) have resulted in new perspectives on the labour process and the meaning of work which have challenged previously established stereotypes, such as that of an omnipotent capitalism unilaterally dictating the labour process, a homogeneous propertyless proletariat, or a working class diverted from socialism by an inert, conservative 'labour aristocracy' of elite workers. The heterogeneity and diversity of work, themselves the product of the slow, uneven and complex development of industrialisation, have been underlined in much recent research – for example that of Joyce (1990) and Benson (1989). Core elements of the Marxist agenda which dominated the social history of work in the 1960s and 1970s, notably the class homogenisation and the deskilling/degradation theses, have come under increasing attack. Feminist historians have made vital contributions, drawing us away from an insular preoccupation with class and into a more nuanced awareness of the importance of gender and class in shaping the labour process, wage payment and relationships at work and the range of identities forged in the workplace (Summerfield, 1998; Savage and Miles, 1994). Workers of both sexes have emerged from recent accounts both as *victims* of an intensely patri-archal and exploitative mode of capitalism in Britain and as *active players*; as an agency in their own right, capable of influencing and regulating working conditions, relationships and the labour pro-cess. One Marxist, critical of Harry Braverman's seminal updating of Marx's own theories of the labour process, has urged the neces-sity of 'bringing the workers back in' (Burawoy, 1985). The aim here is to overview this literature and provide an interpretation of the social history of work over 1880–1950, engaging with and synthesising recent research – both Marxist and 'revisionist' – which has massively expanded our understanding of work and the workplace. This survey of the literature will be supplemented where appropriate with examination and interpretation of original primary material, especially where the published evidence is weak, as, for example, on the interactions between occupation and health in the 1880–1950 period (see Chapter 5). I start with a discussion of some of the ways in which work has been theorised and a survey of the historiography of work in Britain over the recent past.

1

THE HISTORIOGRAPHY AND THEORISING OF WORK

Perspectives on the social history of work have invariably been saturated with political bias. Perhaps inevitably so. This chapter aims to explore some of the most important ways that historians have interpreted work in labour and social history and to identify and evaluate the main theoretical perspectives that have informed and influenced historical accounts. Readers should hopefully emerge with a sharpened sense of the range of viewpoints that coexist within the literature and an understanding of the controversies and debates that characterise this topic. Particularly the fundamental divide between research undertaken in this field in a Marxist tradition and the various strands of revisionism – liberal; feminist; post-modernist – that have come to dominate the research on work published since the 1960s. Readers who are familiar with the literature might care to skip this chapter and move directly on to Chapter 2.

Serious empirical and theoretically informed study of the inner world of the workplace was really only the product of the opening up of social history as a sub-discipline in the 1960s and 1970s. The development of social history drew attention to the labour process and the workplace as a site of culture, conflict, the forging of social relationships and the incubation of working-class consciousness. Much of this work was influenced by Marxist theories. In *Capital*, published in 1867, Marx placed the labour process at the very centre of his analysis of society and social change. Capitalism, he posited, was characterised by a specific relationship of exploitation between those who owned and controlled the means of production – the raw materials and the tools and technology – and the producers, or proletariat. Such a change came incrementally, Marx posited, through three phases: *simple co-operation* (or traditional craft production), *manufacture* and *machinofacture*. Worker independence, control, ownership of tools and relative autonomy over the organisation of work was replaced as capitalism developed with a set of relationships that Marx conceptualised as *formal subordination* and *real subordination*. Bringing workers together in a factory or workshop (the *manufacture* phase) enabled capital to extend their dominance over labour in a formal sense, by, for example, dictating working hours and more effectively monitoring production. However, this still left workers with much autonomy. The logic of competition within capitalism and the urge to maximise return on investment led employers into new strategies to strip maximum profit from their labour force. The culmination of such subordination came with the development and utilisation of science and technology in the labour process. There were physiological and other limits to the exploitation of workers under traditional work regimes (for example fatigue and short life expectancy where work hours were long) characterised by what Marx called the extraction of *absolute surplus value*. Investment in more sophisticated tools and machinery provided an alternative, more intensified mode of profit maximisation (the extraction of *real surplus value*). In effect, until machinery was introduced (Marx's *machinofacture*, or *modern industry* phase) workers retained much knowledge and skill, and thus effective control over the processes of production, methods and training. With technological change came a more detailed division of labour; crafts were subdivided and work became more specialised. In other words, work under capitalism had a deskilling or fragmenting dynamic: 'in place of the hierarchy of specialised workers that characterises manufacture there appears in the automatic factory the tendency to equalise and reduce to an identical level every kind of work that has to be done by the minders of machines' (Marx, in Littler, 1982, pp. 23–4). Moreover, the authority and control of capital became more direct and subordination of workers more *real* (as opposed to *formal*). Capitalist authority was enhanced because employers were now less reliant upon relatively scarce skilled labour. Moreover, the displacement of artisans undermined their collective capacity to resist (and to sustain effective trade unions). Capital, in effect, became omnipotent. Marx was fond of the term 'despotic control' to describe such an outcome.

The ramifications of this transformation of the labour process and social relations at work were cataclysmic. Marx theorised that such developments led directly to the creation of a homogeneous mass of unskilled workers. Alienated from the means of production and subject to close capitalist control, the proletariat developed interests diametrically opposed to the employers. In time, such workers became conscious of their exploitation within this system (a transition Marx conceptualised as movement from '*a class in itself*' to '*a class for itself*') and, hence, within the dominant capitalist mode of production lay the seeds of its own destruction. The relationship that existed between the dominant and exploited social classes was inherently antagonistic and conflictual. Inevitably, according to Marx, as exploitation and its attendant alienation progressed, the proletariat would rise up and the ensuing revolution would see capitalism replaced with communism – a mode of economic and social relations which would return ownership and control over the means of production to the workers. Given that Britain was the most advanced capitalist nation in the mid-Victorian period when Marx was writing, it was here that such a revolution was first expected to occur.

Within British Marxist historiography E. P. Thompson's seminal *The Making of the English Working Class* (1963) constituted a key turning point. Exploiting a formidable range of untapped sources, *The Making* brought the experience of workers at the point of production during the eighteenth century into centre stage. Thompson's argument was that the process of capitalist industrialisation in England destroyed traditional craft skills, drew independent craft workers into the rigid, regularised regime of the factory and this heightened subordination and exploitation of workers contributed (though was not necessarily the critical factor) to the forging of a recognisable working-class consciousness by the early years of the nineteenth century. Handworkers prone to the competition of mechanisation and factory workers subject to the time discipline of the factory and more draconian management thus became more amenable to the radical ideas emanating both from within Britain and across the continent. What Thompson did for the eighteenth century, other Marxists, for example Foster, Hobsbawm and Price, did for the nineteenth, exploring the nature of work within British capitalism. They also directly addressed one of the key questions that has obsessed British Marxist historians: why a socialist revolution did not occur as Marx hypothesised. In Hobsbawm's classic thesis, working-class consciousness in Britain was 'retarded' by a combination of factors amongst the most significant of which was the political conservatism of the 'labour aristocracy'. The aristocrats were the most well-paid manual workers; usually craftsmen but including many miners (such as the hewers) and cotton workers (such as the mule spinners) in the mid-Victorian period. Rather than challenging capitalism, such 'natural leaders' accommodated themselves to it, absorbing and internalising the values and attitudes of the middle classes, as Crossick (1978) and Gray's (1976) studies of the craft artisan elite in London and Edinburgh demonstrated. Later, fundamental changes in the nature of work over *c.* 1880–1914, linked with intensifying economic competition, politicised the artisans whilst simultaneously contributing to the organisation and increased militancy of lesser skilled workers epitomised in the concept of 'new unionism'. Thus Hobsbawm located the key developments in working-class consciousness later, in the period *c.* 1880–1914. Building on such traditions, Richard Price has further emphasised the importance of the labour process in explaining shifts in worker militancy, political awareness (for example the formation of the Labour Party) and class consciousness. Rather than conceptualising a unilinear process, Price posits that working-class consciousness was subject to composition and decomposition depending upon prevailing economic, political and other circumstances.

Thompson, Hobsbawm, Foster, Price and other Marxists' detailed and nuanced evaluations of the work culture of groups such as the stockingers, weavers, dockers, gasworkers, shoemakers and building workers brought the capitalist labour process into sharper focus. Such writing successfully challenged the dominant 'whig' interpretation, pervaded by the facile notions of unproblematic and linear progress, improvement and the concept of a 'neutral' process of technological change bestowing benefits and rewards to all. The new Marxist-inspired historiography raised critical awareness and helped kick-start a proliferation of empirical 'bottom-up'analyses of the nature and meaning of work in people's lives (Stedman-Jones, 1971; Joyce, 1980).

Marxist labour process theory, in turn, was subject to much reiteration, reformulation and revision, influenced in part by a search for the causes of industrial militancy and the radical political struggles in Europe in the late 1960s and the 1970s (Thompson, 1983, pp. 68–71). The pivotal contribution came from Harry Braverman's *Labor and Monopoly Capital* (1974). In essence Braverman updated Marx, suggesting an additional phase of monopoly capitalism in the twentieth century which took the dynamic of deskilling even further than Marx hypothesised, hence further dehumanising and degrading the experience of work. Indeed, Braverman implies that Marx exaggerated the extent of capitalist control and worker subordination in Britain by the 1860s. Such developments, Braverman theorised, only occurred in the twentieth century and the engine of such transformation was the combination of automatic machinery and the diffusion of Taylorite 'scientific management' ideologies of work organisation and labour control. This effectively separated conceptualisation from execution of tasks, the thinking and planning from the 'doing'. Such processes were epitomised in the multinational companies and especially in the flow production motor car manufacturing techniques of Henry Ford, with his preoccupation with division of labour and the minimisation of work cycle times into minute repetitions. However, Braverman claimed the universal applicability of such degradation beyond manufacturing, indeed across the economy, including within service sector employment, arguing that office automation and modern work study created a mass of relatively unskilled clerical workers, such as copy typists and filing clerks. This, Braverman posited, transformed the nature of work in the twentieth century, facilitating the *real subordination* of labour and the dominance of *monopoly capitalism* and hence completing the process of *alienation* of workers within this system of production. The result was the incubation of class consciousness and a class-conflictual mode of social relations (see Littler, 1982; Thompson, 1983).

Other theorists contributed to this reformulation and modification of Marxist labour process theory (see Friedman, 1977; Edwards, 1979; Burawoy, 1985) and a clutch of affirmative historical case studies appeared which claimed to demonstrate the broad validity of Braverman's model (such as Berg, 1979; Zimbalist, 1979; and, in many respects, Joyce, 1980). Marxist sociologists further demonstrated the validity of the degradation thesis (for e.g. Beynon's (1973) penetrating *Working For Ford*), some developing the argument further into the notion that work under capitalism was inherently detrimental to people's physical and mental health and well-being (see Navarro, 1978). Others have broadly supported the notion of a deskilling dynamic inherent within capitalism (Thompson, 1983; Knox, 1999).

The seminal work of Braverman and the other Marxist labour process theorists generated a heated debate on the changing nature of work under capitalism. Much of this was critical of Marxist claims to have discovered universal laws or models and, specifically, of Braverman's assertion of an inherent deskilling and dehumanising dynamic within modern capitalism. The 'revisionist' backlash challenged the theoretical appropriateness and the validity in specific historical contexts of such concepts as alienation, class-conflictual social relations, unilateral capitalist control, and workers' impotence, as well as the deskilling and related class-homogenisation trends. Braverman's assumption of the centrality of Taylorism in such processes has also been heavily criticised. Many remain unconvinced that Braverman's thesis fits the historical reality of Britain's experience in the nineteenth and twentieth centuries.

Empirical research challenged the validity of Marxist theory in relation to the degree and the impact of deskilling. Much recent research has emphasised the slower, more uneven and incomplete process of change by any given point across what was a heterogeneous economy. In the 1950s, Lockwood argued that Marxist theory failed to fit the historical reality of clerical work where tendencies towards mechanisation and bureaucratisation were limited, workers remained relatively secure, workplaces small, paternalist relations prevailed, and class-consciousness muted. As a consequence, British non-manual workers retained a sense of superiority, identifying more with management and employers than with manual workers. Hence the relative weakness at mid-twentieth century of non-manual trade unionism (see Chapter 8). Braverman and other Marxists have quite reasonably been taken to task for utilising a rather romanticised notion of traditional handicraft work as their benchmark for analysis when, in reality, the majority of work was not highly skilled at all or did not develop within the craft tradition (for example in transport, food processing, chemicals, shopwork, domestic service, and much of the extractive sector). Hobsbawm estimated that the skilled labour elite – or 'aristocracy' – constituted around 15 per cent of the male labour force in the mid-Victorian period of its heyday. Moreover, some of these workers had 'socially constructed' the designation of their occupations as skilled, with commensurate financial rewards, through strong collective organisations, whereas in reality the actual job involved little genuine skill (as defined by such factors as task range; discretionary content; autonomy; and training and experience necessary). The cotton mule spinners are the classic example. This use of an erroneous historical benchmark has several implications. It leads Braverman into an exaggeration of the extent of actual deskilling from this base and, as Paul Thompson (1983) has commented, it underestimates similar pressures in the direction of job fragmentation and work intensification within the more numerically dominant non-craft sector (such as dockwork). A further criticism of Braverman has been that his theory was not adequately gendered, failing to recognise the divergent experience of male and female labour (Beechey, 1982; Crompton and Jones, 1984; Cohn, 1985).

The historiography of work in the engineering industry has reflected these fundamental divisions. Hinton, Holton and Burgess are amongst those writing in the Marxist tradition who have, in the main, provided affirmations of the deskilling thesis in relation to the British engineering sector. In a classic thesis, Hinton explained the syndicalist radicalism of skilled engineers in regions such as Clydeside during World War One as a consequence of challenges to the craft tradition associated with the wartime emergency 'dilution' of labour by the importation of unskilled and female labour to work previously monopolised by men. However, More, Penn and, in particular, Zeitlin have likewise argued trenchantly against the applicability of Marxist deskilling notions in this heterogeneous industry. In his evaluation of the changing nature of skill over the period 1870–1914, More indicates that both apprenticeship and genuine skill remained important in engineering because of the nature of labour and product markets (More, 1982, p. 121).

Roger Penn has made a similar plea for the persistence of skill, aided by trade union activism (which we will return to later), in engineering throughout the twentieth century (see Penn, 1985). However, Zeitlin has provided the most sustained and most impressively grounded critique of Marxist theory in relation to the British engineering industry. Here there was no simple uni-linear deskilling trajectory, rather British engineering employers missed the opportunity to transform the labour process, despite pivotal victories against the trade unions in national lockouts in 1897–8 and 1922 (Zeitlin, 1991). This was because employers were reliant upon craft skills as demand for bespoke production remained high up to the middle of the twentieth century, because of residual craft union power (especially at workshop level) and because of the relative conservatism of British management. A similar scenario of tenacious skill retention and weak, prevari-cating management tactics emerges in relation to shipbuilding in the research of Alastair Reid. This author also finds the general notion of deskilling invalid, because of the limitations of technolo-gical change, the strength of the unions to resist changes and the attitudes (and weakness) of British employers (see the critique in Reid, 1992, pp. 27–31).

Perhaps the main weakness in Marxist labour process theory lies in its assumption of workers' inability to *significantly* influence the organisation of work or mediate the process of deskilling in the face of powerful capitalist pressure. Whilst both Marx and Braverman recognise the possibilities of collective organisation and strike action, neither conceptualise the workers – skilled or otherwise – as a *significant* agency in the structuring of the labour process. This view has been criticised by both Marxist and non-Marxist historians and, as Reid has noted, 'as a result there is now a broad consensus, even among those who still see a long-run tend-ency towards deskilling and subordination, that well-organised groups of workers can not only rebel but can also delay and modify these pressures' (Reid, 1992, p. 7). In other words, workers retained rather than lost their independence and autonomy in the workplace. Whipp's research on the Staffordshire potters provides a good example: 'the pottery workers neither uniformly accepted nor endorsed the owners' attempts to construct dominant values and codes of behaviour'. 'The potters', Whipp continued, 'erected their own ideologies from their own experience' (Whipp,

1990, p. 193). Burawoy, Samuel, Zeitlin, Tolliday, Reid and Price are amongst those who have argued strongly and persuasively that workers (and not exclusively the skilled) have successfully resisted capitalist tendencies to deskill and intensify work. Through their trade unions they successfully intervened to raise levels of real earnings, reduce working hours and otherwise to 'humanise' work conditions. This is explored further in Chapter 8.

What has emerged from such empirical research is a much more sensitive evaluation of the roles of capital and labour in different industrial contexts and a sharp sense of the prevailing organisation of work being the product not just of an omnipotent managerial hand, but rather the outcome of a process of conflict and compromise, struggle and accommodation between management and workers. Clearly, economic and political circumstances affected such outcomes and need to be drawn into the equation. For example, whilst there were countervailing tendencies, workers' power to influence the organisation of production was enhanced during the 1910s, due to economic prosperity, war and the extension of the franchise. Conversely, the inter-war economic depression and mass unemployment facilitated an employers' 'counter-attack' against organised labour. This may have stopped short of the extirpation of trade unions but resulted in a successful drive to cut labour costs, increase productivity and reformulate managerial power and authority – a regaining of control in the workplace.

One of the most dynamic areas of recent research into the social history of work has been the exploration of employer and managerial attitudes and behaviour. The main thrust of such work in the 1980s and 1990s has been heavily critical of Marxist conceptualisations of an omnipotent and monolithic capitalist class exercising despotic modes of control and effectively subordinating labour, supported by a pro-capitalist government. The literature now emphasises the internal divisions within employers' ranks which worked to constrain employers' class-consciousness, the wide range of labour control and labour relations strategies exploited by capital and the neutrality of the state in dealing even-handedly with both labour and capital in the twentieth century. Economic determinism has given way to a conception of employers with 'strategic choices' (Tolliday and Zeitlin, 1991, pp. 18–22), operating as active agents with a variety of attitudes and strategies, rather than the hapless victim of market forces. Hence, similar external constraints produced a range of responses, not one given, prede-termined strategy. The empirical evidence from north-west Eng-land suggests that employers' organisations developed their own internal dynamic and could formulate collective policies which appear contradictory in the light of market developments. This is evident, for example, in the markedly different responses of cotton employers in north and south Lancashire to the industrial relations crisis of 1910–14 and in the quite considerable (and ultimately decisive) pressure generated within employers' organi-sations to sustain collective bargaining during the interwar years. Weberian models have become more popular in conceptualising class structure, with an emphasis upon internal hierarchies and status division within both the working class(es) and the bour-geoisie (for example, Trainor, 1993; Johnston, 1997).

Product and labour markets affected the relative power of organ-ised capital and critically influenced the formulation of employers' labour management strategies. Howard Gospel has argued this case consistently and developed the most sophisticated model for understanding and conceptualising the interactions between employer strategy and markets (Gospel, 1992, pp. 1–36). Gospel adapts the theories of Alfred Chandler, arguing that Britain's characteristic nineteenth-century pattern of heterogeneous and fragmented product markets for manufactured goods facilitated entry and consolidated a pattern of large numbers of relatively small firms, with a high degree of competition and perpetuated family ownership. Overstocked labour markets also retarded technological innovation and the development of more sophisti-cated internal labour management systems, as occurred in the USA, Germany and Japan. Lacking resources and organisational structures, British firms were thus more likely to externally deleg-ate labour management to employers' associations whose ability to effectively regulate the labour contract and labour markets was critically influenced by the relative homogeneity or heterogeneity of the industry's product markets (Gospel, 1992). This is a soph-isticated and persuasive model which helps to explain labour man-agement strategies. Certainly in northern England, differences in product market structures made the construction of consensus policies by employers much more difficult in the engineering sector than in the much more homogeneous (in terms of techno-logy and markets) building construction sector. The cotton industry lay somewhere between these two, with important product and process divisions, though much technological convergence and product specialism within particular towns (McIvor, 1996). Employer organisation and regulation of labour markets prior to World War Two was undermined by a lesser or greater degree by the competitive relationship which existed between employers and the characteristic heterogeneity of British product markets. Centrifugal rather than centripetal tendencies were already discernible prior to World War Two. Thereafter, the decline of multi-employer regulation of the labour market and atomisation of industrial relations accelerated markedly, as the Donovan Report documented in the mid/late 1960s (Donovan, 1965–68, pp. 196–202).

The existing literature incorporates quite a wide range of views and perspectives on employers' organisations and labour management strategies. Some 'revisionist' commentators have emphasised the impotency of British employers' associations, the persistence of disunity between capitalists, fragmentation and fractured collective consciousness. Many of the most recent studies have been articulated in terms of the adverse impact of British industrial relations institutions – weak employers and powerful trade unions – upon economic performance (Tolliday and Zeitlin, 1991; Reid, 1992; Phelps Brown, 1983). This was because of the diversity of product market experience, widely differing attitudes to trade unionism, variations in company size and structure, and inter-firm competition and rivalry. The individualist ethos promulgated by the persistence of the family firm 'fostered an inward looking attitude' (Phelps Brown, 1983, p. 113). Employer combinations thus lacked centralised control and authority over their members. As Zeitlin noted: 'British employers were rarely willing to subordinate their individual autonomy to the demands of collective action on a long-term basis' (Zeitlin, 1987, p. 175). The historical record, Tolliday and Zeitlin (1991) argue, confirm no unilinear trajectories, rather a wide variety of experience and divergent patterns in labour management and employer organisation both through time and across the national boundaries of developed capitalist nations. Diversity existed because of unique historical contingencies and because management, employers and their organisations exercised conscious choice over strategy, albeit influenced by structural factors and, most significantly, by the actions of two key 'interlocutors' – the state and the trade unions. The notion and dynamics of class, Tolliday and Zeitlin imply, have very little relevance as explanatory tools. British employers, they assert, have failed to exert direct control over the labour process, failed to develop sophisticated supervisory and managerial hierarchies and failed to construct powerful and effective employers' organisations to articulate their class interests.

Against the grain of 'revisionism', other research emphasises the power and effectiveness of employers' associations and the important role they played in British industrial relations prior to World War Two (Clegg *et al.*, 1964; Clegg, 1985, 1994; Price, 1980; Burgess, 1975; Gospel, 1987, 1992; McIvor, 1984, 1996). Richard Price has postulated in *Masters, Unions and Men* (1980) that powerful local employers' organisations in the building industry played a key role in undermining autonomous craft regulation, creating a niche for employers who contained labour costs and exerted control over work through joint regulation of the labour market by the late nineteenth century. Rodgers has recently argued that between the wars the National Confederation of Employers' Organisations (NCEO) was 'one of the formative agents in modern British social policy' (Rodgers, 1988, p. 314). I have also argued elsewhere for the strategic importance of employers' organisations in strike-breaking in the late nineteenth century, in the dissemination of pro-capitalist political propaganda between the wars and in the development of a formalised industrial relations system based on union recognition and collective bargaining (McIvor, 1984, 1988, 1996; see also Johnston, 1997; Magrath, 1988). Middlemas possibly represents the extreme view of this positive interpretation. He argues that both employers' associations and trade unions were pivotal institutions within British society, incorporated by the state into decision-making from the 1930s, thus contributing to a state of equilibrium in British industrial relations until the 1960s.

The capitalist class in Britain was neither omnipotent nor monolithic. There coexisted, often with some tension, an organised and an unorganised segment of capital. The competitive relationship and individualist ethos, combined with the heterogeneity of business structures, provided significant restraints, made collective organisation amongst employers and the forging of a consensus strategy invariably difficult. However, lack of centralisation – on the Swedish model for example – does not necessarily imply lack of power and influence (Tolliday and Zeitlin, 1991, pp. 296–322). The power of British employers and their organisations was primarily located at the local rather than the national level pre-1914, and they often operated with a great deal of flexibility and pragmatism in order to reconcile conflicting interests (Bullen, 1988; Magrath, 1988; McIvor, 1996; Johnston, 1997). A recognition of divisions of interest and sectional fragmentation within industrial capitalism should not necessarily imply a virtual rejection of the validity of class as an explanatory concept altogether, nor prompt the virtual dismissal of organised capital as a force in British industrial relations. In this respect I think the revisionist interpretation rather oversteps the mark, exaggerating the weakness and disunity of British employers' organisations, presenting, in my view, an overly sanitised, negative view of such bodies. This is predominantly because such accounts concentrate upon the relationship between employers and their skilled, well-organised workers and because this interpretation has been too narrowly focused on the issue of economic performance. This has obscured a broader and more rounded analysis of the aims, activities, genesis and functions of employers' organisations.

The relationship between capital, labour and the state merits a brief comment at this stage. Increasing government involvement at a local and national level in social, economic and industrial matters clashed head on with a business ethos which stressed the prerogative of capital alone to make decisions which affected profitability. The Conciliation Act (1896), Workmen's Compensation Acts (1897, 1906), the Trade Disputes Act (1906), National Insurance (1911), Trade Boards (1909), Labour Exchanges (1909) and legal regulation of working hours (1908) and minimum wages (1912) in coal mining are all examples of state encroachment into labour markets and the labour contract. The success of these elements of the trade union/social reform agenda suggests that the state was responsive to labour's needs and, in turn, were powerful stimulants upon individual employers to organise and provide a counterpoise. A clear lead from the state in promoting collective bargaining from the early 1890s undoubtedly also curtailed the options of employers, undermining the more coercive and authoritarian responses to strikes that characterised earlier years (see Chapter 6).

The influence that organised capital attained in the corridors of political power in the twentieth century has been the subject of quite intense debate. Some commentators postulate that the state consists of an amalgam of interests and reject any inordinate influence for business (organised or unorganised) in the political sphere (Turner, 1984; Lowe, 1987). Other scholars have argued a more explicitly corporatist line, elevating both trade unions and employers' organisations to extra-parliamentary governing bodies, 'estates of the realm', with the government acting as a neutral and honest broker between these factions to assure social stability (Middlemas, 1979). Marxists regard the state as a reflection of dominant economic interests, with businessmen calling the tune. I hope to sustain the argument here that employers and their organisations could influence policy, not least through active involvement in the implementation process in the workplace itself. Organised employer action could subvert the aims of legislation – for example factory and workmen's compensation legislation (Bartrip and Burman, 1983, pp. 190–214; McIvor, 1989) – whilst formal state intervention in labour markets could provide employers with additional leverage, neutralising the dominance of skilled, well-unionised groups of workers. The creation of labour exchanges from 1909 provided employers with an alternative mode of recruiting labour, bypassing skilled subcontractors such as the cotton spinners and the overlookers. Savage has demonstrated the importance of such developments and the ways in which some employer organisations in north Lancashire exploited state regulation of employment to undermine their reliance upon powerful clusters of craft workers (Savage, 1987, pp. 89–90).

Another pivotal theme that has been massively developed in recent literature on the social history of work has been the study of gender and gender relations. Preoccupied with class divisions and struggle, little of the early work on the social history of the workplace in the 1960s and 1970s explored the specific experience of female workers. Indeed Hobsbawm was heavily criticised for such neglect and for his assumption that the official decennial census of occupations accurately represented female economic activity (Alexander *et al.*, 1979). To many feminists, Marxist theory was sex blind and failed to adequately explain female subordination at work. Directly influenced by the revival of feminism, the first wave of women's historians proceeded to address this neglect, exploring 'herstory' – focusing on the role of women in the home, workplace and the public sphere. A whole range of previously untapped sources were exploited to shed insights into women's experience of work and the institutions linked to the workplace, whilst the methodology of oral history was also applied extensively to redress this gap in the literature, notably by Elizabeth Roberts and Braybon and Summerfield (for a useful guide to sources see Beddoe, 1983). Such historians were reacting not just to neglect, but also to an 'optimistic' viewpoint which saw women's status positively transformed, especially as a consequence of female involvement in the two world wars. Hence the notion of a 'quiet revolution' in women's lives, associated with the extension of the franchise, the removal of legal impediments to equality, declining gender wage differentials and the breakdown of sexual segregation in occupations (see Myrdal and Klein, 1956; Marwick, 1988, 1991; Marshall, 1983).

Feminist critiques tend to stress continuity rather than fundamental change in their evaluations of women at work in the 1880–1950 period (e.g. Lewis, 1984; Roberts, 1984, 1987; Walby, 1986; Braybon and Summerfield, 1987) and the idea that gender had an independent impact upon the nature of work. Patterns of segmentation, gender apartheid in employment and the under-valuation of female labour persisted, whilst some historians identified significant differences in experience between women across social classes (see Gordon, 1990; Lewis, 1984). Over time, emphasis has switched from an interest in women's experience *per se* to a closer focus upon gender and gender relations, including the meaning of femininity and masculinity (Tosh, 1999; Baron, 1991; Simonton, 1998). Approaches to the topic diversified as feminism itself fractured. The most valuable analyses explicitly tested feminist theory against empirical evidence, focusing upon the nature of patriarchal society, gender inequalities and women as agency (e.g. Glucksmann, 1990; Summerfield, 1998; Gordon, 1991; Tosh, 1999). Hence Sylvia Walby's nuanced and sensitive evaluation of the interplay between patriarchal attitudes at home and work within what she argues was a *capitalist patriarchy*, where gender inequalities were perpetuated by employers, state and trade unions. Disagreement exists, however, on the relative importance of patriarchy and capitalism in the process of subordinating women. Some observers argue that patriarchy preceded capitalism and stress the home and family as the primary site of oppression and a transference of patriarchy from the domestic sphere to the workplace. For example, where occupations repli-cated 'domestic' style tasks – such as nursing, cleaning and teach-ing – they tended to be feminised. However, there is also strong evidence to suggest patriarchal notions and structures developed independently in the workplace, as Walby and Beechey have argued, and for crossover in the other direction, with patriarchal attitudes and structures in the workplace spilling over into the domestic arena. The workplace and the worker, as Simonton has argued, were gendered: 'The workplace was increasingly con-structed in a male idiom' which downgraded female labour, 'iden-tifying women as not workers, and specifically female tasks, including activities at home, as not work' (Simonton, 1998, p. 261). The deskilling of work could lead directly to it becoming feminised, as, for example, in clerical work, electrical engineer-ing, clothing manufacture and much light assembly-line production (Glucksmann, 1990). In reality, perhaps, both of the interlocking structures of patriarchy and capitalism coalesced to reinforce the subordination of women throughout the period.

In much of this literature the British trade unions emerge as part of the problem, rather than a progressive force responsible for humanising work in the interests of labour irrespective of gen-der. Trade unions absorbed the dominant values of the day and pursued sexist strategies, which only changed slowly and hardly fundamentally by 1950. Recent research has shown how unions excluded women from membership, helped to keep women out of the most highly skilled and highest paid work and failed to address the needs of women as workers, neglecting the key issues such as equal pay, job discrimination, childcare, health and wel-fare (Walby, 1986; Lewenhak, 1980; Boston, 1980; Gordon, 1988, 1991; McIvor, 1992).

The impact of such structural subordination at the point of production, however, has been the subject of much debate. On the one hand it has been argued by Savage and Miles that the gendering of the work experience retarded the development of class-consciousness amongst women. However, against the pre-vailing view that women were unorganised and passive (ideas that derive partly from neoclassical 'rational choice' theories that perceive women as consciously opting out of employment because of their lesser value in the labour market), recent research has shown that levels of female involvement in collective action and resistance to exploitative working conditions were high (Walby, 1986; Gordon, 1991). What tended to happen though was that such activity took place through more informal channels, outside of the parameters of the chauvinist trade unions. Strikes tended to be unofficial and spontaneous, with high levels of picketing (Gordon, 1991). There has also recently developed an effective critique of the notion that women were less committed to work than men. Despite ghettoisation in the lowest levels of the labour market – conceptualised as a 'secondary' labour market in contrast to the male-dominated 'primary' labour market – the oral testimonies of female workers indicate a great deal of camaraderie and bonding within the workplace as well as a strong identification by women with their paid work; a pride and respectability and independence of spirit little different from that exhibited by male employees (see Glucksmann, 1990; Brown and Stephenson, 1990). Moreover, the long-term historical transition over 1880–1950 from employment in domestic service and the 'sweated' clothing sector to employment in shops, offices and lighter manufacturing cannot be adequately explained within a deskilling/degradation of work thesis. War work undoubtedly involved increasing autonomy and more personally enriching and rewarding work for women. As one woman poignantly noted of her move from domestic service to a munitions factory during World War One: 'it was like being let out of a cage' (cited in Braybon, 1981). Penny Summerfield has perhaps developed the most nuanced and sophisticated analysis of gender relations and gender identities in her most recent history of the impact of World War Two on women's lives (Summerfield, 1998). However, the wartime changes proved to be transitory, and quickly overturned. Throughout the period under review it is the continuity of patriarchal subordination that should be stressed, with fundamental change only coming in the second half of the twentieth century.

Several other key elements of Marxist explanations of the dynamics of work and the effects of industrial capitalism in Britain have come under close critical scrutiny. Reid and others have criticised the assumption that industrial capitalism led to an impoverishment of the mass of workers whilst the 'labour aristocrats' alone prospered pre-1914. Rather, real wages rose across the board and a complex hierarchy of wage levels existed with many shades of grey existing between the extremes (Reid, 1992, pp. 31–5). Joyce has developed a trenchant critique of the assumption that social relations within capitalism are necessarily characterised by conflict. The textile factory employers of northern England earned consent and deference from their employees by their paternalist strategies, so that relationships were normally and typically peaceful, punctuated only occasionally by episodic industrial discontent (Joyce, 1980). Divisions within the labour force were considerably more complex and the old craft–labourer divide was already disintegrating in the second half of the nineteenth century with the rapid growth of the semi-skilled worker (for example in transport). Security in employment, it has been demonstrated, was not necessarily the sole prerogative of the skilled. Lummis (1994) has shown how the uniformed post-office and railway workers – his 'company men' – achieved a high degree of social standing comparable to the artisans. Nor were the skilled necessarily immune from loss of employment, either in recessions or during industrial discontent (McIvor, 1984). Moreover, the 'lumpenproletariat', Stedman-Jones has argued, could often be amongst the most politically conservative in the Victorian and Edwardian periods. At the other extreme, a number of observers have documented the long traditions of political radicalism amongst the skilled artisans and the marked leftward drift in their political consciousness, partly influenced by skills erosion and work intensification (Knox, 1990, 1999; Gray, 1981; Price, 1986).

Nor is it adequate to simply denigrate trade union leaders as traitors, betraying the interests of a more radical 'rank and file'. Against a strong and well-established Marxist critique it has been countered that the unions were relatively democratic, leaders were broadly representative and in pursuing relative narrow, economistic aims the unions were broadly reflecting the consensus favouring the regulation and improvement of workers' position *within* capitalism (Zeitlin, 1987; Tolliday and Zeitlin, 1985; Whipp, 1990). Arguably, this has facilitated a more positive overall appraisal of the key role that the unions have played in ameliorating exploitative working conditions and raising real wage levels, whilst recognising that some groups (e.g. *male skilled* workers) have fared rather better than others (see Chapter 8).

For many observers, the meaning of work has extended beyond such issues. Marxists have argued strongly for the centrality of work experience in forging the modern class system, theorising that job fragmentation and work intensification incubated trade unions and socialist politics and that deskilling led directly to a homogenisation of both the working class and the owner class (Hobsbawm, 1964, 1984; Price, 1982, 1986; Burgess, 1975, 1980; Hinton, 1973, 1983). Increasingly, such ideas have also come under fire as research on the social history of work and working-class politics has proliferated. Drawing upon increasingly sophisticated local and regional case studies, other researchers have persuasively argued against the assumption that developments in the economic sphere – in this case the labour process – necessarily have political connotations (Winter, 1985; Savage and Miles, 1994; Knox, 1990, 1999). The politicisation of workers was clearly the product of a combination of factors, with much regional and occupational diversity, and differences in experience based on class and gender.

Recent research has also tended to characterise the British working class as heterogeneous rather than homogeneous. Benson has graphically illustrated the considerable differences in miners' work culture across British coalfields and the internal stratification that characterised the British working *classes* pre-1939. This has developed into a questioning of the very concept of class. Much influenced by the thought of Foucault and the post-modernist school, historians such as Joyce and Stedman-Jones have argued that 'class' was largely a subjective social construct, imposed by the Marxist historians of the 1950s and 1960s as part of an explicit political agenda. Indeed, Joyce talks dismissively of 'propagandistic' accounts of work (Joyce, 1987, p. 4) and has been the foremost protagonist of a new approach to the study of work which rejects Marxist frameworks and focuses upon the meanings of work, looking beyond the economic into the social and cultural connotations of employment. By concentrating specifically upon the language used at the time (hence the phrase 'the linguistic turn' to describe such theorists) such writers suggest that work had a multiplicity of meanings, that there were rarely unilinear trajectories (homogenisation; deskilling; politicisation, etc.) and that in reality class meant very little to ordinary working folk before World War One. Only relatively rarely and episodically did people identify themselves directly in that way. A multiplicity of identities and relationships coexisted within a diversified and pluralistic framework most of which cut across class, such as gender, religion and national identity. As Joyce confidently asserted:

> In Marxist terms 'struggle' is seen as the defining mark of class. ... By contrast, 'populism' points to a set of discourses and identities which are extra-economic in character, and inclusive and universalising in their social remit in contrast to the exclusive categories of class.... Extra-proletarian identifications such as those of 'people' and 'nation' are involved.... Identities and discourses are in fact never coherent but always cross-cutting and contradictory.... People are husbands, mothers, voters, members of classes or of football teams, or whatever, and these do not necessarily form within them coherent wholes. Whether 'deconstruction' takes these 'soft' or 'hard' forms it raises valid questions about supposedly coherent social identities (Joyce, 1991, pp. 11–12).

Joyce's edited collection, *The Historical Meanings of Work* (1987), develops such a new history of work, challenging older discourses, especially Marxist approaches, and highlighting the cultural dimensions of employment.

Historical research on work has, therefore, massively proliferated over the recent past. The debates across this particular 'contested terrain' have sharpened considerably our understanding and helped to place the work experience in perspective. Few would now argue for a mechanistic reading off from the economic to the political spheres, and the rich mosaic of working-class experience, incorporating occupational, regional, ethnic and gender *differences*, must be recognised. This can be taken too far, however. There has been a reaction from the left, some reassertion of the significance of concepts such as class conflict, work intensification and subordination, renewed pleas for the importance of class as an explanatory framework and, to some degree, a move towards a post-revisionist synthesis on the part of such writers as Melling, Kirk, Savage and Miles. Whilst consent and collaboration were important in employment relationships, nevertheless, as the foremost protagonist of the post-modernist approach has admitted: 'the stick ought not to be lost sight of for concentration on the carrot' (Joyce, 1987, p. 7). Readers are exposed in what follows to such debates and perspectives, and whilst this account is broadly critical of much Marxist-inspired economic determinism, it will also be suggested that revisionist and post-modernist perspectives have, in some respects, zealously overstepped the mark. There was much continuity, but also, it will be argued, significant transformations in the context of employment, the experience of work and social relations in the workplace in Britain over 1880–1950. Class and gender, moreover, were of critical importance. Work was central to people's lives – as recent culture-driven accounts have emphasised – only losing such significance as work was rapidly transformed in character in the second half of the twentieth century.

2

THE CHANGING LABOUR FORCE

This chapter outlines the changing occupational profile of Britain, asking the questions who worked, where did they work and how did the shape of the labour force change over the period 1880–1950? Recently, it has become popular amongst historians to stress the uneven, slow process of industrialisation and hence to emphasise the heterogeneous nature of labour markets and the mix of traditional and modern sectors of employment in the mid-Victorian period (Joyce, 1990; Benson, 1985, 1989; Samuel, 1977). The pace and extent of change up to the mid-twentieth century have also been critically scrutinised, with 'revisionist' historians such as Zeitlin and Tolliday suggesting that any notion of a transformation of work linked to deskilling and the decline of manual work needs to be treated with extreme caution. Much of this is persuasive. Some accounts have tended to exaggerate the extent of transformative change, failing to balance this against the evidence of heterogeneity, continuity or, indeed, alternative trajectories to the Marxist paradigm. Nevertheless, it will be argued here that a number of *significant* changes did occur in occupational composition between *c*. 1880 and the mid-twentieth century.

The main source material used by social historians of work to analyse the changing structure of the occupied population has been the decennial Census of Population. Whilst this is invaluable in assessing patterns of employment, there has been a tendency to exploit such a source uncritically, whereas in reality the Census has a number of inherent weaknesses. It is important that this material is treated sensitively and that we are fully aware from the outset of the flaws in such impressive statistical series. If you are not really familiar with the sort of information that the Census provides, you might like to cast your eye over the several tables provided in this chapter before moving on.

The most important problems with the Census are linked to lack of consistency over time, classification errors, the 'snapshot' nature of the exercise and the under-recording of certain groups. As one critic has commented, it is 'static and incomplete' (Treble, 1988). Occupations were reclassified at each ten-yearly interval as the recording of jobs became more sophisticated and hence comparability over time must be undertaken cautiously. In the building industry, for example, some masons were 'lost' to the quarries category and some carpenters recategorised in timber working. The nineteenth-century Censuses also classified producers and distributors together in their relevant industrial group. Thus a man selling bread in a shop would be classified in food processing. Thus numbers in 'distribution' registered in the 1881 Census figures in Table 2.3 are seriously deflated and a comparison with the figures for 1951 erroneously suggests a much more significant shift in employment towards shopwork than actually occurred. There was a major break at the 1911 Census. From 1911 workers were classified by occupation and industry, whereas before they were categorised solely by industry. This meant that groups such as clerks were separately identified from 1911. More accurate definition of occupations also meant that over time workers were more precisely placed in the aggregated tables. Note from Tables 2.3 and 2.4 how the proportion of the total labour force enumerated as 'not classified' fell from 8.7 to just 0.1 per cent between the 1881 and the 1951 Censuses. Errors also crept in due to evasion and exaggeration. This was an issue, for example, in relation to child labour in the late nineteenth century, which, if we accept other evidence such as autobiographies, was more extensive than the official statistics indicate. Higgs has noted a tendency on the part of workers to inflate their occupational status – accountants' clerks, quack doctors and unqualified vets and dentists, for example, claiming professional positions (see Higgs, 1989). Dual occupations, such as farming and fishing, or clergymen-teachers – albeit much less common by the late nineteenth century compared to earlier – were rarely accurately recorded. Census enumerators instead usually classified only what was the 'main' source of employment. Moreover, the Census was taken in the spring at ten-year intervals and the figures are thus a reflection of the state of the economy at that particular time (for e.g. of 'boom' conditions in 1911, and 'slump' in 1921 and 1931).

Adult male workers are most consistently recorded in the Census and, for a number of reasons, female workers, children, casual, seasonal and part-time workers are under-represented, especially pre-1914. This was partly the product of the 'snapshot' nature of the Census, which missed, for example, the seasonal expansion of employment in agriculture at harvest time or in the building industry in the summer. Benson has made the point that the 'black economy', cash-in-hand employment was undoubtedly under-represented, and probably seriously so, in the pre-World War One Census (Benson, 1985). The most serious under-representation, however, occurred in relation to married female labour as Higgs and Thane have shown. Affected by the dominant chauvinist and patriarchal values of the day, the 'household heads' who completed the forms failed to accurately record the economic activity of wives and mothers within the family home, whilst Census enumerators were not particularly vigorous in ensuring that such participation was recorded. Much of the work that married women did within the home – childminding; taking in lodgers; washing; 'sweated' manufacturing, such as matchbox making – went undeclared. Over time, however, such under-recording was minimised. It was much less of a problem by 1951, which may be considered a fairly accurate depiction of the British female labour force (see Beddoe, 1983; Hakim, 1994; Lewis, 1984).

The Census, therefore, has its flaws and weaknesses and its limitations as a source need to be emphasised. By its very nature it can shed few insights into attitudes and behaviour at work, social relationships and interactions, the labour process, work culture, politics, the impact of work upon health and well-being, control and authority structures or power at the point of production. Nevertheless, used sensitively and carefully, with a critical eye upon its drawbacks and omissions, the Census sheds much light upon the changing structure of the British labour force over a relatively long time period. For these reasons it is the rational starting point for the social historian of work. Whilst some scepticism towards the apparent 'solidity' of statistics is good, on the other hand explicit quantification (incorporating an awareness of the distortions, biases and flaws of the primary source material) is preferable to vague implicit quantification or no counting at all, especially where we are dealing with masses of people. A measure of the utility of the Census lies in the considerable number of social and economic historians, economists and sociologists who have quarried this particular seam. On the positive side this source tells us much of value about labour markets, industrial change, the age and gender profile of the workforce, and local/regional variations in experience. In other words it can get us much nearer to answering questions about who worked and where they worked over the period under review, *c.* 1880–1950.

Tables 2.1 and 2.2 provide a breakdown of the occupational structure at the very broadest level by major industrial groups. In comparative terms Britain's status as an advanced economy and as 'workshop of the world' by *c.* 1880 is clearly indicated here, demonstrated in a markedly smaller proportion of total employees engaged in the primary sector – that is agriculture, forestry and fishing and the extractive industries – and larger manufacturing and services sectors than other developing economies in Europe and the USA. This representation of the UK as a modernised economy can be misleading, however, and should not be exaggerated or taken out of context. Samuel, Berg, Sabel and Zeitlin, Joyce and others have recently noted how small-scale, handicraft production continued to proliferate through the nineteenth century, resulting in a more diversified labour force than suggested by Census figures and one characterised by the coexistence of traditional with modernised modes of production (see Chapter 3). It has been pointed out that in 1911 there were still a larger number of agricultural workers than textile manufacturing workers, and more female domestic servants than male miners, and that this had significant implications for social relations because there was a close association between employers and workers in these 'traditional' sectors (Savage and Miles, 1994, pp. 22–3). By 1951, the international differences are considerably less marked, reflecting the slower pace of industrial change in Britain in contrast to elsewhere over the post-1880 period, especially the more dynamic economies of the period: the USA and Germany.

Changes took place over 1880–1950 both within and across these major industrial groups. Jobs in agriculture continued to decline. Employment in the towns proved attractive to rural labourers, as Alfred Williams indicated in his *Life in a Railway*

30

Table 2.1 Economically active population by major industrial groups (expressed as a percentage of total employment), *c.* 1880

	Agriculture, forestry and fishing	Extractive industry	Manufacturing	Construction	Commerce, finance, etc.	Transport and communications	Services	Others occupied
UK	13.2	5.5	36.5	6.8	2.8	6.9	21.7	7.3
USA	50.1	1.8	18.2	4.8	7.8	4.9	12.1	1.1
Germany	46.7	3.4	26.7	5.4	4.8	2.5	9.2	1.3
Italy	51.4	0.4	19.6	5.4	1.7	1.9	9.3	10.5
France	47.0	1.5	19.6	4.6	8.5	1.8	17.1	0.0
Belgium	39.7	4.3	28.8	3.2	8.8	1.1	14.2	0.0
Netherlands	32.9	0.9	22.5	6.9	9.3	6.8	19.3	1.5

UK = 1881; USA = 1880; Germany = 1882; Italy = 1881; France = 1886; Belgium = 1880; Netherlands = 1889.

Sources: B. R. Mitchell, *European Historical Statistics, 1750–1975* (2nd series, 1980), pp. 161–71; B. R. Mitchell, *International Historical Statistics: The Americas, 1750–1988* (2nd edition, 1993), p. 103.

31

Table 2.2 Economically active population by major industrial groups (expressed as a percentage of total employment), *c.* 1950

	Agriculture, forestry and fishing	Extractive industry	Manufacturing	Construction	Commerce, finance, etc.	Transport and communications	Services	Others occupied
UK	5.1	3.8	39.0	6.3	14.0	7.7	23.7	0.5
USA	11.9	1.6	26.7	6.3	21.3	6.3	23.3	2.6
Germany	18.7	3.2	32.9	8.8	10.3	5.5	18.2	2.3
Italy	42.2		24.6	7.5	0.9	4.0	20.8	0.0
France	27.0	1.9	27.2	7.2	11.1	5.3	20.3	0.0
Belgium	12.5	5.6	37.8	5.2	14.0	7.3	17.5	0.2
Netherlands	19.3	1.4	28.0	7.5	14.2	6.7	21.4	1.4

UK = 1951; USA = 1951; Germany (West) = 1950; Italy = 1951; France = 1954; Belgium = 1947; Netherlands = 1947.
Sources: B. R. Mitchell, *European Historical Statistics, 1750–1975* (2nd series, 1980), pp. 161–71; B. R. Mitchell, *International Historical Statistics: The Americas, 1750–1988* (2nd edition, 1993), p. 103.

Factory (1915). Rural wages rose in response as farmers struggled to compete with urban wage levels. 'Push' factors were also important as mechanisation spread and the sector became less labour and more capital intensive, latterly with the increasing use of motorised tractors and other mechanical equipment such as the combine harvester. Numbers employed in agriculture, forestry and fishing in Britain fell from 1.6 million in 1881 down to just over 1 million in 1951 during a period when total employment within the economy increased by 74 per cent. Still, at mid-twentieth century almost one in 20 British workers were employed on the land, and this sector was the seventh largest of the 26 industrial classifications.

The numbers employed in mines and quarries grew steadily through the nineteenth century to a peak of 1.4 million in 1921 (when one in every 11 male workers in Britain were employed in this sector). Extractive employment expanded as demand rose for the product in export markets, in domestic industry and in homes as a fuel. Contraction followed as demand for coal fell dramatically in the inter-war recession. British producers found it difficult to compete due to a number of factors: the working out of the most productive seams; slower diffusion of mechanisation – notably cutters and conveyors; the overvaluation of sterling; fragmented and relatively small-scale business structure; archaic managerial practices; poor industrial relations. Numbers employed in mining and quarrying fell to 847 000 by 1951 (two decades later this had fallen even more dramatically to just 256 000).

Obsolescence and renewal went hand in hand. The labour force in manufacturing doubled from 3 to 6.1 million between 1881 and 1951, reaching a historic peak of around 40 per cent of total UK employment. Significant changes in job opportunities were taking place, however, *within* manufacturing, with the decline of the more traditional 'staple' industries of iron manufacture, heavy engineering, shipbuilding, clothing and textile manufacture after World War One. This led to mass unemployment between the wars, particularly in the regions where such industries were heavily concentrated: Clydeside, Tyneside, Lancashire and Merseyside, South Wales and Northern Ireland. Job losses in these sectors of manufacturing were balanced by the continuing expansion of some well-established manufacturing sections, such as paper, printing and wood manufacture and the mushroom growth of the early twentieth-century 'sunrise' industries: chemicals, food processing, light and electrical engineering, vehicle manufacture, plastics and artificial fibres. There was also significant growth in employment in the public utilities and in communications, both in absolute numbers and in relative terms. Such changes are clearly illustrated in Tables 2.3 and 2.4. The most dynamic industries were located in the English Midlands, the South, London and the South-East. These acted as a magnet, with migration from the so-called 'depressed areas' to the more prosperous regions in search of work in the 1920s and 1930s. By 1950, older workers tended to cluster in the staple sectors with younger workers increasingly drawn to the newer, expanding industries and to clerical and shopwork.

The most striking change occurring over 1880–1950 in the composition of the British labour force was the growth of the non-manual sector. The expansion of employment opportunities in the services: in public administration, commerce, finance, in scientific and technical work, the professions and shopwork was quite dramatic. By 1911 around 20 per cent of the labour force were non-manual and by 1951 around 30 per cent (see Tables 2.5 and 2.6). The expansion of jobs in clerical work and in shops was especially marked. The number of clerical workers alone rose to 887 000 in 1911 and to 2.4 million by 1951 (60 per cent of whom were female).

The age profile of those in employment had also changed significantly by 1950. The lifetime work period had been shortened by later entry to paid employment, with the rising school leaving age (11 in 1893; 12 in 1896; 14 in 1918 – Lewis, 1984, p. 148) and legislation bringing child labour under control. The last vestiges of child labour were removed in 1918 when the 'half-time' working system – common in the textile mills – was abolished. The introduction of pensionable retirement from 1906 (initially age 70) also led to a drawing back of the age at which full-time paid work terminated. By 1950, the pension age was set at 65. Together, these changes had reduced the typical lifetime work span by eight to ten years by 1950. It was no longer a case of children prematurely forced to work, or of people having to work until they dropped. The other significant change in regard to age was a marked increase from the 1930s in the participation rate of

Table 2.3 Employed workforce in Britain by industry, 1881

	Total	%	Females	%	Males	%
Agriculture, forestry, fishing	1 590 641	12.5	119 169	3.1	1 471 472	16.6
Mining and quarrying	619 133	4.9	7 738	0.2	611 395	6.9
Food, drink, tobacco	592 898	4.7	98 454	2.5	494 444	5.6
Chemicals	77 052	0.6	6 832	0.2	70 220	0.8
Metal manufacture	475 252	3.7	10 887	0.3	464 365	5.3
Mechanical engineering	204 230	1.6	1 696	0	202 534	2.3
Instrument engineering	31 355	0.2	1 366	0	29 989	0.3
Electrical engineering	2 600	0	26	0	2 574	0
Shipbuilding/marine engineering	72 572	0.6	135	0	72 437	0.8
Vehicles	66 954	0.5	452	0	66 502	0.8
Miscellaneous metals	161 176	1.3	33 525	0.9	127 651	1.4
Textiles	1 298 748	10.2	744 819	19.2	553 929	6.3
Leather and fur	88 728	0.7	16 225	0.4	72 503	0.8
Clothing	1 031 498	8.1	655 568	16.9	375 930	4.3
Bricks, pottery, glass	137 292	1.1	26 363	0.7	110 929	1.3
Timber, furniture	204 942	1.6	20 758	0.5	184 184	2.1
Paper and printing	186 859	1.5	53 090	1.4	133 769	1.5
Other manufacture	38 858	0.3	10 255	0.3	28 603	0.3
Construction	873 035	6.9	2 286	0.1	870 749	9.8
Utilities	28 725	0.2	198	0	28 527	0.3
Transport and communications	792 313	6.3	14 107	0.4	778 206	8.8
Distribution	133 461	1	56 736	1.5	76 725	0.9
Insurance, banking, finance	48 444	0.4	419	0	48 025	0.5
Professional and scientific	439 796	3.5	198 550	5.1	241 246	2.7
Other services	2 199 206	17.3	1 761 442	45.2	437 764	5
Public administration and defence	231 148	1.8	8 521	0.2	222 627	2.5
Not classified	1 103 301	8.7	37 440	1	1 065 861	12.1
Total employed	12 730 012	100	3 887 057	100	8 843 160	100

% = percentage of total employed in each row.

Table 2.4 Employed workforce in Britain by industry, 1951

	Total	%	Females	%	Males	%
Agriculture, forestry, fishing	1 126 119	5.1	115 142	1.7	1 010 977	6.6
Mining and quarrying	841 014	3.8	13 779	0.2	827 235	5.4
Food, drink, tobacco	742 092	3.4	275 575	4.0	466 517	3.0
Coal and petroleum processing	40 483	0.2	3 269	0.0	37 214	0.2
Chemicals	394 981	1.8	112 265	1.6	282 716	1.8
Metal manufacture	570 565	2.6	61 764	0.9	508 801	3.3
Mechanical engineering	932 198	4.2	138 976	2.0	793 222	5.2
Instrument engineering	111 483	0.5	34 922	0.5	76 561	0.5
Electrical engineering	557 260	2.5	200 424	2.9	356 836	2.3
Shipbuilding/marine engineering	276 803	1.3	10 644	0.2	266 159	1.7
Vehicles	734 616	3.3	99 016	1.5	635 600	4.2
Miscellaneous metals	503 627	2.3	168 165	2.5	335 462	2.2
Textiles	985 562	4.5	548 228	8.0	437 334	2.9
Leather and fur	78 436	0.4	27 782	0.4	50 654	0.3
Clothing	675 898	3.1	476 336	7.0	199 562	1.3
Bricks, pottery, glass	313 660	1.4	73 220	1.1	240 440	1.6
Timber, furniture	325 964	1.5	52 884	0.8	273 080	1.8
Paper and printing	515 274	2.3	181 285	2.7	333 989	2.2
Other manufacture	264 207	1.2	103 147	1.5	161 060	1.1
Construction	1 388 128	6.3	40 162	0.6	1 347 966	8.8
Utilities	357 214	1.6	31 454	0.5	325 760	2.1
Transport and communications	1 704 195	7.7	214 941	3.1	1 489 254	9.7
Distribution	2 673 680	12.1	1 152 288	16.9	1 521 392	9.9
Insurance, banking, finance	435 121	2.0	149 754	2.2	285 367	1.9
Professional and scientific	1 523 606	6.9	893 339	13.1	630 267	4.1
Other services	2 339 076	10.6	1 369 465	20.1	969 611	6.3
Public administration and defence	1 704 831	7.7	271 123	4.0	1 433 708	9.4
Not classified	18 596	0.1	6 318	0.1	12 278	0.1
Total employed	22 134 689	100	6 825 667	100	15 309 022	100

% = percentage of total employed in each row.
Source: Lee (1979).

Table 2.5 Manual and non-manual workers in Britain, 1911–51 (in thousands)

	Manual	Non-manual
1911	13 685	3 433
1921	13 920	4 094
1931	14 776	4 841
1951	14 450	6 948

Source:　Bain and Price (1980, pp. 41–2).

Table 2.6 Non-manual employees by industry group, England and Wales, 1951 (%)

Agriculture, forestry, fishing	5.8
Mining and quarrying	5.2
Manufacturing	17.6
Construction	9.7
Gas, electricity, water	23.6
Transport, communications	25.1
Distribution	34.2
Insurance, banking, finance	87.7
Professions, scientific	72.4
Miscellaneous services	15.5
Public administration	46.9

Source:　Noble (1981, p. 200).

Table 2.7　Age profiles of occupied women, 1901, 1931, 1951 (%)

	15–34	35–44	45–49
1901	77	13	11
1931	72	14	14
1951	55	20	25

Source:　Lewis (1984, p. 154) (from Hakim, 1979, p. 12).

married women, which increased the participation of women aged 30–50 in paid employment (see Table 2.7).

One of the problems with the Census is that it fails to record the quite cataclysmic changes in the labour force which occurred during the two world wars. Both wars witnessed a transformation in labour markets, with the loss of millions of workers to the armed

Table 2.8   The industrial workforce during World War One (000s)

	Industrial workforce (excluding government workers)		Workers employed in government factories	
	Male	*Female*	*Male*	*Female*
July 1914	6160	2180	76	2
Oct. 1915	5350	2330	160	4
Oct. 1916	5100	2580	223	119
Oct. 1917	4950	2710	254	216
Oct. 1918	4860	2740	257	225

Source: Lawrence (1994, p. 153).

forces and the influx of replacement 'dilutee' labour to produce munitions and war-related products. Table 2.8 gives some sense of the quite dramatic, if short-lived upheaval in employment which war created.

At the beginning of our period, *c.* 1880, the British labour market was characterised by acute segmentation where job choices were sharply constrained and largely dictated by class, gender and ethnicity. Social class was very significant in influencing job choice, with little movement across the dividing line between manual and non-manual employment. Minority groups also invariably found themselves in a disadvantaged position. The clustering of the Catholic Irish into the least skilled and poorest paid jobs would be an apposite example. The prevailing deeply entrenched Victorian cult of domesticity determined sharply defined gender roles and the development of dual labour markets based on gender. Several salient characteristics of female employment in the 1880s are evident. According to the Census a much smaller proportion of adult women were 'economically active', or 'participating' (around 35 per cent) in the 'formal' economy than men (around 90 per cent). However, the points made earlier about under-representation need to be borne in mind here. What is clear is that the vast majority of female employees in full-time paid employment were young – between the ages of 14/15 and mid-twenties. Social convention and in many industries a marriage bar ensured that few women continued to work after marriage in the formal economy. On marriage it was normal for women to reorientate their lives around the domestic sphere. Hence, whilst

Table 2.9   Female employment by marital status, 1911–51 (expressed as a percentage of total females employed)

	England and Wales			Scotland		
	Married	Single	Widowed/ divorced	Married	Single	Widowed/ divorced
1911	14	77	9	5	87	7
1921	14	78	8	6	87	7
1931	16	77	7	9	86	6
1951	40	52	8	23	69	7

Sources: Lewis (1984, p. 152); McIvor (1992, p. 142).

there were quite wide regional variations (with a larger proportion of married women continuing in work in the textile manufacturing towns), the Census in 1911 recorded only 14 per cent of married women in employment in England and Wales and in the even more patriarchal society north of the border in Scotland the Census recorded only 5 per cent so employed (see Table 2.9). The situation changed quite markedly in the 1930s and 1940s, as an increasing proportion of married women entered the formal economy. These changes were stimulated by rising consumerism, changing attitudes, some ameliorative employment rights legislation (notably in 1918), feminist campaigning, and the demands of the war and post-war economies for female labour. The growth of part-time employment for female workers was also evident by 1950 and would expand massively thereafter.

Patriarchy at work was clearly reflected in wide gender wage differentials and in the gender composition of British occupations indicated in the Census. Table 2.3 illustrates how women were ghettoised into a narrow range of occupations, with over 70 per cent of female employees in 1881 located in just three sectors: domestic service, clothing and textile manufacture. Within these sectors, moreover, a fairly rigid sexual division of labour existed, with women occupying the lower echelons and invariably the lowest status, least responsible and poorest paid work, irrespective of genuine skill content. Over 1880–1950 all these traditional areas of female employment declined, none more rapidly than indoor domestic service, where a staggering 1.5 million jobs were shed. Female workers moved increasingly into shopwork and

Table 2.10   Women employed by region, England and Wales, 1931

	Percentage of total employed
Lancashire, Cheshire	41.9
South-East	36.1
Greater London	39.9
Midlands	35.0
West Yorkshire	35.4
Cumberland, Westmorland, Yorkshire, East and North Ridings	27.5
South-West	27.4
East	26.4
North Wales	24.8
Durham, Northumberland	23.1
South Wales	19.5
England and Wales	34.2

Source: Glucksmann (1990, p. 44).

clerical work, and the lighter, new manufacturing industries. However, undervaluation of labour and occupational segregation based on gender transferred over into these 'modern' occupations (see Chapter 7). There remained quite wide differences in experience across the country in female participation in paid employment, as Table 2.10 shows.

From 1911 the introduction of classification by occupation (rather than industry) enables a somewhat different breakdown of the labour force by socio-economic status groups, indicated in Tables 2.11 and 2.12. Several points about the nature of the British labour force are worth highlighting from these figures. Firstly, they confirm a picture of a highly stratified and quite heterogeneous labour force: a more complex structure emerging from the industrialisation process. Secondly, the evidence here is ambiguous, even contradictory, on the issue of deskilling and degradation (see Chapter 3). Within the manual sector there does appear to have been a relative loss of skilled workers (expressed as a proportion of total employees) and a quite substantial rise in absolute and proportionate terms of the unskilled category. On the other hand the proportion of the total labour force located in the higher status categories (1A; 1B; 2A; 2B; 4) rose significantly (from 15.5 to 19.8 per cent of the total). The largest expansion

Table 2.11   Occupied population by class, 1911 and 1951 (in thousands)

		1911	1951
1A	Higher professions	184 1.0%	434 1.9%
1B	Lower professions	560 3.1%	1059 4.7%
2A	Employers and proprietors	1232 6.7%	1118 5.0%
2B	Managers and administrators	629 3.4%	1246 5.5%
3	Clerical workers	887 4.8%	2404 10.7%
4	Foremen, inspectors, supervisors	236 1.3%	590 2.6%
5	Skilled manual workers	5608 30.6%	5616 25.0%
6	Semi-skilled manual workers	7244 39.5%	7338 32.6%
7	Unskilled manual workers	1767 9.6%	2709 12.0%
	All	18347 100.0%	22514 100.0%

Source: Routh (1987, p. 28).

occurs, as one might expect, within the clerical sector. The majority, by 1951, were female and this leads us on to perhaps the most important feature of the British labour force thrown up by these statistics on the occupied population by class and gender. Tables 2.4 and 2.12 clearly demonstrate on the one hand the limited penetration of female employees into some previously male-dominated occupations – notably clerical and shopwork, and significant entry into light and electrical engineering, paper and printing. However, what is also clearly illustrated here is the lack of any fundamental change by the mid-twentieth century in the sexual division of labour. The input of women into the formal economy during wartime had indicated the potential of female labour power and raised confidence and expectations on the part of female workers. However, the effects of the wars proved to be

Table 2.12 Occupied population by class and gender, 1951 (in thousands)

		All	Male	Female
1A	Higher professions	434 1.9%	399 2.6%	36 0.5%
1B	Lower professions	1059 4.7%	492 3.2%	567 8.2%
2A	Employers and proprietors	1118 5.0%	894 5.7%	223 3.2%
2B	Managers and administrators	1246 5.5%	1056 6.8%	189 2.7%
3	Clerical workers	2404 10.7%	990 6.4%	1414 20.4%
4	Foremen, inspectors, supervisors	590 2.6%	511 3.3%	79 1.1%
5	Skilled manual workers	5616 25.0%	4733 30.4%	884 12.8%
6	Semi-skilled manual workers	7338 32.6%	4294 27.6%	2805 40.5%
7	Unskilled manual workers	2709 12.0%	2215 14.2%	733 10.6%
	All	22514 100.0%	15584 100.0%	6930 100.0%

Source: Routh (1987, p. 38).

transitory and in 1950 a system of gender apartheid still existed, with a glass ceiling effectively operating, seriously constraining job opportunities for women. Table 2.12 shows this quite starkly with the marked under-representation of female workers in skilled manual jobs and in the higher status ranks of employers, managers, administrators and higher professions. Where women were clustered was in the intermediate, semi-skilled grades of manual work, in personal service (cleaners, waitresses, etc.) and in lower status grades in shop and clerical work. In this context, Catherine Hakim has made a very valid point about the persistence of gender segregation in Britain's labour markets in the post-World War Two era.

By 1951 Britain's labour force had changed in a number of important respects and such developments had wider ramifications outside of the workplace. There was a long-term growth in the number of non-manual occupations and sharp decline in several 'traditional' sectors of work, including agriculture, mining, domestic service, textiles and clothing manufacture. The professions, managerial and supervisory jobs also expanded very significantly, providing opportunities for upward mobility, though this was almost exclusively for male workers. An increasing proportion of married women were entering the formal economy and, towards the bottom of the employment hierarchy, there were about a million more unskilled manual workers in 1951 compared to 1911. The picture, therefore, is a mixed one, though as Savage and Miles have pointed out, there was clearly an increasing tendency over this period for male members of the working class to be located in 'blue collar' manufacturing work, where numbers rose from 3 to 6 million. This had important ramifications, facilitating class cohesion and consciousness, whilst the experience of women within the labour market was somewhat different. Savage and Miles (1994, p. 25) note:

These trends forged a complex and interacting set of boundaries between the genders and the classes. In general, shifts in employment led to the decline of forms of work allowing ready 'inter-class' relations. However, there was an important exception to this among working class women. The occupational world of men became more firmly class-divided, while women continued to occupy a rather more shadowy, ambiguous position, thereby complicating and undermining tendencies towards social cleavage.

The failure of the male-dominated labour movement to respond adequately to the demands of female workers added to their sense of exclusion and a markedly different experience in the workplace. Such issues are examined in more depth in Chapters 7 and 8.

3

THE *EXPERIENCE* OF WORK: DESKILLING, INTENSIFICATION AND ALIENATION?

This chapter explores the continuities and the main changes that took place in the way that work was organised and in the labour process in Britain between 1880 and 1950. 'Labour process' might be defined as the actual performance of work, involving the interaction of workers with the tools, technologies and materials necessary to manufacture goods or provide services. Social historians of work have focused much attention on this theme. Marxist labour process theorists and historians, much influenced by Braverman's updating of Marx in *Labor and Monopoly Capital* in 1974, have hypothesised that work in a capitalist framework inevitably led to *deskilling* and a concomitant degradation, or dehumanisation, of work. Other social historians have rejected the validity of Braverman's model as inappropriate in the British context, arguing against a straightforward, unilinear trend towards deskilling. This chapter will argue a case for a more complex process of change and development in the *experience* of work over the period 1880–1950. Deskilling through job fragmentation was occurring over these years, but was limited by the nature of British product markets, business and managerial structures and attitudes, as well as labour resistance, exercised increasingly through powerful trade unions. Moreover, upward job mobility and recomposition of skills – or skill specialisation – also occurred. The 'dilution' of male skilled craft labour during the two wars may have been lamented by the engineers, but this represented an opportunity for advancement and in many cases heightened job satisfaction for the many workers who flooded out of domestic service and heavy manual labouring jobs into munitions. What was more pervasive, perhaps, was the *intensification* of work, which occurred through a variety of forms and mechanisms as employers and managers were forced to react to a considerably more hostile product market as competition cranked up and Britain found itself increasingly losing its pre-eminent position as 'the workshop of the world'. There is now something of a consensus amongst social historians of work that such intensification occurred. What should be stressed, however, is that the pace and process of both deskilling and work intensification were uneven, and contingent upon a series of factors and circumstances. The alienation this engendered was tempered, to a degree at least, by worker resistance and collective organisation, and by the compensations provided by employment: the camaraderie; the reduction in work time; more regular and secure work; and rising real wages, facilitating improvements in the quality of life, at least for those fortunate enough to sustain themselves in employment.

Skill and the Organisation of Work in Late Victorian Britain

There is a tendency in some of the literature to look back to a 'golden age' when workers controlled their own production, dictated the pace and rhythm of work and enjoyed a deep job satisfaction through the exercise of their craft. The increasing exploitation of labour under advanced capitalism is thus deemed to have destroyed this. However, the fundamental flaw in such an interpretation is that it uses as a benchmark a mythical notion of 'craftsmanship', conflating this experience when, in reality, the great majority of workers in the late Victorian British economy lacked access to skilled work, craft wage rates, or such workers' autonomy and power at the point of production. The Census of 1911, as we have seen, defined less than a third of all the occupied population as 'skilled manual workers'. Most workers were engaged in dull, repetitive, hard physical toil over a very long work day, week and year (with only a few days off as official, unpaid 'holidays'). Moreover, the extent and pace of 'modernising' change have also been exaggerated, a consequence of the traditional emphasis on the industrial 'revolution'. Historians have tended to construct their arguments by reference to only the experience of large employers, primarily in manufacturing and mining. In the 1880s around 60 per cent of the employed workforce in Britain were still employed *outside* manufacturing and mining, in services, agriculture, administration, transport, construction and elsewhere. Samuel, Joyce, Sabel and Zeitlin, Reid, Benson and others have recently postulated that the process of industrialisation was extremely uneven. The factory did not dominate the economy even by the mid-Victorian period, and other modes of production were equally significant: the workshop, the household (domestic service), the sweatshop, the office and the farm, for example.

Around 1880, after a century of industrialisation, the experience of work in Britain was bewilderingly diverse. At one extreme there were many industries and sectors where working methods had changed relatively little and still relied heavily on physical strength and dexterity. Agriculture provides an example, where labour-intensive rather than capital-intensive methods predominated. In 1880, over 1.5 million rural workers (more than the numbers employed in mining or textiles) toiled on holdings which remained relatively small and where technology remained rudimentary. They exploited the strength of their bodies and simple hand tools such as the hoe, the scythe and the hand trowel. Much of the work was physically debilitating, dirty and subject to the vagaries of the weather and the strong discipline of the farm overseer. Harvesting continued to demand an ever-increasing army of labourers. The Irish labourer Patrick MacGill (1914) provides an evocative account of such back-breaking employment in potato picking in Scotland in this era (see also Holmes, 1997). There was more widespread use of mechanical reaping machines in the last two decades of the century, and these machines did reduce demand for casual labour during harvest-time, as Armstrong has shown, and changed the nature of the work somewhat, though their diffusion across the land was fairly slow. This was partly because of the small scale of farming and reluctance to increase investment levels (Armstrong, 1988, pp. 112–13, 123). This round of technological change facilitated a noticeable drift away from female employment of the land, into peripheral tasks and back into unpaid homemaking (see also Snell, 1985). More fundamental changes, brought by the coming of tractors, occurred much later, between 1920 and 1950.

At the other extreme was a modernised, factory-based, highly mechanised sector. Metallurgy and textile manufacture exemplify this, whilst many engineering works, breweries and shipyards also exploited high levels of steam power as a form of motive power in the mid-Victorian period. The cotton textile workers were amongst the first modern factory workers, interacting with sophisticated power-driven machinery in relatively large-scale enterprises – the average cotton factory employed around 200 workers by the 1880s. For most, the work involved repetitive machine-tending tasks in a continuous process; for spinners the monitoring of hundreds of spinning spindles and repairing – or piecing – of broken threads; for weavers the frequent replenishing of the loom shuttles so that the warp could be interlaced with the weft. Such workers might most appropriately be described as semi-skilled machine minders – what one historian has termed 'part artisan, part proletarian' (Joyce, 1990), though the spinners had managed, through strong trade unions, to maintain high wage levels and thus a status equating to the skilled craft artisans, or 'labour aristocracy'. The coal hewers also fall into this sort of rough classification as semi-skilled. These were toilers who performed a highly ardous manual task, undercutting the coal at the face using hand tools (the pick), then ripping the seam down and loading the broken coal into the tubs for transportation to the pit shaft and hence to the surface. The big difference, however, is that the hewers used hand tools whilst the cotton workers minded power-driven machinery. The application of power to the coal pit applied largely to pumping and winding, and affected the labour process of actually hewing the coal in only a minimal fashion. By c. 1880, less than 1 per cent of all coal in Britain was cut by mechanical means, despite the first cutting machines being developed two decades earlier. In many other occupations (such as dockwork and navvying) the premium was upon physical strength, where any significant interaction with mechanical aids remained unusual prior to 1880. Sharp contrasts in experience existed within sectors, such as transport, where large-scale employment on the railways coexisted with the largely solitary employment of the carter or the canal barge operator.

This is an important point. Obsession with the modernised sectors – with steam power and factories – has led to an underestimation of the extent to which handicraft labour and hard physical toil and smaller, alternative forms of capitalist enterprise continued to dominate the economy in 1880. Booth's massive study of work in London *c.* 1880 outlines a diverse mixture of mostly small-scale production units – sweatshops, self-employment, subcontracting, factories, workshops – operating in an intensely competitive environment, in a chronically overstocked labour market. The result was irregularity of employment, poor conditions, excessive working hours and endemic poverty. In a seminal piece of Marxist revisionism, Raphael Samuel made this point emphatically in a panoramic survey of the nature of work in the mid-Victorian period published in 1977. Samuel emphasised the uneven nature of capitalist development, the parallel expansion of small workshop and outwork, or domestic, production – what he termed 'sweating' and 'back-yard industries and trades' concurrent with the growth of large factories; the combination of hand and steam-powered technologies; and the persistence of skill based on the predominance of hand tool production. 'Nineteenth century capitalism', Samuel argued, 'created many more skills than it destroyed, though they were different in kind from those of the all-round craftsmen, and subject to a wholly new level of exploitation' (p. 59). Samuel's kaleidoscopic survey identifies handicraft, non-mechanised styles of work dominant in food processing, clothing – where the sewing machine exacerbated the concentration of the industry in homes and small sweatshops – building, pottery, glass manufacture, woodworking, leather manufacture, boots and shoes, and light engineering, of the type that predominated around Birmingham and the Black Country. One major omission which should be added to this list is domestic service, where over 2 million workers toiled, in relative isolation, undertaking a range of very labour-intensive and predominantly gender-specific tasks (see Burnett, 1974, pp. 135–48; McBride, 1976). Moreover, what appears evident is that even in large-scale enterprises and within the factory mode of production, groups of workers continued to maintain their independence and exercise time-honoured handicraft skills. Indeed, the Victorian expansion of engineering, shipbuilding and metallurgy created new opportunities for the expansion of such skills, as that of the smith, the patternmaker, the cooper, the shipwright and the iron moulder. The pattern of demand for many British manufactured products – especially in engineering – remained largely for quality, tailor-made, 'bespoke' production and this continued to place a heavy premium on skilled labour pre-1880.

Many years ago Hobsbawm identified the existence of an 'upper stratum' of highly paid, skilled craft workers in the Victorian economy, whilst the work of Gray, Crossick and others, has confirmed the growing importance of this 'labour aristocracy' in the second half of the nineteenth century. Latterly, the topic has become an important issue of controversy and debate. Recent research has persuasively challenged the notion that such craft artisans were intrinsically conservative and the concept that the artisanal elite necessarily monopolised skill and job security in the late Victorian era (Lummis, 1994; Harrison and Zeitlin, 1985; Knox, 1990, 1999). However, few commentators dispute the existence of such a relatively privileged group with genuine skill, much autonomy at work and considerable control over their own labour process.

Skill has been defined by More as a combination of manual dexterity with knowledge (of materials and tools) and discretion acquired through a long training period, traditionally of several years, commonly through apprenticeship. Knowledge of the craft was retained by the workers in nineteenth-century Britain, even invariably with the transition into factory production. This was tied up with a tendency on the part of British employers to manage indirectly and hence to allow many such privileged workers this independence and not encroach into their labour process or into the quite intimate, personal process of transmitting craft knowledge, through on-the-job training, traditionally via the apprenticeship system. Skill was widely regarded in this culture as the capital of the craftsman, almost as an art form, to be closely protected as part of a workers' property to be passed on to their sons, or other male kin. Moreover, invariably such workers owned their own means of production, and the possession of a craftsman's toolbox was the outward symbol of his autonomy and status. The high earnings of such workers – which in 1880 included building craftsmen, printers, engineering fitters and turners, smiths, shipyard platers, boilermakers, coopers, moulders, bookbinders, iron puddlers – also marked them from the rest.

Typically, craft artisans could earn around double the wages of labourers and the regularity of their earnings over the year cushioned such workers from the boom and slump nature of the economy and enabled artisans to save, to contribute to friendly societies and unions and to enjoy a relatively high standard of living compared to others. Moreover, their pivotal role in the production process, their relative economic security and their exercise of authority in the workplace influenced their standing within the community, where they were positioned at the top of the status hierarchy. They were amongst the most respectable, aloof and dignified of workers. Whilst not a closed caste, nonetheless pre-1880 intermarriage *within* the group was common and entry to the craft was primarily preserved for the kin of artisans. Movement across from the rough, unskilled labouring work to craftwork was very unusual.

However, to see even this group of skilled craft artisans as a homogeneous group, with common values, politics and attitudes would be an oversimplification. There existed a major divide between the modern and the traditional crafts and between the quality and rough, or 'degraded' ends of production. The latter is evident, for example, in the tailoring trade and some sections of building, such as house painting, where skills could be 'picked up' relatively easily. The experience of traditional craftsmen, such as hand-loom weavers, saddlers, watchmakers, cabinetmakers, wheelwrights, masons, smiths, millwrights, coopers and shipwrights, could diverge significantly from the rising modern occupations, much in demand, especially in metalworking and engineering (such as boilermakers, fitters and turners). The group incorporated declining, 'obsolete' crafts, where mechanisation and factories led craft workers into a loss of self-employed status, as with the wheelwright (see Sturt, 1923). Some skilled work, such as in shipbuilding, was so subject to the vagaries of the trade cycle that the security of the craftsmen was seriously threatened. By contrast, as recent research has demonstrated, some non-craft groups of workers enjoyed regular work and were better paid than many artisans, including what Lummis has termed the 'uniformed working class' (railwaymen and post office workers are examples). In some trades – for example food processing – the craft tradition was weak and there clearly existed gradations of skills and aptitudes, rather than a stark distinction (as in building) between the craft artisans and the labourers (Harrison and Zeitlin, 1985).

Nonetheless, it was the craft artisans who were the group of workers most able to sustain collective organisation pre-1880. Their mid-Victorian trade societies played an important role in enhancing job security, protecting workers' control over the labour process (resisting piecework, for example), and providing insurance in the eventuality of unemployment, victimisation, injury or illness (as well as death benefits to allow a respectable funeral). Crucial was control over the numbers of apprentices taken on, because this restriction enabled craftsmen to maintain their market scarcity and hence their value and capacity to maintain high earnings. Whilst not as strike-prone as later organisations associated with the notion of 'new unionism' from the late 1880s, the craft unions did perform a significant protective role, creating and extending sets of 'trade rules', bargaining collectively with employers and initiating industrial action to preserve craft rights, as in engineering in 1852. Their organisation and agitation through the Trades Union Congress succeeded in creating a firm framework of labour law in the 1870s which facilitated further trade union expansion. The point has also been made that collective organisation facilitated the social construction of skill. Powerful trade unions allowed some groups of workers to maintain their earnings, relative scarcity and 'aristocratic' status, even after technological and organisational change had effectively deskilled the job, such as the cotton spinners. Whilst strong unions could also help to create high wage levels thus allowing groups of workers to aspire to higher status – such as railway engine drivers and coal hewers – so-called 'contrived' aristocrats (Gray, 1981). The role such organisations played in the regulation of work and labour markets will be explored further in Chapter 8.

Thus, by 1880, it is reasonable to argue that the first phase of industrialisation had a more limited impact upon the nature of work than traditional accounts stressing the revolutionary and transformative impact of economic change, mechanisation and factorisation in the nineteenth century have suggested. The nature of the enterprise and the work environment varied considerably and the work itself ranged from labouring, domestic service and clerical work, through semi-skilled tasks, to the combination of conceptualisation and execution that characterised most artisanal activity. However, probably less than a third of all workers could be considered as skilled craftworkers in the late nineteenth century, defined by access to a considerable range in tasks requiring long training and a degree of autonomy and independence exercised at work. Samuel (1977, pp. 58–9) describes this heterogeneity in the mid-Victorian work experience quite beautifully:

> If one looks at the economy as a whole rather than at its most novel and striking features, a less orderly canvas might be drawn – one bearing more resemblance to a Bruegel or even a Hieronymus Bosch than to the geometrical regularities of a modern abstract. The industrial landscape would be seen to be full of diggings and pits as well as of tall factory chimneys. Smithies would sprout in the shadows of the furnaces, sweat-shops in those of the looms. Agricultural labourers might take up the foreground, armed with sickle or scythe, while behind them troops of women and children would be bent double over the ripening crops of the field, pulling charlock, hoeing nettles, or cleaning the furrows of stones. In the middle distance there might be navvies digging sewers and paviors laying flags. On the building sites there would be a bustle of man-powered activity, with house-painters on ladders, and slaters nailing roofs. Carters would be loading and unloading horses, market women carrying baskets of produce on their heads; dockers balancing weights. The factories would be hot and steamy, with men stripped to the singlet, and juvenile runners in bare feet. At the lead works women would be carrying pots of poisonous metal on their heads.... Instead of calling his picture 'machinery' the artist might prefer to name it 'toil'.

However limited, change was still significant and it would be quite erroneous to give the impression in this 'snapshot' of working life *c*. 1880 of a lack of dynamism in the workplace. The competitive nature of the capitalist economy in the nineteenth century had ramifications, leading to a regularisation of work and increased intensity of production, in both larger and smaller enterprises. However, this was a long-drawn-out, incremental process which E. P. Thompson recognised and somewhat exaggerated in his analysis of the early phase of industrialisation (Thompson, 1963). Undoubtably, the emerging factory sector placed pressures on the workshop and domestic sector, as Behagg demonstrated in his study of Birmingham (Behagg, 1979). Traditional crafts, such as the hand-loom weaver, were undermined, 'obsolete' tradesmen dishonoured by unemployment, job security diminished by over-stocked urban labour markets – the result, Joyce has commented, was that 'the tempo and quality of workshop life was altered' (Joyce, 1990, p. 155). Nonetheless, the pace of change was much more dramatic over the following two generations which consti-tuted, over 1880–1950, something of a transformation in the *experience* of work in Britain. The rest of this section considers the evidence for what has been termed 'deskilling' and the 'intensi-fication' of work up to the mid-twentieth century. These develop-ments are related to changes in control and authority structures, which are analysed in the next chapter.

Technology, Organisational Change and Deskilling

Change in the nature of work over 1880–1950 was linked intim-ately to economic forces, changes in business structure and organ-isation and the introduction of technology. From the 1870s, Britain progressively lost her pre-eminent position in the world, as other countries, starting with Germany and the USA, industrial-ised. External competitive pressures intensified and whilst pro-duction continued to rise, Britain's market share contracted, productivity in many sectors declined, labour costs rose and, as a consequence Britain's relative economic position worsened. This process of economic retardation has been examined in detail elsewhere. Our concern here is how this impacted upon the experience of work. Several related tendencies can be discerned. Employers responded by developing company structures, creating the modern form of business enterprise. Over 1880–1950, as Hannah has shown, Britain underwent a transition from an eco-nomy based on the small-scale family firm, to one charactererised by the large-scale joint-stock limited liability company. By 1950, the factory predominated as the basic unit of production and around 26 per cent of all manufacturing output was produced by the largest 100 companies (Cronin, 1984, p. 154; Savage and Miles, 1994, p. 48). With this change, the more paternalist relationships between master and man gave way to a more depersonalised industrial relations and collective bargaining conducted between the representatives of companies and workers. Employers and managers responded to more hostile product markets and the escalating profit squeeze with attempts to cut production costs and increase efficiency, rationalising work processes and extending managerial control more directly over production processes. As skilled work was amongst the most costly form of labour, inevitably there was an attack upon the skilled.

For Britain over 1880–1950, there is much evidence to support the view that deskilling was, as Paul Thompson puts it, 'the major tendential presence within the development of the capitalist labour process' (Thompson, 1983, p. 118). In mining, the 'independent collier' with all-round skills, gave way with mechanisation and the longwall method to more specialised hewers performing a narrower range of much more specific tasks – essentially undercutting the coal, ripping down and filling, sometimes in three separate shifts. In building construction there was an expansion of the intermediate grades of labour – for example, crane-drivers, asphalters and scaffolders. The growth of the semi-skilled group was evident in many industries before World War One – by 1911 around 6.3 million workers, around a third of all employed, were categorised as semi-skilled – and this blurred the distinction between labourers and craftsmen. Zweig (1952a, p. 28) defined such a worker thus:

> The semi-skilled man is basically a machine operator usually trained for a few weeks or months in factory schools or training departments or, more often, while working. In this semi-skilled work dexterity, care, alertness, and interest in the work are the greatest assets. Neither skill in the strict sense of the word nor physical strength are needed, but first of all the ability to stand the monotony of repetitive operations.

In manufacturing as a whole there was an incremental shift towards larger-scale production of standardised parts, exploiting first semi-automatic and then fully automatic machines and flow production techniques. In London, the process was well under way prior to 1880, with displaced craftsmen forced into casual work, including the docks (Stedman-Jones, 1971, p. 75). Task range and discretionary content in manufacturing jobs were both lessening, and apprenticeship declining. In engineering, skilled craftsmen engaged in nodal modes of production c. 1880 gave way to the increasing employment of male and female machinists, handymen and semi-skilled assemblers, performing much more specialised jobs, with a narrower task range. In the mid-1890s an engineering worker commented on the demise of the millwright and the coming of 'subdivision of labour':

All mechanics will agree with me that the introduction of machinery has not raised the standard of skill among workmen. Nay, on the contrary, it has enormously increased the mono-tony of their toil, and limited the scope for the exercise of their ingenuity. It must of necessity dull their artistic perceptions, and tend to reduce them to the mere level of machines capable only of repeating one operation so many times per day (Galton, 1896, p. 106).

Complex craft jobs were broken up as new machinery was intro-duced – such as the turret and capstan lathes and specialised grinding and boring machines – and as the new ideas associated with Taylorism and Fordism diffused across the Atlantic. Increas-ingly popular from the 1900s, Taylorist managerial philosophy encouraged managers to subdivide labour after undertaking a systematic analysis of the labour process, using the stopwatch. Developments at the Singer Corporation at Clydebank near Glasgow provide an example. Here the imposition of American management techniques, extensive mechanisation, reduction in squad sizes, manipulation of staffing levels and monitoring with the stopwatch all combined to alienate the Scottish workforce, resulting in a major all-out strike in 1911 (Glasgow Labour History Workshop, 1989; Kenefick and McIvor, 1996). At Weirs, another Glasgow factory that experimented with American 'scientific man-agement' methods, one worker, Harry McShane, commented bit-terly on this trend towards deskilling: 'every morning each man knew the job he was going to do during the day. The jobs were so ridiculously simple that anyone could do them' (cited in Knox, 1999, p. 146). In engineering and shipbuilding there was increasing employment of young workers, replacing time-served journeymen.

Deskilling was clearly occurring prior to World War One, though the pressures of wartime, followed by the crisis of the inter-war economic recession, provided more fertile ground for the attack on skill. The expansion of flow production processes in the war industries, and especially in munitions manufacture, did much to popularise the benefits of division of labour and provided a platform for further rationalisation. This was encouraged in the post-war period by the main employers' organisations, including the Federation of British Industries, the Engineering Employers' Federation (EEF) and by the government through the newly formed Department of Scientific and Industrial Research. The trends are evident in engineering and epitomised in the transition between 1920 and 1950 in motor car manufacture from small-scale craft-based production to assembly-line, flow production methods, where work-cycle times were driven down to the absolute minimum according to Fordist principles. Ford UK was a pioneer in this respect, initially at Trafford Park, Manchester, from 1911, and at Dagenham, London, from 1931. Apprenticeship eroded rapidly in engineering between the wars: one survey in 1938 found that only 16 per cent of engineering firms took on apprentices (Penn, 1982, p. 97). In Scotland, as Knox has shown, apprenticeship was subverted, with few being given full training in the craft. Apprentices were being replaced by 'learners', or sacked on attaining journeyman status and the right to the full wage rate (Greenwood, 1933, 1939). In all, there was a net loss of some 150 000 skilled engineering workers in the inter-war period alone (McIvor, 1996, pp. 255–6). Statistics compiled by the EEF indicate this marked decline in skill in the industry, and a noticeable expansion of the semi-skilled group (Table 3.1). At the same time the number of female workers in engineering proliferated from around 2 per cent of total employed in 1900, to around

Table 3.1   Workers classified by skill in member firms of the Engineering Employers' Federation, 1914–33 (%)

	Skilled	Semi-skilled	Unskilled
1914	60	20	20
1921	50	30	20
1926	40	45	15
1933	32	57	11

Source: Gospel (1974, p. 50).

15 per cent on the eve of World War Two and to 23 per cent by 1951 (see Table 2.4). Female workers were engaged especially on the assembly lines in the light and consumer engineering companies (see Glucksmann, 1990).

Elsewhere technological and organisational change, including the spread of automatic machine tools, led directly to deskilling and job fragmentation, resulting in the further division of labour. This process proceeded from a craft and a non-craft basis. Mass production methods occurred especially, though not exclusively, in the newer industries: light and electrical engineering (e.g. the American-owned plants: Ford, Singer, Westinghouse), chemicals (notably ICI), food processing (Lyons, Tate and Lyle), artificial fibres (Courtaulds) tobacco (Wills, Players) and newspaper production. The more rapid diffusion of mechanical cutters and conveyors in mining resulted in an extensive reorganisation of traditional working methods, extending deskilling, and resulting in miners' work becoming more physical. In his autobiography published in the late 1930s, B. L. Coombes, a South Wales miner, graphically describes such changes and his inability to keep up with the pace of the coal cutters and conveyors (Coombes, 1939). By 1950, 84 per cent of coal produced in Britain was being cut and almost 90 per cent conveyed by machine. With mechanisation, miners were being transformed into specialised labourers (Knox, 1999, p. 205). In his 1948 study of miners, Zweig detected an appreciable loss of interest in the work as a result of such changes:

An old miner took pride in his work...the getting of coal by hand, with all the cutting, shovelling, ripping, packing, drawing off, etc., was a craft, an art, while now all the jobs are specialised, and have become monotonous....The collier of today in a mechanised colliery is doing practically nothing but shovelling – shovelling all the time. How can you expect him to take an interest in his job? An old collier could take his time; there was not such a rush and strain as there is now, with the conveyor and the twenty four hours' cycle (Zweig, 1948b, p. 21).

In the building industry, prefabrication replaced much on-site craft work – e.g. with pre-dressed stone, pre-formed joinery (windows and doors), pipes (plumbing) and concrete. In common with other industries, this created a larger group of specialised semi-skilled workers. As one builder informed an investigator in 1908:

> Specialists are largely taking the place of the ordinary artisan and navvy. His foreman told me that things were getting very specialised now, the idea of 'one man, one job' being carried to an extreme, and each having his own particular sphere. This is largely the result of the new processes and materials replacing the old familiar methods (cited in Meacham, 1977, p. 142).

Similarly, printing and woodworking were subject to erosion of skill with the diffusion of machine woodworking and new printing technology in the monotype and linotype machines. One indication of the extent to which this affected skilled labour in printing can be found in the evidence of labour replacement during strikes in the 1890s. Surprisingly for such a skilled sector, almost half of all strikes in printing between 1888 and 1899 were settled by employers simply replacing the striking labour force with substitute labour (McIvor, 1984). The adoption of a shorter three 8-hour shift system in the gas industry in 1889 was followed by extensive reorganisation of work in the 1890s, with massive investment in new technology in more efficient, larger gas retorts and increased job specialisation (Hobsbawm, 1964). In the boot and shoe industry the transition to the 'American system' of flow production was rapid after the employers' victory in the 1895 lockout. The new work regime replaced craft with mechanical production, with detailed division of labour under flow production principles, and workers largely paid by results. Similarly, in the clothing sector large factories, mechanisation and flow production principle replaced working with the needle in the classic Victorian 'sweatshop'. The first clothing factory using a conveyor system opened in 1918. The secretary of the Amalgamated Society of Tailors reflected back over such changes in work methods in 1937:

> I can remember working in shops where even a sewing machine would not have been tolerated and every stitch had to be done by hand. I have lived long enough to see almost every process usurped by the machine, among them cutting, pressing, seaming, felling, padding, basting, buttonholing and buttoning

and with the conveyor belt to carry subdivided portions of the work from one operative to another (cited in Stewart and Hunter, 1964, p. 197).

Other occupations and industries identified by historians as having a deskilling dynamic over 1880–1950 include agriculture (with extensive tractorisation), metallurgy and shopwork (with the decline of the traditional grocery apprenticeship) (Knox, 1999, pp. 273–5; McGuffie, 1985).

From World War One one of the most important mechanisms of job specialisation and deskilling was the spread of Taylorism in Britain. Littler has argued that the Bedaux system, first introduced to Britain in 1926, was the most influential conduit of Taylorist ideas. About 250 British firms experimented with aspects of the Bedaux system between the wars, including a number of very large companies (ICI, Wolsey, Ferranti, Avery, Goodrich, Lucas, Lyons). The spread of the system attracted the interest of the TUC, which produced a report on Bedaux in 1933. The upshot of the diffusion of Taylorite and Bedaux ideologies, according to Littler, was more detailed division of labour: 'a divorce of "direct" and "indirect" labour and job simplification. Those who worked within the framework of the Bedaux system lost a large part of their autonomy and initiative. On the job analysis, exploiting the stopwatch and motion study, enabled craft knowledge to be transferred to management and planning departments and jobs to be routinised and fragmented' (Littler, 1982, pp. 140–1). This is discussed in more detail in Chapter 4.

As Paul Thompson, Littler and others have argued, there also occurred a parallel movement – job fragmentation from a non-craft basis. This was the trend in chemicals and food processing over the course of the first half of the twentieth century, and, arguably in clerical work. Office employment had no well-established craft tradition, though a minority of Victorian male clerks had been articled apprentices (see Anderson, 1976). The period 1920–50 witnessed a long process of task subdivision and increasing specialisation in clerical work, associated with the diffusion of the typewriter and other mechanical aids (such as the calculator). This facilitated the feminisation of office employment, with ghettoisation of women into the subordinate grades of typists and filing clerks (Anderson, 1988; Zimmeck, 1986; Cohn, 1985).

Whilst the evidence suggests that deskilling was an important tendency within developed capitalism, whether what occurred in Britain over 1880–1950 constituted a wholesale collapse in skills and radical transformation of the labour process is debatable. Much recent research has been highly critical of this concept in relation to the timing, extent and degree of change. What emerges from this work is a clear need to refine and modify the degradation hypothesis to take into account countervailing tendencies, contrary evidence and the diversity of historical experience.

New technologies were capable of creating new skills as well as destroying crafts. In line with deskilling went a recomposition of skills, and what More has termed 'reskilling' (More, 1996). The new work regimes associated with Taylorism, Ford and Bedaux created opportunities for planners, supervisors, maintenance workers, technicians and statisticians. More argues that job specialisation concentrated skills within a narrower task range: dexterity, 'tricks of the trade', knowledge of the quirks of a particular machine and grudging respect for the complexity of new technology remained much in evidence. The wars also created new skills, as did technical education and company retraining programmes, like that at the Singer Corporation in Clydebank (More, 1996, pp. 104–10). Hirst has argued that the shift from wood to iron shipbuilding enhanced rather than diminished skills. In short, this was not a one-way process. Paul Thompson's conceptualisation of 'cycles of deskilling' is a useful one (Thompson, 1983, pp. 106–7). Whilst the inter-war depression facilitated an attack on craft skills, the late 1930s and the 1940s represented a period when rearmament, the war economy, tight labour markets, the revival of trade unions and the growth of shop stewards, combined with a changed political framework, may well have slowed deskilling tendencies markedly. Indeed, World War Two led to widespread acquisition of many new transferable skills as the labour market was radically shaken up by the removal of millions from the workplace to the armed forces. In some cases work groups managed to recompose lost skills and extend controls over production. A good example would be the Coventry engineering and car-making factories (Thompson, 1983, 48; Thompson, 1988).

Moreover, many jobs were not deskilled *per se*, because they never had a craft foundation in the first place. This would apply to much work in the transport and agricultural sectors, in sweatshops, distribution, food processing and domestic service. In the latter sector, the albeit slow diffusion of labour-saving technologies, notably from the 1930s on, removed much of the physical drudgery of this particularly debilitating occupation, character- ised as it was by *very* long working hours. The same could be said of dockwork between 1900 and 1950 with the development of mechanical conveyors and cranes. Benson has argued persuas- ively that the extent of change in shopwork has been exaggerated by an overemphasis on the rise of the big department store: 'Of the estimated 747 000 shops that were trading in 1938, all but 90 000 remained in the hands of small firms with fewer than ten branches: the overwhelming majority were still single shops with working proprietors' (Benson, 1989, p. 26).

The validity of the deskilling thesis, moreover, is much stronger when applied to male than female labour, and to manual than non-manual work. The long-term shift from domestic service and sweated home and workshop production across into clerical work, light engineering and shopwork did not necessarily represent a *downgrading*. Indeed the weight of women's own oral testimony suggests quite the opposite, though the picture is a complex one, which we will return to (Braybon and Summerfield, 1987; Summerfield, 1998; Glucksmann, 1990; Brown and Stephenson, 1990). Such experience of job enrichment is rarely directly docu- mented – writing by unskilled and female workers is much less common than the skilled. However, in a revealing article in the Workers' Union journal in 1914 George Shann commented that deskilling through scientific management would open up oppor- tunities for more fulfilling and better paid work for labourers, and regarded the breaking down of craft monopoly over areas of work as a positive development:

> Any man of average intelligence and initiative can pick up and do the relatively simple process required. This fact has several results. In the first place the division between the skilled and the unskilled is breaking down. Apprenticeship is going out of fashion, and a youth which is supposed to be specially trained has only a knowledge of one or two processes. On the other hand, in a machine shop a sharp unskilled youth can move from one process to another until we find a so-called skilled man working side by side in the same job as a so-called unskilled

man, both getting the same rate and earning the same money. And the more the division of processes takes place the more this result will come. Thus there seems to be a conflict of interest between the skilled and the unskilled, and it is a fact, I think, that on the whole the unskilled man rather welcomes the change that has come, whilst the skilled man condemns it root and branch (Shann, 1914).

Lockwood's classic thesis on clerical work noted a tendency towards loss of status as the work became increasingly feminised, and indicated that there was a 'modernised' sector of very large offices, where work was bureaucratised, mechanisation quite extensive and employment relations were impersonal by the 1950s in Britain. Government departments are examples (Lockwood, 1958, pp. 92–3). However, his research showed that such work environments were atypical:

> Physically clerks were scattered among a large number of small offices, working in close contact with employers, and divorced from the factory workmen. Their working relationships were largely determined by personal and particular ties, which meant that there was little uniformity in standards of work and remuneration, and that individualistic aspirations to advancement were strongly encouraged (Lockwood, 1958, p. 207).

Taking issue with Klingender's Marxist interpretation, which equated office mechanisation with factory deskilling in the 1930s, Lockwood showed that detailed division of labour and 'production-line methods', such as the typing pool, were relatively uncommon with machinery mostly used in an 'ancillary' fashion (as an aid to calculation, for example). Whilst recognising the tendencies towards job fragmentation and machine operation, Lockwood emphasises the variation in experience within the heterogeneous clerical sector and the limited extent to which mechanisation and rationalisation had transformed the nature of work and social relations: 'the most advanced developments in the field are likely to divert attention from the normal division of labour' (Lockwood, 1958, p. 92). Lockwood tended to overconcentrate on the male experience in clerical work. Nonetheless, recent research on female clerical workers pre-1950 has tended, I think, to confirm such an interpretation. Gender segregation and poor promotion prospects characterised such work, but clerical work was better paid, more secure and regarded by women as of higher status than both domestic service and factory work (Zimmeck, 1986; Sanderson, 1986; Lewis, 1984; Anderson, 1988).

Most importantly, perhaps, the deskilling thesis has been criticised – including by Marxists – because it fails to recognise across the wide range of work contexts the limitations operating upon capital or the ability of labour itself to prevent, constrain and mediate tendencies towards the degradation of work (see Burawoy, 1985; Price, 1986; Tolliday and Zeitlin, 1991; Reid, 1992; McIvor, 1996). Employers were not omnipotent, nor workers powerless. Thus workers have emerged from recent research as a much more active agency in this process. There is much empirical evidence to indicate that the organisation of work and the labour process itself was rarely imposed unilaterally from above, rather this was the product of joint regulation between labour and capital. As trade unionism developed, moreover, so too did the capability of unions to protect their members' interests at the point of production expand, notably from the regulation of wages and conditions and provision of benefits into work organisation and the labour process. This could curtail employer attempts to destroy skills, as shown in case studies of the engineering, metalworking, printing, shipbuilding and textile industries (Lazonick, 1979; Zeitlin, 1985, 1991; Harrison and Zeitlin, 1985; Reid, 1992; McKinlay, 1996). In their struggle to produce good quality yarn from increasingly cheaper, inferior, short staple fibres on the mule spinning machine, the skills of spinners probably became even more advanced between 1920 and 1950 (Lazonick, 1979). Similarly, concerted trade union opposition retarded the spread of the more looms system in weaving – in 1950 still 75 per cent of weavers in England were operating the traditional complement of four looms or less (McIvor, 1996). Printers also regained control over the new technologies after defeats in the late nineteenth century and, by 1950, were amongst the highest paid and most powerful of craft groups (Zweig, 1952a; Zeitlin, 1985). Littler has also shown how the Taylorite Bedaux system was met with considerable resistance in the 1930s – including, significantly, from some foremen and supervisors – and how industrial action in a number of cases (such as at Wolsey, and at Johnson and Nephew) resulted in the proposed work reorganisation being abandoned or radically modified. The warrening of manufacturing industry in the 1940s with shop stewards was also significant, in that this facilitated tight control over the job, as for example, in the car industry in the West Midlands. Paul Thompson's research on Coventry car workers (1988) and Alan McKinlay's work on Clydeside shipbuilding (1991), using oral history techniques, have both demonstrated the long-run persistence of skill, as well as high levels of work control by wage earners.

There were other limits upon the process of deskilling. Not least of these were the nature of British labour and product markets and employers' own views and strategies. On the land, the progress of mechanisation was relatively slow. Whilst in 1950 about 250 000 tractors were in use, there remained more working horses – 335 000. Armstrong has argued that the result was a balance between continuity and change, rather than a cataclysmic transformation of working methods in agriculture precipitated by mechanisation (Armstrong, 1988, pp. 223–7). The key changes were the contraction of harvesting time to one or two days, mechanical milking and the subcontracting of hedging and ditching. The great gangs of farm labourers dragooned in for the harvest withered and farmwork became more isolated, with a diminution of the 'social' aspects of rural labour. This represented a regularisation of the rural work regime and an elimination of many long-standing rural customs, practices and rituals. However, Armstrong's work shows that variety and job satisfaction remained high, the time-honoured seasonal rhythms of agricultural life remained significant and workers benefited from machinery that took much of the back-breaking toil out of farming. Moreover, many farmworkers identified with their new machinery and took pride in modernising techniques. Tractors and other farm equipment differed significantly, moreover, in that workers still had to exercise a great deal of discretion, control and guidance, in marked contrast to the stultification of factory assembly lines. The drift of labour from the land, Armstrong argues, was as much the product of alienation with relatively low wages as it was the product of capital-intensive technological change (Armstrong, 1988, pp. 227–31).

Overstocked urban labour markets continued to work as a disincentive to capital investment in new technology and work

reorganisation (in contrast to the USA) and employers characteristically grumbled about the high administrative costs of Taylorism.
Reid has made the point that British manufacturing employers
exhibited a long-running preference for quality production,
'bespoke', differentiated (as opposed to standardised) products
made to order (as in many branches of engineering and shipbuilding) and as a consequence there remained a heavy reliance
upon skilled and knowledgeable workers (Reid, 1992, p. 30;
More, 1980, p. 171). The statistics compiled by the EEF cited earlier
in this chapter (Table 3.1), indicating significant deskilling in
engineering, may well be a distortion of reality. As these are figures based on EEF membership, they represent only what
occurred in the largest engineering companies and they incorporate the employers' own notional 'downgrading' of skilled tasks.
A 1938 survey of the engineering industry as a whole suggests a
significantly slower rate of deskilling, with 51 per cent of all workers
still classified as skilled, 36 per cent semi-skilled and 13 per cent
unskilled (Zweig, 1952a, p. 38).

There was also reluctance on the part of British management to
eschew customary rule of thumb labour management and a com-
placency which fossilised traditional work practices, leaving workers
with much independence at the point of production. This is
reflected in the abhorrence towards scientific management in
some of the engineering employers' journals prior to World War
One. For example:

> There is much to be said for, but in our opinion . . . more to be
> said against Taylorism. . . . There are fair ways and unfair ways
> of diminishing labour costs, ways sportsmanlike and ways
> unsportsmanlike, ways humane and ways inhuman. We do not
> hesitate to say that Taylorism is inhuman. As far as possible it
> dehumanises the man for it endeavours to remove the only
> distinction that makes him better than a machine – his intelli-
> gence. . . . For heaven's sake let us leave the free man who works
> for us something on which to exercise his intelligence . . . and to
> give him a right still to call himself a man. (*The Engineer*, 19 May
> 1911, p. 520).

In engineering, the main changes were in the assembly processes,
but there was little change pre-1914 in the foundry, the smithy,

the pattern shop or the boilershop. It has been estimated that at most, assembly-line production accounted for just 2 per cent of the entire British workforce as late as 1940 (Savage and Miles, 1994, p. 50).

British employers developed a whole range of strategies designed to manage and control labour, and hence facilitate the maximisation of profit, and work reorganisation including technological change which involved deskilling was one, though not necessarily the most significant, of these. This conclusion is supported by the most comprehensive of all occupational surveys; the decennial Census and by studies of occupational mobility. Tables 2.11 and 2.12 suggested a mixed picture. There were a million more workers classified officially as unskilled in 1951 compared to 1911, whilst the number of skilled manual workers (at around 5.6 million) remained constant and fell from 31 to 25 per cent of total employed. On the other hand, the number and proportion of professionals, managers and administrators rose sharply from 1.4 (7.5 per cent) to 2.7 million (12.1 per cent) between 1911 and 1951. Studies of social mobility, as Savage and Miles have shown, also suggest a more complex picture, rather than sustaining an argument of unilinear downgrading. Miles's work has shown that *c*. 1880 intergenerational occupational mobility was relatively rare, either across the working class to middle-class occupations, or between the categories of unskilled, semi-skilled and skilled. By 1914, there was less rigidity and more movement within the working class, with *both* the upgrading of unskilled workers and demotion of skilled in evidence (by 1914 around a third of all skilled workers' sons were downwardly mobile, descending into unskilled status). Later studies confirmed this fluidity in both directions. By *c*. 1950, roughly an equal proportion of sons from an unskilled background found themselves in skilled jobs, and vice versa. An important new development, however, was in cross-class intergenerational mobility. By 1950, around 20 per cent of workers' sons (predominantly from the ranks of the skilled) had moved across the divide from manual occupations upwards into non-manual, middle-class jobs (Savage and Miles, 1994, pp. 35–9). The altering pattern of job opportunities and rising educational standards were pivotal factors in these developments. With these changes went a marked erosion in wage differentials between skilled and unskilled work: around 1900 skilled workers earnt almost 70 per cent more than the unskilled, whereas by the 1940s they earned around 40–50 per cent more (Savage and Miles, 1994, pp. 28–9).

The tendency within British capitalism to deskill and fragment work tasks should not, therefore, be seen in isolation, nor its significance exaggerated. Arguably, what was at least as important over 1880–1950 were attempts by management to increase discipline and control, and intensify work *within* the parameters of the existing technology and division of labour. This could occur with technological innovation and deskilling, but the extent to which British employers continued to concentrate on more labour-intensive and skilled types of production is striking. Management looked to enhance systems of workplace authority and supervision, increased the speed of machines and the pace of production, slashed direct labour costs and introduced new wage systems, particularly payments by results and bonus systems as incentives to work harder and increase productivity. These tendencies towards work *intensification* were widespread and may well have been more significant an experience for more workers within the British economy over *c.* 1880–1950 than deskilling.

The Intensification of Work

In marked contrast to the thesis of linear improvement in working conditions over time, a number of social historians, including Hobsbawm, Benson, Cronin and Richard Price, have argued quite persuasively that the period from *c.* 1880 witnessed an increasing intensification, rationalisation and regularisation of work. Referring to the two decades before World War One Cronin has commented: 'almost all workers perceived some deterioration and intensification of their work . . . industrial concentration and management strategy were working to their disadvantage' (Cronin, 1979, p. 59; see also Knox, 1990; Kenefick and McIvor, 1996). To improve competitiveness and maintain healthy profit margins many employers experimented with a wide range of techniques to cheapen production costs. This drive to reduce costs incorporated an attempt to reorganise traditional work methods by speeding up machinery, tightening supervision and discipline on the shop floor, extending payments by results wage systems and introducing novel types of bonus payments in an attempt to cajole, motivate and manipulate workers to increase effort and raise levels of productivity. It is possible to detect such tendencies across almost all sectors of the economy, though the timing, extent and mode often varied considerably. Cumulatively, this radically altered the experience of work over these years.

In part this was a product of the changing nature of business enterprise as family firms gave way to the limited liability companies and big corporations. An iron founder noted in 1908:

> These firms have vanished, and have been replaced by the strictly business hustler on their side, and the animated dividend producer on ours.... Working conditions can be summed up as follows: The speeding up of both human and inanimate machinery intensifies all along the line. Men complain of a multitude of petty tyrannies and humiliations in the course of workshop life. The pace grows hotter... (cited in Meacham, 1977, p. 138).

As working hours shortened (to an average of around 55 hours a week in 1900, a 48-hour week by 1920 and 44–45 hours by 1950) management sought to utilise the working day more systematically, regularising the time actually spent in production. For example, in the Royal Ordnance Factories and Royal Docks the changeover to the shorter eight-hour day was combined with the introduction of clocking in and out, a more draconian fining system and greater shop-floor supervision with the employment of what were appropriately termed 'workchasers'. A Portsmouth dock worker commented:

> Much dissatisfaction is being expressed in the dockyard concerning the working of the eight hours day. The men find that they really have to work all their time in the yard. Much of the idling has been stopped, and it is probable that more work is being turned out per man than ever before (*The Engineer*, 3 August 1894).

Similarly, an engineering worker made the point that 'the severity of the labour is increased by it being compressed from nine hours into eight' (*The Engineer*, 4 May 1894). Workloads of railway workers were increased as rail traffic grew without commensurate staffing increases, leading to systematic overworking (Bagwell, 1963). Williams's account of working in the Swindon railway factory before World War One has repeated references to speed-up and increased workloads. Similarly, the alienation wrought by the pressure of work, combined with craft deskilling in the building trade, are recurrent themes in the social realist novel *Ragged Trousered Philanthropists* by Tressell. Here the labour process is the dominant theme and the foreman, 'Nimrod', personifies the driving and speeding supervisor.

Some employers, as in the boot and shoe industry, used the opportunity of successful lockouts in the 1890s to initiate extensive reorganisation of working methods. Others, as in cotton textiles, increased the size or the number of the machines operated by the workers (more spindles, more looms), speeded up existing technology, 'cribbed' time by starting earlier, encroached into breaks and finished later than legally regulated working hours. Most significantly, perhaps, mill-owners purchased cheaper, poorer quality raw materials which, because of more yarn breakages in the mule and loom, significantly increased workloads. The extent of this problem with 'bad material' can be gauged by the fact that this issue accounted for more than 75 per cent of all the disputes going through the cotton industry conciliation machinery over 1900–14. Such work intensification could have detrimental effects on workers' health. Allan Clarke in *The Effects of the Factory System*, published in 1899, argued that cotton workers were habituated to repetitive and monotonous work tasks, were mentally drained, stunted and debilitated in physique, and resorted to a vast array of pills, potions, self-medication, herbal remedies and quack doctors in an attempt to ameliorate their exhaustion. This has been seen as somewhat sensationalised stuff, written by a socialist-journalist who was somewhat removed from the mills (a teacher). However, Clarke's portrayal was largely confirmed by Britain's foremost occupational health specialist Thomas Oliver who noted in the 1900s that cotton workers suffered constant speeding-up of work and identified female cotton workers, often bearing the double burden of running a home and paid employment, as being most fatigued and overstrained (these issues are explored more fully in Chapter 5).

The imposition of direct wage cuts, combined with the spread of payments by results and premium bonus systems of remuneration across a number of occupations – including engineering, cotton, boot and shoe, printing, ironfounding, woodwork and furniture, in the period before World War One also exacerbated problems of fatigue and overstrain. Wage cuts – usually imposed in periods of economic recession or downturn – encouraged workers to increase their effort, in an attempt to enhance their employability. This led to a redefinition of what constituted a fair day's work, with rewards for labour more directly tied to effort. Moreover, management could use the simplest of pretexts to cut established piecework or bonus rates, with the result that workers were driven on to intensify their effort to maintain the earnings level to which they had become accustomed. This, the Trades Union Congress argued in 1910, resulted in a vicious spiral of speed-up, work scamping, declining product quality, together with worker fatigue and ill health, and a draining of 'human capital' (TUC, 1910). In the massive Singer sewing machine plant in Clydebank near Glasgow such conditions provoked a major all-out strike in 1911. As one Singer worker bitterly commented: 'They were the best organised firm in Britain. . . . It was all piecework and if you didn't make it, you didn't get it. . . . If you said a word to a gaffer you just got chucked out. . . . Singers had a bad name. I myself thought as a boy that they should blow it up' (Bill Lang; see Glasgow Labour History Workshop, 1989, p. 13).

The spread of piecework modes of wage payment occurred across manufacturing – cotton, mining, woodworking, printing, ironfounding, boot and shoe manufacture – but was particularly rapid in engineering. Whereas 5 per cent of workers in the industry were paid by results in 1886, the proportion of engineering fitters and turners on piecework rose to 46 per cent and 37 per cent respectively by 1914 (Knox, 1999, p. 149). By 1950 it has been estimated that around 70 per cent of all engineering workers were paid by results (Zweig, 1952a, p. 39). The defeats of the engineering workers in the lockouts of 1897–8 and 1922 facilitated this process. In all areas of manufacturing, some 38 per cent of employees were on piecework by 1950 (Cronin, 1984, p. 155). Bonus wage payment systems, such as the premium bonus, also spread, as employers looked towards new incentives to raise productivity. These new wage payment methods, as Graham argued in 1921, were explicitly designed to intensify workers' effort by removing 'the tendency to limited effort which was characteristic of flat rate remuneration' (Graham, 1921, p. 35).

On the docks, the arrival of the steamship led to pressure upon dockers to load and unload more rapidly, so that vessels could be turned around and the return on higher capital investment recouped quickly. At the same time the size of dock squads was reduced to cut costs, breaching customary, time-honoured working methods (Kenefick and McIvor, 1996, p. 29). Everywhere, it seemed, the intensity of exploitation was being cranked up and customary work patterns were being fractured. Indeed, this process was one of the main underlying causes of the growth of trade unions and the wave of strikes that engulfed Britain during the 'labour unrest' of 1910–14. Williams's account of work in the Great Western Railway factory again provides an insightful view of such processes. He observed how workers' control over the pace and rhythm of production was progressively diminished in contrast to previously when workers were not 'watched and timed at every little operation' (Williams, 1915, pp. 304–5):

Everything was designed for the man to start as early as possible, to keep on mechanically to and from the furnace and hammer with not the slightest pause, except for meals, and to run till the very last moment. His prices were fixed accordingly. Every operation was correctly timed. The manager and overseer stood together, watches in hand (Williams, 1915, p. 183).

World War One and the economic recession of the inter-war years saw such intensification of work cranked up further. The connections between piecework, speed-up and deteriorating health were affirmed by Cole in 1917, by the wartime Health of Munitions Workers Committee, by Graham in 1921 and in several reports of the Industrial Fatigue Research Board and the Industrial Health Research Board in the inter-war years. Whilst real wages rose on average, wage cuts bit deep into earnings in the hard-hit 'staple' sectors of the economy: notably cotton, coal, heavy engineering and shipbuilding. It was in these declining sectors where the pressure on work pace was most intense. Miners had to keep pace with mechanical cutters and conveyors and were also subject to increased monitoring and supervision. Whilst

Supple has rather downplayed the significance of such developments, Mcintyre has emphasised how miners' work was significantly intensified between the wars (Mcintyre, 1980, p. 63). Indeed, the nature of mining work was radically transformed by 1950, with longwall working and the diffusion of coal cutters and conveyors. Similarly, the Depression underwrote and energised a resurgence of unilateral managerial control in the textile mills and a new round of work intensification which the weakened textile unions found hard to effectively resist (McIvor, 1996, pp. 188–9). One female weaver noted:

> Work inside the factory is much harder than it used to be owing to the great speeding up of machinery. The toil is now almost ceaseless; the machinery demands constant attention. Thirty years ago this was not the case; the machinery ran very much slower and the operatives had a little leisure during working hours, but all this has been abolished... whether spinner or weaver, the textile operatives are on their feet from the first turn of the wheel in the morning till the last turn in the evening (Pollock, 1926, p. 234).

The Depression enhanced the ability of employers to impose unilateral work intensification. As one cotton employers' association official commented in 1927: 'We claim the right as employers to employ whom we think fit, and also the right to make a change without being compelled to give a reason' (McIvor, 1996, p. 188). Similar changes affected the clothing industry, where conditions in the early 1930s led one worker to equate work to slavery: 'the long hours, the high speed, the monotony, the low wages, the inability to move from one's seat until a given signal, the stress and strain makes one feel like a galley slave' (*Amalgamated Society of Tailors, Journal,* 1931, cited in Stewart and Hunter, 1964, p. 197). The inter-war speed-up thus affected many industries. The Workers' Theatre Movement savagely caricatured the intensification of work during the recession in an *agitprop* skit:

> *Capitalist*:
> Speed-up, speed-up! Watch your step.
> Hold on tight and show some pep.

Move your hands and bend your body.
Without end and not so shoddy.
Faster, faster, shake it up,
No one idles in this shop

Worker:
We are humans, not machines.

Capitalist:
You don't like this fast routine?
Get your pay and get out quick,
You speak like a Bolshevik.

Woman worker:
My head, oh, my head! I can't go on.

Capitalist:
You want time off, that's your game.
Get your pay and get out quick,
There's no place here for the sick.
Here's a youngster strong and willing.
Will not find the pace so killing.
(*Redstage: Journal of the Workers Theatre Movement*, September
1932, p. 7)

In engineering and metalworking, the employers' organisations played a pivotal role in facilitating work intensification – in
some cases in northern England the workloads of fitters and
turners were doubled, on the pretext of returning to pre-war
practices (McIvor, 1996, pp. 252–8). Job insecurity in the
depression facilitated work intensification, as one steelworker
noted: 'the workers were scared and took risks rather than lose
their jobs' (Stirling, 1938, p. 86). A Foundry Workers' Union
organiser (Harry Sinclair) noted how 'the pace is so hot' the
workers 'are fit for nothing . . . this is living to work not working
to live' (cited in Fyrth and Collins, 1959, p. 211). Arthur Exell's
experience in Morris Motors in the 1930s provides another
example of such practices. He emphasises the tyranny of managers, foremen and inspectors, the constant pressure of payments by results and having to keep pace with the production
line:

> My brother went straight into the Press Shop...and I could
> have cried when I saw him coming home. There were blisters
> on his hands, all across. The blisters stood right up, where he'd
> blistered them picking up this metal and putting it in the press.
> That's what they had to do, one hundred every hour, nearly
> two a minute. And that's how you'd go, all day, like that (Exell,
> 1977, p. 28).

Exell was a communist and might be expected to be excessively
critical of the capitalist labour process. However, more 'neutral'
observers also noted these tendencies, including the factory
inspectors. It was noted in the 1935 *Factory Inspectors' Report* (*FIR*)
that 'speed is the essence of present-day industry' and the
Inspectorate also identified a higher incidence of accidents at
work amongst young employees under 18 as a consequence of
intensification (*FIR*, 1935, pp. 6–7; also see *FIR*, 1934, p. 8). In his
1937 study of such workers in British industry John Gollan
argued that lack of training was the main cause, and that this was
linked to the all-pervasive intensification of work which the economic depression exacerbated:

> It becomes clear that many of our youth are being mutilated,
> mangled by the machinery, simply for lack of training. It is not
> enough to stop at this explanation, however. We must go fur-
> ther and ask why are the youth not properly trained and why
> are they not properly supervised? The answer is to be found in
> a phenomenon noticed in chapter after chapter of this book –
> the terrific drive for increased output through speed-up which
> has come in the train of rationalisation and mass production.
> Every nerve has to be concentrated under modern conditions
> on the keeping up of the output; is there any wonder that the
> more pressed adult has not time to give to training the inexperi-
> enced youth? (Gollan, 1937, pp. 196–7).

The pressures of wartime only served to further heighten the
pace of production, resulting directly in a marked rise in fatigue,
occupational injuries and mortality. In this work context, age was
a significant factor and advancing years continued to mean more
insecurity and a downward spiral into lower paid employment.
Zweig noted in 1952:

Demotion affects the vast majority of working men at a certain age. A man's strength and resilience grows less, his speed declines, and he cannot keep up with the requirements of the job. And when he loses his job in a firm he cannot find as good a job as the one he held before, and he often has to throw away his union ticket and start again as a labourer on a light job. A faceworker in a mine will go on to haulage, a craftsman in the building trade may become a night-watchman, a skilled man in the workshop may become a commissionaire on the gate (Zweig, 1952a, p. 23).

Older workers' expectations were also affected by having experienced the insecurity of the interwar recession at first hand. Younger workers entering the economy from the late 1930s were markedly less content and considerably less willing to tolerate unilaterally imposed speed-up and deteriorating conditions (Zweig, 1952a, pp. 54–62).

Again, however, it is important not to exaggerate such tendencies. The extent and nature of work intensification varied greatly between and even within industries. Where employers operated in relatively protected markets the cold blast of competition failed to have the necessary enervating effect, and work conditions and pace varied little. The scale of production remained relatively small in many sectors, including building, pottery, printing and agriculture. The small master painter, plumber, printer and potter remained much in evidence (Benson, 1989, pp. 19–20). Over the period the state also assumed some responsibility to curb excessively exploitative practices (this issue is explored in more detail in Chapter 6). Moreover, as with deskilling, workers themselves reacted and resisted new work regimes, not least through industrial action and collective organisation – even in some cases in the worst years of the inter-war Depression (e.g. cotton weavers' strikes against 'more looms'). Recent research has clearly demonstrated that employers were rarely able to act unilaterally and that in well-unionised sectors and in periods of tight labour markets the effects of work intensification could be mediated, as Zeitlin, Price, Stearns and others have argued. This was particularly true of the 1940s, as trade union strength grew and workers became more confident of their market power. Zweig noted in 1952:

The status of the worker has risen considerably in recent years. He does not regard himself simply as a means of production, as a profit-making piece of machinery. He regards himself more as a junior partner entitled to voice his opinions on all basic issues which involve conditions of work or the prospect of employment. The workplace on which his lot depends is *his* (Zweig's emphasis) workplace; it is a social unit of the first importance. He has acquired a new sense of his importance and he asks that his dignity shall be respected. The rules of work or the discipline of work cannot be imposed on him without consultation with him or his representative. . . . Autocracy in British industry belongs to the past. An employer cannot do what he likes; he must not only conform to the rules and regulations – and there is a profusion of them in the collective agreements and trade union rules – but he must also be prepared to consult his men on all basic changes in his workplace (Zweig, 1952a, pp. 122–3).

The trade unions did provide a bulwark against unscrupulous, profit-maximising employers. However, trade union effectiveness was patchy across the economy, relatively few of the unskilled or female workers were organised and the capacity of the unions to protect members against work intensification was critically undermined by mass unemployment and a massive haemorrhage in membership between the wars. Trade unions' strategic emphasis on the wage packet also limited their potential to significantly blunt the inexorable thrust of work intensification. Nonetheless, their presence and their capability were considerably greater by 1950 than 1880 (see Chapter 8). Significantly, though, employers increasingly organised as a counterweight against the unions and despite being beset by internal divisions, the evidence suggests that strong industry-wide employers' organisations were effective in bolstering the efforts of companies to increase workloads (McIvor, 1996, pp. 126–30) and erode craft controls in industries such as building and engineering (this is explored in more depth in the next chapter).

Conclusions

What occurred over 1880–1950 was the slow, uneven, but clearly evident transition from traditional towards modern forms of work where the pace of production was intensified and skills were fragmented. Recent research has emphasised the more evolutionary and patchy nature of industrialisation. Late into the nineteenth century traditional modes of work survived, where workers toiled for very long hours in relatively small workplaces, but retained much control. The rhythm of work was slow and irregular and subject to many interruptions and breaks. There already existed a modernised sector, but its importance, by the mid-Victorian years, should not be exaggerated. The new work regimes which evolved over 1880–1950 were characterised by regularity, a curtailment of worker independence, closer and more direct managerial control, intensification of work pace and shorter work hours, in a context of increased scale and more mechanised production, which fragmented work tasks leading to more specialised skills. Unskilled and semi-skilled manual jobs were increasing faster than skilled ones, and jobs in the more mechanised industries were undoubtably less skilled than the all-round artisanal crafts of the mid-Victorian period. In the most in-depth analysis of the changing nature of work in Scotland over the nineteenth and twentieth centuries, Knox has argued persuasively in support of such a deskilling dynamic:

> The independent craftsman symbolised in the ownership of tools, the extensive system of workplace rituals and ceremonies, which served to emphasise his status in the workplace and underpin the values of craft pride and solidarity, disappeared with the arrival of the stop watch, quality control, planning offices and modern technology. In his place emerged the semi-skilled assembly worker and the technician, more specialised and subject to greater managerial discipline. Other workers outside the realm of skilled work also experienced the passing of established working habits and customs, indeed, a whole way of life (Knox, 1999, p. 278).

Against the dynamics of deskilling, intensification and the depersonalisation of work, however, must be weighed the compensations and countervailing tendencies. The application of science and technology could reduce the physical burden of work – as it did in mining, the docks and in domestic service. Younger miners in the late 1940s accepted mechanisation and many recognised the benefits. One noted: 'There is no sense in getting coal with our bare hands. . . . In the old days it was all brute force and ignorance: thank God it isn't now' (Zweig, 1948b, pp. 22–3). A considerable number of workers experienced job enrichment, retraining, the acquisition of new skills, promotion to the increasing technical and supervisory jobs and extended their control over work organisation (not least through their unions), whilst the material rewards of labour (in real wages – see Chapter 9) had increased massively. Already, in 1952, Zweig discovered the widespread existence of an instrumental attitude towards work: high wages and increased job security since the 1930s Depression, he asserted, went a good way to compensating workers engaged in relatively monotonous work (Zweig, 1952a, pp. 96–114).

The picture, therefore is a mixed one. Some groups of artisans clearly experienced deskilling, though this was not a uniform process and could be mediated. This was partly because workers were not powerless, and they reacted and adapted to change. In several industries, many groups of skilled workers were successful in maintaining their craft identity and skilled status, including engineering, printing, cotton spinning and building. Moreover, the tight labour markets of the 1940s enabled even the unskilled and semi-skilled to significantly extend controls over and enhance the status of their jobs, including dockers and car workers (see Price, 1982, 1984). It is difficult to sum up these disparate and sometimes countervailing tendencies in work organisation and the labour process. Clearly, the pace and extent of change were uneven, across skills, genders, age groups and occupations. Expressions of dissatisfaction with work need to be balanced against much evidence that work was rewarding, not least in oral testimony (e.g. Summerfield, 1998; Brown and Stevenson, 1990). Job satisfaction, however, was less evident for female workers and labourers, and Zweig has identified important differences between industries, with more alienation in the declining staple trades – including mining and cotton by 1950, than engineering and construction (Zweig, 1952a, pp. 99–100). However, he concludes his survey by emphasising the interest most workers found in their employment: 'a review of the industries in the country does not suggest that in the majority work is dull and repetitive' (Zweig, 1952a, p. 112). Whilst the gap between skilled and unskilled workers narrowed, diversity remained – there was a kaleidoscopic variety of different work tasks in 1950. An important continuity, however, lay in the markedly different experience of paid employment of men and women. Arguably, the fundamental experience of female paid labour changed little between 1880 and 1950 with women excluded from skilled and well-paid work, segregated into the most routine jobs, lacking the collective strength to socially construct higher status (as the contrast between male cotton spinners and female cotton weavers demonstrates). This did not, strictly speaking, represent a deskilling of work, rather a persistent tendency, within an intensely patriarchal capitalist society (and largely with the collusion of the trade unions) to subordinate female labour (see Chapter 7).

Cumulatively, however, the evidence does indicate a marked transformation in the nature of work over the period 1880–1950, as a consequence of a number of related changes, amongst the most important of which were the tendencies towards deskilling and a marked intensification and regularisation of work. These developments were connected to significant changes in the economy and in business structure and organisation as competition increased, and in employers' attitudes, strategies and the exercise of authority in British workplaces. As labour management methods became more sophisticated, levels of exploitation were intensified and the workplace became increasingly bureaucratised. We turn to an examination of these developments in the exercise of control at work in the next chapter.

4

EXERCISING CONTROL: EMPLOYERS AND THE MANAGEMENT OF LABOUR

Almost all work involves elements of management and discipline. Labour has to be recruited, work has to be organised and as capitalist enterprises became larger, so methods of labour management and control became more sophisticated. As Marx noted, labour is an elastic property and within a capitalist framework requires subordination and control in order to fully exploit its potential for generating surplus value, or profit. Marx argued that by the 1860s in Britain employers had achieved such dominance and control – the real subordination of labour – through the spread of the factory system and mechanisation. This interpretation, however, has been challenged by Marxists and non-Marxists alike and a series of new perspectives have now emerged, providing us with a more nuanced, sensitive picture of managerial methods and the uneven nature of control mechanisms within developed capitalism. The concept of the omnipotent capitalist has been modified and what has emerged from recent research on the exercise of authority at work is recognition of a wide range of strategies utilised by employers to manage labour – the coexistence of direct and indirect, subtle and coercive, simple and complex, bureaucratic modes of control. There were, it appears, many ways to skin the cat. What is clearly evident, is that over the period 1880–1950 employers adjusted and adapted their policies. The imperatives of profit maintenance within the context of more hostile product markets from the 1870s, as we have seen, led to attempts to intensify and fragment labour, fundamentally altering the wage-for-effort exchange. New supervisory and management structures were necessary to facilitate such changes. The reactions of workers and the incubation of strong trade unions also forced employers to modify their management styles and strategies. There was a general transition (though uneven and certainly not unbroken) over 1880–1950 from authoritarian modes of management towards more conciliatory and incorporative strategies: working with the unions, rather than trying to root them out by coercive methods, such as the lockout, eviction and victimisation. This necessitated new management structures, with both an extension of internal management bureaucracy as well as a tendency to externally delegate elements of management to employers' organisations, especially the job of dealing with the demands and actions of the growing trade union movement. Within the company, anachronistic modes of employer paternalism declined, whilst employers embraced welfarist, technical and more bureaucratic modes of controlling labour (see Fitzgerald, 1988; Littler, 1982), becoming more committed, in the process, to methods of 'manufacturing consent' (Burawoy, 1985) and to more direct forms of managing the labour force, initially through the foremen and latterly with a move towards Taylorite, 'scientific' methods of management. All this constituted, by 1950, a marked change in the nature of labour management in Britain.

Exercising the Right to Manage in Late Victorian Britain

Labour management occurred at a number of levels, both internal and external to the firm. However, around 1880, internal management mechanisms predominated. Victorian entrepreneurs were, in the main, fiercely independent believers in the free market, imbued with the notion that the provision of capital conferred the right – often articulated as the 'prerogative' – to manage their enterprises as they thought fit, without interference. At the extreme, this meant authoritarian hire and fire management, with iron discipline on the shop floor. The authoritarian work regimes of mid-Victorian railway companies, ironmasters, coalmasters, shipping lines, engineering companies and textile mills are well documented (Dutton and King, 1982; Melling, 1982; Fraser, 1974; McIvor, 1996). Witness, for example, James Naysmyth's draconian regime in his steam hammer works near Manchester, the arbitrary works rules and regulations in Lord Penryhn's North Wales slate quarries and the rigid conformity to discipline expected of workers in Coats' mills and Dixons' collieries in west Scotland (Cantrell, 1985; Knox, 1995; Melling, 1982; Merfyn-Jones, 1982). The factory system itself represented a shift towards more effective managerial control over labour. Here labour was centralised and subject to the work times and rhythms dictated by employers and their overseers (Thompson, 1963; Burawoy, 1985). By the early 1870s some 23 000 factories existed, employing around 2 million workers (Crouzet, 1982, pp. 80–1). In cotton textiles, perhaps the most advanced sector, mill-owners were already exploiting modern methods of controlling labour, combining technical control and machine pacing with payments by results wage systems. The extensive use of piecework wage payment systems provided a direct and personal inducement upon key workers, such as the mule spinners, to maximise productivity.

We have already noted, however, the dangers of over-extrapolating from the basis of the modernised factory sector. This can also lead to a distorted perspective on the exercise of authority at work. More than 10 million workers – five out of every six in 1880 – worked outside of the factories. Even within the factories, as recent research has shown, it would be quite wrong to assume that late Victorian employers always exercised *direct* control over their labour.

What we now know about the nature of work suggests, as we noted in Chapter 3, that change proceeded at an uneven pace and that there were both centrifugal and centripetal tendencies operating in the second half of the nineteenth century. The domestic, or putting-out system – where merchant-manufacturers provided the raw materials and workers undertook the labour process within their own homes – left workers themselves with almost full control over their pace and rhythm of toil. This system was in decline in face of competition from factory production. Nonetheless, as Schmiechen and Stedman-Jones have shown, it died slowly and persisted into the twentieth century in a number of trades, notably clothing, footwear, hats and other 'sweated' sectors in the big cities. The advantages to employers were numerous: the system required minimal capital investment, spread risks across a great many operating units and relieved employers of the need and cost of directly recruiting, supervising and maintaining a labour force.

In other industries, employers showed a tendency to avoid direct management of labour by the use of subcontractors. This was widespread in building, civil engineering, railways, mining, iron and steel, engineering on the docks and in many of the smaller metalworking trades. On the docks, for example, teams of workers, led by a gang boss, contracted directly for work. This was one of the many grievances of the London dockers which led to the famous 1889 strike. Subcontracting, as Littler has shown, involved employers internally delegating their authority to these intermediate workers, who hired and supervised the labour. For the employer this spread risk and saved the cost and trouble of managing workers. To maximise profit, employers squeezed the subcontractors and they in turn drove their labour harder or cut wages to increase effort (Littler, 1982).

The main embodiment of managerial authority in the workplace around 1880, however, were the foremen – the 'non-commissioned officers' of industry (Melling, 1980). These supervisory workers were directly employed by the firm and were usually promoted upwards from the ranks of the workers. They were primarily responsible for hiring and firing workers, discipline on the shop floor, handling grievances, planning work and controlling the pace of production and determining wage rates. Managerial power was thus effectively designated to this key cadre of supervisory workers, who virtually controlled workers' destinies in this period. Favouritism was rife, with much depending upon a worker's standing with the foreman. Those in favour would be allocated the best-paid work and would be most secure, the last to be paid off during recessions. The basis of the foreman's authority lay in his wide-ranging discretionary powers, delegated down to these supervisors by employers and higher management. Some groups of supervisors retained sympathy and some allegiance to fellow-workers and others earned respect and loyalty through fair treatment and their superior knowledge of tools and processes (see Williams, 1915). An example would be the textile overlookers. Nonetheless most foremen operated by 1880 as the executive arm of management, acting as petty despots driving workers through direct and coercive methods. To some extent the skilled artisans were above this. For most unskilled, female and semi-skilled workers, the late nineteenth-century work regime was one based on fear and intimidation, shading over into sexual harassment, usually from male workers in positions of authority.

What is also significant is the extent to which craftsmen and other privileged groups of workers (such as the spinners and hewers) supervised themselves, retained a great deal of independence over their own labour process and also sometimes recruited and directly controlled their own subordinates, or 'helpers'. Such craft autonomy was common, as we have seen, in metalworking, engineering and shipbuilding. Witness, for example, the extensive work controls of the iron puddler, the toolmaker and the iron moulder. For artisans, much of this control over the labour process was bound up with the desire to maintain craftsmanship and emanated from the fact that only the craftsman had direct knowledge of how a job could be done, imparted through long experience, training and apprenticeship. In the mines, in the bord and pillar system, direct supervision of the miners' work was virtually impossible, hence the reputation of the 'independent collier'. Moreover, pivotal workers such as textile spinners, coal hewers and iron puddlers often hired and controlled their own assistants, who, more often than not, were kin. The 'butty' and 'little marra' systems in the mines and the employment of 'big' and 'little' piecers in cotton spinning are examples. One upshot of this was that the authority structures in late Victorian capitalism were somewhat diffuse. For a great many employees it was fellow-workers and subcontractors who were seen to be the exploiters, rather than the masters themselves, whilst many craftsmen were left with the space to perform their work with minimal interference from employers or their managerial agents.

Having said this, again it is important not to lose a sense of perspective. The craftworkers were, as we have noted, in the minority. In other workplaces, on the land, in domestic service, in transport, in offices and in shops, the hierarchy of supervision and management could be extensive and stultifying, whether via the chargehand, overseer, manager or the foreman. The generally overstocked labour markets of the main urban centres in this period also facilitated managerial control, exercising an invisible but real disciplining force. The mentality of the survival of the fittest is perhaps best expressed in the custom in some docks of throwing brass tallies into the throng of unemployed gathered at the dock gates and employing only the individuals who emerged with them. This reminds us of the degrading and insecure nature of much work for most folk in this era and the draconian methods through which many employers and managers exercised their authority. The sack, together with possible eviction from company housing and blacklisting, faced many workers who failed to toe the line. Power could be exercised brutally.

That is not to suggest, however, that late Victorian masters controlled labour solely through coercive methods. Work regimes varied enormously. Invariably, there was a judicious integration of the carrot and the stick. In periods when labour markets were tight, employers' attitudes mellowed and more consensual as opposed to conflictual strategies prevailed. The long traditions of worker agitation, protest, riot and organisation were partly responsible for tempering employer policies and attitudes. Moreover, whilst paternalist attitudes and policies may well have eroded as industrialisation developed through the nineteenth century, nonetheless they remained, as Joyce and Fitzgerald have demonstrated, very widespread and very effective mechanisms for extending employers' influence, control and authority in the workplace.

Many employers, across a range of industries, continued to act as paternalistic bosses, providing a plethora of welfarist benefits to their employees which, to some extent at least, blunted the harsh realities of low wages and job insecurity which characterised the Victorian labour market. The longer persistence of relatively small-scale, family-owned enterprises facilitated the survival of paternalism in Britain. In his seminal study of northern England, Joyce has demonstrated how mill-owners incubated loyalty to their work regimes and deference to authority through a matrix of compensatory welfarist benefits and company social provision, including pension schemes, sick clubs, mill schools and libraries, savings clubs, factory football and cricket teams and mill socials and sports days (Joyce, 1980). Railway companies and the Quaker food processing companies (Cadbury and Rowntree) offered a similar range of welfarist benefits, amenities and 'perks' (Fitzgerald, 1988). The provision of company housing, as Melling (1981, 1982) has shown, was one of the most pervasive of welfarist

benefits, common in shipbuilding, mining and the railways, especially in more remote locations away from the big cities. Whilst the
degree of acquiescence of workers to such regimes has probably
been exaggerated, still, prior to 1880 the evidence does support
the view that such mechanisms helped management to attract
and maintain their labour force, to increase efficiency and bolster
workplace discipline. It was very difficult to grumble, or down
tools when the result could be the loss of pension rights, or eviction from the company-owned family home. From the employers'
point of view, it was this that made the invariably heavy capital
investment in welfarist schemes (such as housing provision)
worthwhile. Paternalism was also quite blatantly selective. The
father figure of the Victorian entrepreneur had his favoured children. The supervisors, clerical staff and skilled workers were the
major beneficiaries of company largesse around 1880, though,
significantly, there was usually something for all workers within
the embrace of the paternalist employer. This undoubtedly
helped to stabilise industrial relations, incubating a closer association between masters and men, whilst cementing a bond of
loyalty to the company. Whilst rarely complete (as the record
of strike activity shows), acquiescence to employers' authority in
the workplace could be enhanced by this extension of capital's
influence deep into the community.

Management Structures and Employers' Strategies, 1880–1914

Important changes took place in management structures and
employers' strategies in the three decades preceding World War
One as employers reacted, albeit slowly and unevenly, to a series
of developments – increasing competition, eroding profits and
more hostile product markets; tighter labour markets; the germination and growth of trade unions and heightened state intervention.
This period witnessed the consolidation of the foreman as the
central figure of authority in the British workplace and the commensurate decline of the subcontractor. Traditional modes of
company paternalism atrophied and the ability of paternalist
employers to exert control over their labour force waned. The
factory system increased its dominance in manufacturing and
the scale of production rose markedly, with a related increase in

the use of payments by results wage systems. The shift to limited liability corporations introduced the professional works manager, responsible to a board of directors, whilst family-owned, paternalist-inclined firms declined. Industrial relations became more deper-sonalised. With increased capital expenditure on mechanisation and larger factories, employers became more sensitive towards recouping such capital, and as a consequence tightened work-place discipline. In turn, these changes elicited responses from labour, manifested in a surge in collective organisation and the opening out of trade unionism from the artisans to the lesser skilled (see Chapter 8). Where unions gained a foothold, the power rela-tionship between capital and labour was inevitably affected, with a discernible undermining of the ability of the individual entre-preneur to exercise unilateral control within the workplace. As a consequence, employers increasingly formed and joined their own collective organisations. Revisionist historians have attempted to seriously play down the influence, power and unity of these employers' organisations and it is true that employers were not an all-powerful, monolithic block (Tolliday and Zeitlin, 1991; Phelps-Brown, 1983). Nonetheless, by 1914, these employers' organisations were playing a significant role in labour management and the regulation of industrial relations, operating with much success as the guardians of managerial prerogative (Gospel, 1992; McIvor, 1996).

The scale of business enterprise in Britain increased markedly over 1880–1914 as family firms gave way to the modern business corporation. This brought the modern works manager and, in the larger plants, a more sophisticated managerial hierarchy of func-tionalised supervisors, coordinated through the planning and personnel departments (Hannah, 1976; Littler, 1982). Singer in Clydebank, Westinghouse and Ford in Manchester provide examples. Over the economy as a whole, the number of supervi-sors and managers increased (see Tables 2.11 and 2.12). There were limits to this process, however, as Chandler and others have shown that family dynasties often managed to retain control on the new boards of directors and the emergence of a group of professional managers was slower in Britain than either the USA or Germany. There was a tendency, noted in the last chapter, for British employers to eschew new methods, to favour *ad hoc* managerial techniques and labour-intensive production methods over capital-intensive ones.

The engagement of subcontractors did, however, decline. Littler has argued that this was both as a consequence of work group and trade union opposition to subcontractors' 'slave-driving' and 'because new ideas, new methods and new technology influenced many employers to reach down for more control over the shop floor' (Littler, 1982, p. 79). The squeeze on profits facilitated this move towards eliminating the middlemen, who had all but disappeared from the British workplace by World War One. The foremen became the pivotal managerial agent at the point of production. Indeed, this period marked the peak of the foreman's power in the British workplace. There was a discernible shift over these years, moreover, with the foremen increasingly relating to management rather than to the men. This can be witnessed in the decline in trade union membership amongst foremen and the increased affiliation to employer-controlled welfarist organisations, such as the Foremen's Mutual Benefit Society in engineering and shipbuilding (Melling, 1980; Burgess, 1986). The provision of company housing to managers, supervisors and foremen, as Melling has shown, also helped to solidify their commitment to the company and their place in the hierarchy as agents of capital. A chairman of John Brown's shipyard on the Clyde noted in 1916 that company housing 'was not all philanthropy, but hard-headed business to separate the foremen from the men' (Knox, 1999, p. 152).

At the same time, traditional paternalism was declining as an explicit labour control strategy. Joyce and Knox have charted this transition in case studies of northern England and Scotland. Joyce relates this decline to the rise of the large business corporations and the disappearance of the family firm, together with the close personal relationships that the traditional company structure engendered. Changes in the workforce, the growth of trade unionism and growing class-consciousness also ate into the foundations of paternalist authority before 1914 (Knox, 1999, pp. 152–3, and 1995). Savage has argued the case that over the long term this atrophying of paternalism was also connected to the growth of alternative state welfare services. Important here in the pre-1914 period were the passage of Workmen's Compensation Acts (1896, 1907) and the clutch of Liberal reforms from 1906 which included pensions (1908), the creation of the Trade Boards (1909), Labour Exchanges (1909) and National Insurance (1911). Moreover, whilst *ad hoc* paternalism remained widespread, Littler has shown that only a handful of British firms on the eve of World War One could be considered to be systematic welfarists, indicated in the fact that only 60–70 welfare secretaries were employed in industry in 1914. Workers, unions and foremen were all frequently hostile to company welfarism. Few companies included full job security in their basket of benefits, and lay-offs, underemployment and wage cuts were endemic within manufacturing pre-1914. George Askwith, the government's main pre-1914 industrial relations troubleshooter, observed:

> Although there were many employers with vision who... were continuously out for improvements and who thought of the welfare of their men in and out of the shops, and strove for good ventilation, cleanliness, amenities and recreation, it cannot be said that the majority did more than comply with the bare necessities required by the Factory Acts (Askwith, 1920, pp. 353–4).

Nonetheless, the evidence does suggest that paternalism survived as an important labour control strategy within a significant, if a minority strand of employers, including Lever, Cadbury, Rowntree and sectors where production continued to be small scale, such as the potteries, wool and worsted, brewing and footwear (Fitzgerald, 1988, pp. 10–11). Increasingly, though, employers and managers were looking inward, to tighter workplace discipline and work reorganisation to facilitate control and maximise profit.

In line with reorganisation of production and mechanisation, employers tightened discipline and control. Hence, many workers found themselves more closely watched and monitored at the point of production. As the longwall work methods in mining proceeded, and coal cutters were introduced, so the number of supervisors rose in the pits. Similarly on the railways, where discipline had always been heavily enforced, levels of supervision, fining and testing workers' capabilities and health increased. The same was true of the Royal Ordnance Factories in the 1890s, as we have seen. Everywhere, the intensification of competition led to tighter discipline and surveillance, exercised through an ever-growing army of foremen. Alfred Williams noted such tendencies with disgust in his portrayal of work in the Great Western Railway works in Swindon. To Williams, the new types of supervisors lacked respect for craftsmanship and their bullying methods (combined with blatant bribery and favouritism) sapped workers' morale and energy, extracting all the joy out of work. Tighter supervision facilitated the intensification of work pace. So too did the spread of piecework and bonus wage payment systems, as we saw in Chapter 3. These developments took place in tandem with job fragmentation and work reorganisation which in themselves had a labour control function: a deskilled workforce was not only cheaper to employ, but more flexible, more easily replaced, more directly managed and less autonomous.

The other major change was the growing tendency on the part of British employers to delegate externally elements of labour management and control. The proliferating employers' organisations – which increased in number from 336 in 1895 to 1487 by 1914 – came to strengthen the hands of employers, particularly when dealing with trade unions (Garside and Gospel, 1982; Gospel, 1992; McIvor, 1996). By 1914, a formidable matrix of industrywide federations and local employers' associations existed (see Table 4.1).

The main *raison d'être* of an employers' organisation was to protect managerial prerogatives against the 'encroachments' of trade unions. In the 1880s and 1890s, many employers' organisations bolstered managerial authority by providing what the Shipping Federation termed 'a permanent battle-axe' against the emerging 'socialistic' unions. A plethora of coercive strike-breaking and union-busting weapons enabled employers' associations to root out workers' organisations, or at least limit their influence, thus retaining the essence of the individually negotiated labour contract between master and man, determined by the market mechanism (McIvor, 1984). As trade union power was consolidated, with the capability of unions to sustain long strikes, so employers were forced to rethink their labour relations strategies. Trade unions in the workplace constituted a major challenge to managerial authority and gradually employers in industry after industry shifted from authoritarian modes of control towards more consensual and collaborative behaviour. In essence this represented a shift from unilateral towards procedural forms of control through formalised collective bargaining mechanisms and stage-by-stage disputes procedures designed to neutralise industrial

Table 4.1   Employers' associations in Britain, 1914

Sectors / industries	Number of associations (local, regional and national)	
Building	468	
Food, drink, tobacco	166	
Iron, steel, metals	144	
Paper, printing	116	
Newspapers		4
Textiles	99	
Cotton		35
Wool, worsted, shoddy		24
Finishing		18
Clothing	84	
Tailoring		54
Boot and shoe		23
Transport and communication	69	
Railways		1
Road		40
Water		28
Engineering	56	
Woodworking, furnishing	52	
Mining and quarrying	38	
Coal		24
Personal service	31	
Laundering, dyeing		29
Hairdressing		1
Undertaking		1
Shipbuilding	25	
Bricks, pottery, glass	25	
Agriculture and fishing	10	
Chemicals	2	
Total employers' associations	1 487	

Note: The figures include only associations concerned with labour relations and exclude trade and technical associations, including chambers of commerce.
Source: Ministry of Labour, *Eighteenth Abstract of Labour Statistics*, 1926, p. 191.

conflict. Even areas where there was a particularly entrenched authoritarian capitalist culture, such as Clydeside, witnessed a distinct move in the direction of conciliation and collective bargaining by 1914 (Johnston, 1997).

This enhanced managerial control and discipline in a number of ways. The formalised rules and regulations channelled grievances into procedures which initially favoured the employers' side and muzzled spontaneous industrial action, including 'wildcat' strikes. Union officials, moreover, acted as policemen over the collectively bargained agreements. Unions came to refuse to support industrial action that occurred before the formal procedures were exhausted, and strike pay could be refused if workers downed tools in breach of agreement. The employers' organisations facilitated systematic victimisation of 'troublemakers', through widely circulated blacklists, 'character' notes and the custom of the 'enquiry note'. The lockout and the lockout threat were also used to good effect to curtail the effectiveness of the sectional 'rolling' strike where concessions achieved by the unions at one firm were snowballed throughout a region or industry.

This is not to imply, however, that the pre-1914 employers' organisations were everywhere successful. Indeed, with the emergence of strong trade unions and employers' organisations what occurred was a constant struggle over the control of work, the outcome of which depended upon the relative power of each group, which in turn was much influenced by the prevailing state of product and labour markets, and the attitudes of the state and the public, amongst other factors. The frontier of control and the basis of authority at the point of production was a shifting one. Moreover, the capacity of employers' organisations to regulate working conditions, such as wages and hours, was undermined by internal divisions of interest and competitive pressures, as Zeitlin, Phelps Brown, Reid and others have demonstrated. It was also the case that collective bargaining dealt primarily with wages and conditions, leaving most other areas to the discretion of internal management. Furthermore, the unions also got something out of collective bargaining. It conferred higher status and recognition and a direct say in the regulation of wages and conditions (see Chapter 8).

Whilst such revisionist perspectives, in my view, have rather underestimated the power and capabilities of organised capital, nonetheless the point that capital was no unified and monolithic entity is a valid one. Whilst their powers were limited, nonetheless the complex matrix of employers' organisations that had emerged in Britain by 1914 undoubtedly played a major role in facilitating work intensification and bolstering managerial control at the point of production. This has been shown in the case of cotton and wool textiles, building and engineering and in case studies of Clydeside capitalism (McIvor, 1996; Magrath, 1988; Johnston, 1997). In the 1890s, as Garside and Gospel have argued, the employers' organisations took the initiative in creating industry-wide agreements in cotton, coal, footwear and engineering 'as a means of reasserting managerial prerogatives, constraining trade union activity, and bringing order and stability into their industries' (Garside and Gospel, 1982, p. 105). The extent to which this formalisation of industrial relations had developed is indicated by the fact that by 1910–14, 85 per cent of all strikes were being settled by negotiation, conciliation and arbitration. Employers' organisations thus bolstered managerial discipline, exerting some control over unions and their main weapon – the strike – whilst increasingly becoming a source of formal rules governing employment relations. In response to their authority being threatened in the workplace by the emergence of the trade unions, employers increasingly shifted the determination of basic wages and working conditions from within the firm to the realm of collective bargaining. Despite the prognostications of revisionists, the Engineering Terms of Settlement of 1898 did facilitate deskilling, the subversion of apprenticeship, the spread of piecework wage payment and the staffing of machinery with cheaper semi-skilled and female labour (McIvor, 1996, pp. 125–32). Moreover, collective bargaining pre-1914 helped employers to muzzle spontaneous industrial action and delay change. This proved especially frustrating in periods of tight labour markets. Over 1910–14 workers' grievances over what they regarded as the unfair working of procedure accelerated, and in several cases agreements were formally abrogated (including the Engineering 'Terms' and the 1892 Brooklands Agreement in cotton).

Before 1914 though, the power and influence of employers' organisations ranged widely across the economy. They were relatively strong in coal, cotton, engineering, shipbuilding, printing and construction and weak in iron and steel, transport, distribution, quarrying, chemicals and clothing. This mirrored the patchy coverage of trade unions (see Table 8.3). Whilst employers' organisations were strong at the local level, their powers were undermined by regional and sectional splits, whilst *national* collective bargaining was still relatively weak pre-1914. The majority of employers remained non-members prior to World War One and company-level managerial policies and internal authority structures thus remained of paramount importance.

Towards Rationalisation, Taylorism and *Real* Subordination of Labour, 1914–50

There exists much debate over the extent to which labour management methods were transformed in Britain in the first half of the twentieth century and the nature of this process, which is intimately linked to the managerial philosophies of Taylor, Bedaux and Ford. On the one hand are those social historians of work who emphasise the revolution that occurred in management methods, the deep penetration of scientific management ideas and practices to the British shop floor by 1950 and the related removal of authority and independence from workers and traditional foremen, with power, planning and decision-making transferred to the employers and the office (Braverman, 1974; Knox, 1999; Whitston, 1996). Bedaux may well have played a key role in this process, as Littler has argued, though recent research suggests a more diffuse process, where Taylorite ideas and endogenous managerial innovations (such as premium bonus) spread widely in a piecemeal fashion, through various conduits to the British workplace (see Gospel, 1992; Whitston, 1996). On the other hand, 'revisionist' historians have emphasised the limited penetration of rationalised and functionalised management, the weakness of internal management structures, the survival of craft control and workplace independence and the anachronistic character of British labour management (Zeitlin, 1991; McKinlay and Zeitlin, 1989; Reid, 1992).

In his writings and consultancy work in the USA in the 1890s and 1900s, Taylor challenged employers directly to exercise their authority in the workplace; to reach down and wrest control and power from the workers. His system, enshrined in *The Principles of Scientific Management* published in 1911, necessitated 'a complete revolution in the mental attitude and the habits of all those engaged in management' (Taylor, 1976 edn, p. 131). The main objective of Taylor and the other work study specialists was to replace the *ad hoc* unsystematised 'rule of thumb' managerial techniques prevalent in industry with scientific methods of management and control which would maximise productivity. The methods of the efficiency engineers varied, but usually included detailed analysis of the way that work was performed, with operations being timed with a stopwatch and motions and effort expended closely analysed (the motion experts used film for this purpose). In this way management accrued the knowledge of how jobs were performed which had previously resided with the workers. This led to a restructuring of the labour process along more 'efficient' lines, which invariably involved more detailed division of labour, a curtailment of worker discretion in how the job was performed and a more flexible, adaptable, interchangeable and casualised workforce.

We have explored some of these implications in the previous chapter. What concerns us here are the new structures and strategies of labour management which Taylorism produced – the process by which management took control over the organisation of the work, directing the employees in how to perform their jobs. Invariably, this became the role of the company planning department which directed workers to undertake their specified, standardised tasks, with detailed instructions on how the labour process was to be undertaken, and the allotted time allowed for each task. Job fragmentation inevitably resulted, affecting not only the skilled craft artisans but also semi-skilled 'process' workers, the supervisors and foremen. Taylorite systems broke up the foreman's job, creating a clutch of functionalised supervisors with more prescribed roles – setting-up; 'speed and feed men'; quality inspectors; maintenance and repair – and extracting the powers of hiring and firing from the foremen, which became the function of the personnel department. Incentives were built into the new managerial regime, notably payments by results wage schemes that promised considerable increases in earnings as compensation for work restructuring. Taylor's wage bonus scheme, which incorporated, in principle, the potential to double workers' earnings, was described by one employers' journal as the 'lubricant' (*The Engineer*, 14 Nov. 1913, p. 521). Significantly, Taylor's system had no role for paternalism or any interaction with the worker in the community. Taylor focused solely within the factory gates and upon the point of production to extend managerial control and erode workers' autonomy and authority.

To what extent had Taylorism transformed the management of labour in Britain by 1950? The first point that might be made is that Taylor was a synthesiser of ideas about rationalising management and the efficiency engineering movement was much wider than just Taylor. There were distinct moves in the direction of 'scientific management' within Britain, with a whole genre of management literature and practical experiments in work rationalisation (e.g. in the arms firms) and new wage systems, namely premium bonus, before World War One. Already, in the pre-1914 period, there were the first signs that this was resulting in some erosion of the power of the foreman (Littler, 1982, pp. 96–7) and Whitston noted how the 'fracturing of conception and execution . . . was developing independently in British engineering workshops from the turn of the century' (Whitston, 1996, p. 51). Secondly, the evidence suggests that the initial response to Taylorist ideas in Britain was a lukewarm one: certainly British management were more sceptical and markedly less receptive than their counterparts in the USA, Germany, Italy and France before 1914 (Littler, 1982, pp. 94–5). This was linked to poor management education in Britain and entrepreneurial conservatism, as well as fear of labour opposition in a period of tight labour markets and escalating labour militancy over 1910–14. There were *some* direct experiments with Taylorist methods, such as at the Singer corporation in Clydebank over 1910–14, but these were rare occurrences (Glasgow Labour History Workshop, 1989; for a view to the contrary see Burgess, 1980, pp. 83–4).

Thirdly, notwithstanding this slow start, the evidence overwhelmingly supports the thesis that Taylorist ideas diffused widely throughout British *manufacturing* industry over the period 1914–50. The inter-war Depression and the two world wars acted as incubators of new production management ideas, promoting time and motion study, flow production methods, deskilling and new managerial structures and methods. Around 250 of Britain's largest manufacturing firms directly used Bedaux methods between the wars and 'as a result Bedaux became the most commonly used system of managerial control in British industry' (Littler, 1982, p. 114). What this meant was tighter controls over workers, a loss of discretion and autonomy, closer links between effort and earnings

and more intrusive monitoring and surveillance over work. Glucksmann has noted such tendencies in the inter-war assembly-line
industries in domestic appliances, motor car parts, electrical
engineering, clothing and food processing.

However, Littler may well have exaggerated the pivotal role
played by the Bedaux system. Recent research suggests that the
conduits through which Taylorist ideas spread through to British
management were much more diffuse and the Bedaux system was
not necessarily the most important. Whitston has recently argued
this case:

> The real history of scientific management in Britain is to be
> found in the pragmatic adoption, by engineers and managers,
> of elements of Taylor's system, rather than the 'system' itself,
> and in the development of production engineering which
> removed the planning and control of production from the shop
> floor to the office (Whitston, 1996, p. 48).

This occurred, for example, in Rowntree's works and in the major
car companies without the employment of the Bedaux management consultants. The Industrial Health (previously Fatigue)
Research Board and the National Institute of Industrial Psychology also undertook quite detailed work studies in the 1920s and
1930s and acted as disseminators of scientific management ideas,
albeit in a somewhat more 'humanised' form (McIvor, 1987b).
Whether through Bedaux or in other ways, what is evident is that
many of the largest manufacturing companies and industry leaders
in Britain practised scientific management methods by the end of
the 1940s, including the main car companies (Ford, Austin, Morris),
ICI, Wolsey, Lucas, Westinghouse, Ferranti, Hoover, Morphy-
Richards, Cadbury, Rowntree, Lyons, Courtaulds. By 1950, some
employers' organisations were also directly promoting work
study and scientific management, including in some of the older
'staple' sectors, for example the Federation of Master Cotton
Spinners' Associations.

The increasing sophistication of labour management is demonstrated in the rising number of supervisors, managers and administrators in Britain. Table 2.11 showed how numbers of foremen,
inspectors and supervisors rose from 236 000 (1.3 per cent of the
labour force) in 1911 to 590 000 (2.6 per cent of the total) in 1951.

Similarly, the numbers of managers and administrators doubled from 629 000 to 1.2 million, or from 3.4 to 5.5 per cent of the total labour force. In manufacturing and mining, the number of managers and administrators grew by some 130 per cent between 1921 and 1951 (Whitston, 1996, p. 52). Another clear indicator of the growth of professional management can be found in the formation and membership of professional bodies. By 1939 there were 800 members of the Institution of Labour Management and around 2000 members of the Institution of Production Engineers. At the end of World War Two an organisation representing time-and-motion experts and rate-fixers was also established and the British Institute of Management was created in 1948 (Whitston, 1996, pp. 53, 60). In the industry leaders in British manufacturing, labour management techniques and the organisation of the labour process had been radically transformed. The impact of these tendencies in British industry is clear enough. Here at least, authority at the point of production had been wrested from the workers and control effectively located in the hands of management.

Nonetheless, the extent and the pace of change should not be exaggerated. This all needs to be kept in perspective. Urwick and Brech noted in their survey of the scientific management movement that knowledge of Taylorism was still poor in 1939 and estimated that only around one in ten British companies had actually introduced elements of scientific management. Gospel (1992), McIvor (1996) and McKinlay and Zeitlin (1989) have all emphasised the tendency of employers between the wars to resort to traditional methods of intensifying work with a range of labour relations strategies, including external delegation and institutionalised welfarism (see also Fitzgerald, 1988). Opposition from both workers and foremen and a clutch of strikes retarded the progress of the Bedaux system and modified its impact in the 1930s (Littler, 1982, pp. 117–45).

Unfortunately, we lack detailed research on the spread of scientific management during the 1940s. Nonetheless, evidence suggests that World War Two provided a further boost to the efficiency engineers and the 1940s undoubtedly witnessed further significant bureaucratisation of work, with more sophisticated management structures and a commensurate erosion in workers' independence and discretion at the point of production. Workers' opposition was more muted (the TUC officially supported Taylorism from 1933), whilst the popularity of American productionist ideas was again rising in contrast to the inter-war period, when such ideas were associated with the loss of employment and degradation of skills.

However, management restructuring along Taylorite lines was extremely uneven. It should be stressed that 'scientific management' was still only the practice of the largest manufacturing companies, most evidently in the newer, mass production industries. In 1950, systematic work study and sophisticated management structures were rare in teaching and the professions, office work, administration and the civil service, in construction, transport and communications, in mining, in shipbuilding, in agriculture and only in its infancy in textile manufacture (where it expanded rapidly in the 1950s) (Whitston, 1996, pp. 60–1). Traditional authority structures persisted in these occupations, including the power of the foreman and line supervisor, whilst more reliance was placed on intensification of workers' effort in customary ways, especially during the Depression. Moreover, there were countervailing tendencies. The resurgence of trade unionism and the power of workplace organisation, with the revival of the shop stewards from the mid-1930s, created an alternative locus of power and authority on the shop floor (see Chapter 8).

In tandem with the adoption of elements of Taylorism, moreover, managerial authority was enhanced by other means, notably through company welfarist policies designed to inculcate loyalty to the firm, undermine trade unions and induce better industrial relations. Managerial authority was bolstered further from 1914 by an extension of employers' organisations and a developing system of external delegation whereby more areas of the employment relationship became regulated outside the workplace and subject to increasingly formalised collective bargaining.

Whilst the *ex gratia* form of employer paternalism was increasingly being seen as anachronistic, it continued within some sectors where small-to-medium-scale production persisted, including the potteries, brewing, wool and worsted and footwear. Moreover, more systematic company welfarism expanded, as Fitzgerald has shown, especially in the newer industries from World War One. Company pension provision grew markedly in the 1920s (Gospel, 1987, pp. 179–80). The railway companies and the gas industry

continued to heavily favour an explicitly welfarist labour management strategy and their monopoly position facilitated the finan-
cing of quite sophisticated schemes (Fitzgerald, 1988, pp. 184–5).
Company-based welfarism was also evident in metal manufacture,
glass (Pilkingtons), shipbuilding, tobacco, electrical engineering and
paper manufacture. Also, in some cotton manufacturing companies, notably Coats (Knox, 1995; Jones, 1988). In some cases, institutionalised benefits and company sports and welfare amenities
helped to take the edge off impersonal corporate management
and the stultifying effects of Taylorite work reorganisation and
deskilling mechanisation. The Singer Corporation, for example,
introduced a range of welfarist schemes and provision – including
massive sports facilities and a social club – in the decade after the
1911 strike in an attempt to divert workers from the attractions of
industrial unionism and rebuild a company ethos. Similarly, ICI
sweetened the pill of scientific management by an extensive programme of welfare benefits between the wars. The quiescent
industrial relations records of both plants between 1920 and 1950
testify to the success of such schemes in assuaging industrial
conflict. ICI experienced a drastic fall in union membership, from
around 60 to around 20 per cent of the workforce. Some of the
traditional stalwarts of personalised paternalism, including the
Quaker employers Rowntree and Cadbury, moved in the opposite direction, bolting on a more explicit commitment to Taylorism
to their existing welfarist work regimes. This was indicative of a
growing convergence between the 'human factor' management
theorists and the Taylorists which congealed into personnel management and the 'work study' movement of post-1945. By 1939
there were about 1800 welfare officers employed in British industry, something of an indication of the propensity of British capital
to balance the use of both the carrot and the stick in their
approaches to the management of labour (Gospel, 1987, p. 179).
However, it remained largely the big corporations in the new,
more buoyant industries and/or in monopoly market positions
that had the resources and more sophisticated managerial structures, as well as the profit margins, to sustain a deep commitment
to systematic welfarist labour control strategies.

    Parallel with the evolution of more sophisticated and bureaucrat-
ised internal labour management structures and more formalised
company welfarist policies of labour control, employers increasingly

devolved crucial aspects of labour management, work regulation and industrial relations to external bodies. This trend was clearly evident before World War One, though in 1914 the coverage of employers' organisations remained patchy and their role in regulating industrial relations was uneven and largely confined to the local and regional levels. Outside of cotton textiles, there existed no national system of collective bargaining, though in coal, ship-building and engineering national wage movements were being decided on top of a basic system of standardised district wage rates. During the decade or so from 1914, however, employers' organisations were significantly strengthened and national collective bargaining was rapidly extended. The coverage and membership of employers' organisations massively increased. This occurred vertically, in the sense that existing organisations attracted a larger proportion of their respective industries – and horizontally, with the formation of a plethora of industry-wide federations, specialist employers' agencies (such as the Economic League) and the formation of the first effective employers' confederations – the Federation of British Industries (1916) and the National Confederation of Employers' Organisations (1919). This growth was in reaction to the surge in trade union membership and escalation of industrial conflict in the 'radical decade' starting c. 1910, and a knee-jerk response against the challenge of the war-time shop stewards movement and the spectre of socialism and 'bolshevism' in the workplace. Employers were also encouraged to combine together to more effectively represent the interests of capital in relation to a more interventionist state increasingly encroaching into areas of labour relations and managerial prerogative, especially during the war years. By the late 1930s around half of all British workers were employed in firms which were members of employers' organisations – an organised proportion well in excess of that achieved by the trade unions, which were critically weakened after 1920 by mass unemployment.

Organised capital helped employers to accommodate to and exert some control over the burgeoning trade union movement which was perceived as a direct challenge to managerial authority at the point of production. They strove to protect managerial prerogatives and strengthen workplace discipline, bolstered attempts to cut wages, intensify workloads and rationalise production, and succeeded in extending the system of national collective bargaining across a wide swathe of British industry. However, this process was uneven across different sectors and much influenced by the nature of labour and product markets. During the period 1914–20 employers' organisations were very much on the defensive, forced by tight labour markets, wartime circumstances and government policies into more accommodative, flexible and co-operative relationships with organised labour. The state directly encouraged employers to formally recognise trade unions and regulate working conditions through collective bargaining. This strategy was enshrined in the Whitley Committees from 1917, where the government created collective bargaining mechanisms for many of the least organised industries which lacked voluntary provision. Such changes, together with the encroachments into production management by the wartime shop stewards, were interpreted by employers as a serious infringement into sacrosanct managerial prerogatives and an erosion of the tight workplace discipline and control necessary for the maintenance of competitiveness.

The onset of economic recession from 1920 and the subsequent two decades of depression and mass unemployment provided the opportunity for employers to move on to the offensive. A multipronged 'counter-attack' ensued, with the employers' organisations spearheading a campaign to cut labour costs, victimise labour activists, neutralise industrial conflict and reassert managerial prerogative and employers' unilateral control over production management. This was most evident in the older, most depressed staple sectors of the economy. In cotton textiles the employers' organisations revived a series of coercive weapons to discipline the unions, including the victimisation of activists, labour replacement in strikes and the lockout threat, which was used effectively through the 1920s to circumvent individual mill strikes on at least five occasions (McIvor, 1996, pp. 186–8). The cotton associations successfully resurrected and defended the fining system as an essential element of mill discipline, beating back trade union challenges in 1926–7 and 1929–30. Scathing wage cuts were imposed in cotton manufacture in several waves between the wars, whilst the formal system of collective bargaining was also suspended by the employers' organisations in 1932 to facilitate wage undercutting and speed-up. Such actions underwrote and energised a resurgence of unilateral managerial control in the mills, which, as we argued in the last chapter, bolstered the capacity of individual mill-owners to increase workloads.

Similarly in coal mining, the owners exploited the changed economic circumstances to initiate an attack on what was perhaps the most powerful union within the British economy. In a series of disputes, culminating in the General Strike of 1926 and the miners' lockout, the mine-owners reasserted their authority, forcing the union to accept increased working hours, trenchant wage cuts and a return to district level collective bargaining. Mass unemployment, employer intransigence, industrial defeat and demoralisation led to a collapse in trade union membership in mining between 1920 and 1933 from around 90 per cent to a little over 50 per cent of all those employed. Many contemporary sources, including Coombes' panoramic autobiography, testify to the stultifying control and subordination that miners faced in the pits in the 1920s and 1930s as the mine-owners pressed forward their advantage and reasserted their prerogative to manage their collieries as they thought fit.

Engineering is a less clear-cut case, and has been subject to much debate and disagreement. On the one hand it has been argued that the EEF spearheaded the employers' inter-war offensive against labour because this was where the shop stewards' movement had made the deepest inroads into managerial prerogative during the war (Hinton, 1973; McIvor, 1996). Zeitlin argues, conversely, that engineering employers were weak and divided and patently failed to resurrect workplace discipline, oversee a transformation in work organisation or even significantly influence industrial relations. Engineering was a particularly diffuse industry and outcomes differed across traditional and new sections of engineering. Moreover, the employers' counter-attack in engineering did not go unchallenged. Nonetheless, there remains substantial evidence of employer success in the drive in engineering to re-establish managerial rights. Victimisation and systematic blacklisting were used widely from 1918 to remove those whom the employers regarded as the most dangerous threats to workshop discipline – including many of the leaders of the wartime shop stewards movement. Later, the EEF was one of the main supporters of the Economic League which provided a centralised blacklisting service for British employers for the first time from 1926 (McIvor, 1988). The 1922 engineering lockout

ended with the EEF successfully forcing the Amalgamated Engineering Union to accept a restated managerial functions clause,
which clearly recognised the right of employers to manage production without interference from the unions. Moreover, to press the
point home, the 1922 settlement was unilaterally imposed upon
50 other unions within engineering. This was no hollow success
quickly reversed by strong trade unions, but, as Gospel has shown,
a 'substantial victory' which 'was to undermine the position of
the engineering union, especially at shop-floor level, for over a
decade' (Gospel, 1987, p. 171). Industrial relations were stabil-
ised: time lost through industrial disputes slumped from 17.5
million working days in 1922, to 6 million in 1923, 1.4 million in
1924 and then averaged only 183 000 days lost per year over the
period 1925–34 (Mitchell and Deane, 1976, p. 72). Moreover, the
evidence for north-west England suggests that the engineering
employers' victory facilitated a reassertion of employers' discretionary power and authority. This enabled the intensification of
work, the achievement of significant productivity gains, further
extension of payments by results wage systems, and the erosion of
some time-honoured 'protective' or 'restrictive' (depending on
your point of view) practices (McIvor, 1996, pp. 246–60).

Elsewhere, especially in the newer industries, more progressive
employer attitudes prevailed, as indicated in the Mond–Turner
talks of 1927–9. However, the failure of the talks in the face of
NCEO opposition indicates the extent to which industrialists were
intent on using the recession to minimise trade union influence,
prevent unions having the power to veto or discuss matters relating
to production management and thus retain managerial discretion
and prerogative. Significantly, however, national collective bargaining endured and employers stopped short of using the Depression
as an opportunity to root out trade unionism from the British
shop floor. Indeed, trade union recognition spread downwards to
an increasing number of unskilled, female and clerical workers'
organisations, whilst more and more employers came to realise
the benefits of a formalised industrial relations system in stabilising industrial relations.

All this is not to imply that the power of organised capital did
not go unchallenged. The capacity of work groups and trade
unions to resist may well have been undermined by the recession,
but what is surprising is the extent to which struggle continued in

some sectors, especially when traditional work customs were challenged. An example would be cotton textiles where a series of strikes took place in the early 1930s against work intensification, including the 'more looms' system (despite over 40 per cent unemployment). Clegg (1985) has also argued that the slower rate of wage cuts in the second recession of 1929–32 (compared to 1920–2) was a reflection of employer wariness born from experience of the General Strike of 1926 and the residual capacity of labour to resist, even during periods of mass unemployment. At the local level, moreover, as Zeitlin (1991) has shown for engineering, union branches and work groups were capable of subverting some elements of the 1922 settlement and retaining a degree of control and authority at the point of production. This was especially the case in shipbuilding and the more buoyant newer sectors of light engineering (such as aircraft manufacture) developing between the wars.

Revisionist historians have developed such arguments into an assertion that employers were distinctively weak, divided and ineffectual in imposing their authority upon the unions and within the workplace. This is an over-extrapolation from the experience of a small set of examples, predominantly engineering and shipbuilding. It is one thing to stress internal divisions of interest within employers' organisations and centrifugal tendencies leading to breakaways, disloyalty and a lack of consensus. However, this can obscure fundamental tendencies within British capitalism at this time. Notwithstanding the revisionist arguments, it remains the case that the inter-war years represented a period when employers' power and managerial authority were strengthened. This control was expressed through a revival of more brutal, coercive tactics in the Depression *as well as* a broader commitment to utilising formal national collective bargaining and disputes procedures to neutralise industrial conflict and impose discipline and order to industrial relations. Moreover, whilst clearly not omnipotent, the proliferating matrix of industry-wide employers' organisations clearly played a key role in this process.

In many respects World War Two marked a critical watershed in employer strategies and labour management in Britain. The wartime crisis, state intervention, the revival of trade union power and the return to full employment combined to drastically shift the balance of power in the workplace from capital to labour. This process was already discernible as rearmament gathered pace from the mid-1930s. The challenge to managerial authority at work in the 1940s came from two sources: from the state as it took control of the war economy in the national interest; and from below, as workers' bargaining power, confidence and capabilities revived.

One response was to strengthen employers' collective organisations. Middlemas sees this as a period of consolidation when employers' associations and trade unions came to dominate industrial relations, operating as 'estates of the realm'. More employers and workers were covered by national collective bargaining arrangements in the late 1940s than at any other time, and throughout the period from 1940 to 1951 the state added a further tier of compulsory arbitration (under order 1305). This, and other wartime restrictions such as the Essential Works Order, were as effective as during World War One in extending control over labour and stabilising industrial relations. Perhaps even more so. Strikes and lockouts were technically illegal and whilst the number of strikes did rise, working days lost through strikes remained at a very low level during the 1940s – indeed at around half the level of World War One. Virtually everywhere the employers were on the defensive during wartime. Their position was weakened by a widespread sense, picked up in the Mass Observation studies, of managerial incompetence, nepotism, favouritism and profiteering (Mass Observation, 1942, pp. 233–5). Price has argued persuasively that during the war years managerial prerogatives were sacrificed to maximise production for the war effort (Price, 1986, pp. 190–204). Unilateral managerial control was seriously eroded during wartime and replaced with joint regulation: 'the main effect of the draconian state regulation of the labour contract was to diminish enormously the prerogatives and powers of the employers' (Price, 1986, p. 191).

The Essential Works Order and the creation of joint production committees (JPCs) heralded a change in social relations on the shop floor whereby power was stripped from management and effective joint regulation of work and production matters established. This was on the initiative of Ernest Bevin, Minister of Labour, whose wartime controls and regulations seriously restrained management's room for manoeuvre and had a liberating impact in the workplace. By 1944 there were JPCs in 4500 factories and they were effectively regulating areas of production management that had previously been regarded as sacrosanct to management. From an initial focus on welfare, the JPCs' functions extended to discussion of machine staffing and the organisation of production, wage setting and bonuses, vetos over dilution, and issues of discipline, including absenteeism. As Arthur Exell noted: 'the bosses didn't dare do anything' (Price, 1986, p. 191). Hinton's recent study has shown how the warrening of industry with shop stewards in the 1940s facilitated this drifting encroachment into areas of managerial prerogative and revived concepts of workers' control (Hinton, 1994).

These developments put pressure on the multi-employer-driven industrial relations system. Paradoxically, perhaps, there were already signs of a weakening of the influence of employers' organisations and the control they exercised over their own members. As early as 1942 a Mass Observation study noted the conservatism of employers' associations and their failure to absorb the changes brought by the war, commenting: 'they are generally well behind individual employers in their approach to the present and the future' (Mass Observation, 1942, p. 235). By 1950 there existed a noticeable difference between nationally agreed wages and conditions and the actual working conditions, where the tendency was to pay a premium above what multi-employer bargaining allowed. Here was tangible evidence of slippage in the authority of employers' associations. Whilst still only a tendency, what was already apparent in 1950 was a weakening of the system of externally delegated control through powerful employers' organisations, with the initiative returning to the individual company. The growing scale of business enterprise facilitated this drift back to a more atomised industrial relations system. The bigger corporations were increasingly preferring to tailor their own personnel strategies to their own perceived needs and market niches. This can be seen in the growing popularity of plant-level productivity bargaining as management struggled to find solutions to the main labour problems of post-1945 – the productivity gap, high wage costs, poor work relations and the persistence of what employers regarded as 'restrictive' practices (Gospel, 1996). Many employers were also alienated by the tendency of employers' organisations to abdicate leadership, paralysed by internal divisions and undermined by governments in the 1940s that clearly favoured labour over the managerial interest. Witness, for example, the failure of employers' organisations to stand up to strikes in the good years of the late 1940s and 1950s and in their failure to campaign against the JPCs in the immediate postwar years (Middlemas, 1979, pp. 399–400).

Clearly, the balance of power had shifted quite decisively during the 1940s, resulting in a marked diminution of the authority of employers and management. Zweig's study in 1952 demonstrates this quite clearly:

> There is no doubt that autocracy in British industry belongs to the past. An employer cannot do what he likes; he must not only conform to the rules and regulations – and there is a profusion of them in the collective agreements and the trade union rules – but he must also be prepared to consult his men on all basic changes in the workplace.... The status of the worker has risen considerably in recent years.... He regards himself more as a junior partner entitled to voice his opinions on all basic issues which involve conditions of work or the prospect of employment. The workplace on which his lot depends is *his* [author's emphasis] workplace; it is a social unit of the first importance. He has acquired a new sense of his importance and he asks that his dignity shall be respected. The rules of work or the discipline of work cannot be imposed on him without consultation with him or his representative (Zweig, 1952a, pp. 122–3).

Compared to the prevailing situation in 1880 this represented a quite radical transformation in workplace relations. Nonetheless, there were limits to this erosion of employer authority and control. Whilst many shop stewards continued to campaign for further extension of workers' control after 1945, there exists strong evidence to suggest that neither the majority of workers, nor their union leaders, were willing to press forward the challenge to managerial authority. There continued to be widespread support within the workplace for the idea that employers had the right to manage. The way in which the JPCs fell into disuse after 1945 indicates the prevalence of this attitude. Nor was there much enthusiasm for extended workers' control in the newly created nationalised industries. Here the managerial regime may well have been distinctively more humanised compared to the 1930s (most noticeably, perhaps, in coal and the railways). Nonetheless, the managerial structures of the public corporation were not fundamentally different from private enterprise; whilst top trade union officials were frequently appointed, their role in production management was minimal and there was little real workers' control, in practice, on the boards of public enterprises (Miliband, 1972; Hinton, 1994). Stafford Cripps noted in 1946 that this was because there was little will for this and workers lacked the ability: 'There is not yet a very large number of workers in Britain capable of taking over large enterprises' (*The Times*, 28 Oct. 1946). Thus joint regulation in industry remained essentially prescribed. Workers' representatives were invariably reacting and advising, rather than initiating and directing changes in the labour process. Moreover, employers' attitudes altered less fundamentally in the smaller and medium-sized firms in the private sector than within the larger plants most affected by the wartime changes. Furthermore, there was a move after 1945 by some employers to dismantle the encumbrances of joint regulation (some shop stewards were victimised and workplace organisation declined) which intensified from 1947 (Price, 1986, pp. 200–1). However, as Price concedes, this counter-attack had only limited success. What should be emphasised, in the final analysis, is the extent to which social relations had been transformed and managerial authority and control eroded by 1950. This was particularly evident in employers' relations with the unions, as Zweig observed:

> In the past the employer was the villain of the piece, but those times are over. In the nationalised industries the owner has disappeared completely, and in private industries he is co-operative, recognises the union and grants it its proper place. Many employers prefer their men organised in the union....The employers know that the 'take it or leave it' attitude has nowadays little chance of success since the modern worker would not stand for it (Zweig, 1952a, p. 181).

For the employers, of course, the regulation of industrial relations through collective bargaining offered distinct advantages, allowing the containment of conflict, more order and stability. Moreover, accommodating the unions was made more palatable because employers' intrinsic right to manage was not fundamentally

challenged by a trade union movement that accepted the capitalist mode of production and the hierarchical system of control,
and worked closely with the employers' organisations. 'They piss
in the same pot' was how one worker in northern England
expressed this cosy relationship to Zweig in 1952. Of central
importance here was that most union leaders, as Middlemas has
commented, 'accepted the superior capacity of management,
provided management used it with ... responsibility' (Middlemas,
1979, p. 393).

Conclusions

Between 1880 and 1950, employers' strategies had swung around
fully to embrace more co-operative and consensual modes of
labour management through a dual system of national collective
bargaining and joint regulation at workplace level, supplemented,
in some cases, with institutionalised company welfarism. Here
employers were reacting to the long-term growth of trade unionism (almost half of the British labour force were union members
by 1950), shifts in public opinion and heightened state intervention in labour and production matters, stimulated by the pressures
imposed by two world wars. Workers' consent within this system
was lubricated by relative job security, nationalisation, a more
favourable political climate, trade union recognition and rising
real wages. At the same time, this masked intensified exploitation,
skill fragmentation and tighter control of labour in the workplace
as a consequence of the diffusion of Taylorist principles and more
sophisticated internal labour management structures and modes
of supervision and control.

   However, this process was uneven and labour management
strategies continued to vary considerably. What employers gave up
related primarily to issues around the labour contract – especially
wages and working conditions. Little was effectively sacrificed in
terms of managerial prerogative in relation to the labour process,
the organisation of work and the management of production.
Here workers' influence and trade union or shop stewards' interventions remained marginal across the bulk of British industry.
The changes of the 1940s were significant, producing a markedly
different balance of power involving a deep erosion of employer

authority and the end of unilateral managerial control at the workplace. The trade-off, paradoxically, was in the sphere of production
and supervision. Workers were more directly managed, monitored
and controlled at the point of production by 1950 compared to
1880. The union gains occurred within the parameters of rationalised production and a more intensified work regime where the
wage was increasingly being used as the basic inducement to
maximise productivity. Employers gave ground in terms of the
labour contract and control over labour markets. However, the
procedural control element of collective bargaining should not
be overlooked. Moreover, little ground was conceded on the fundamental issues of capital investment, the staffing of machinery,
the division of labour, production management and the strategic
running of the capitalist enterprise. On balance, whilst there were
countervailing tendencies and much diversity in structure and
strategy, the increasing bureaucratisation of the workplace represented very real erosion of workers' independence and autonomy
in the workplace and a cranking up of *real* subordination of
labour to the imperatives of capital. Employers had come to adapt
and accommodate themselves to the rise of organised labour.
Whilst managerial authority was eroded by the rise of mass unionisation (see Chapter 8), the employers could at least congratulate
themselves that they had largely retained managerial prerogative
in production matters and had kept union influence at a minimum within the workplace.

5

WORK CONDITIONS, OCCUPATION AND HEALTH

The health of workers has long been a subject of serious historical enquiry. Traditionally, the emphasis of such work has focused on the more spectacular public health crises linked to urban conditions and poverty (including the epidemics of cholera, smallpox, tuberculosis and influenza) and the interactions between unemployment and health. The impact of work upon health has suffered serious neglect as a subject of historical study. This oversight perhaps reflects the very low status of occupational health within British society; amongst employers, trade unions and politicians. It is not without significance that no occupational health service was included within the orbit of the NHS when it was established after World War Two. This chapter reviews recent research findings in this area, explores the changing nature of the work environment and analyses the extent to which employment impacted upon workers' health and well-being in Britain over the period 1880–1950.

Historical research on this particular topic is less well developed than other areas of the social history of work, though output is increasing rapidly. Interpretations inevitably vary. On the one hand, there is a tendency in some of the literature to stress the emancipating potential of science, technology, advancing knowledge and political reform to improve work conditions and raise occupational health and safety standards (Hunt, 1981; Hopkins, 1979; Webbs, 1920; Zweig, 1948a, 1952a). In this interpretation, the congruence of medical knowledge, an increasingly interventionist state and growing trade union power achieved a dramatic

111

ameliorative transformation of the work environment over the nineteenth and twentieth centuries. Alternatively, Marxist sociologists such as Navarro, Woolfson and Beck have emphasised the intrinsically stressful, alienating and physically harmful effects of work under capitalist conditions, which critically undermined health and well-being. In a competitive environment, profit was placed above health and safety. Such a 'deterioration' thesis is linked to concepts of the unequal distribution of power within society and the degrading processes of deskilling and intensification of work.

Most recent research has rejected the overarching suppositions behind both the 'Whig' and Marxist interpretations, at least in their undiluted form, and has considerably developed our understanding of the interactions between work and health, as well as the politics of occupational health and safety. Peter Bartrip's seminal work in this area over the 1980s and 1990s stands out and perhaps exemplifies this 'revisionist' perspective. A number of stereotypes in the literature have begun to be challenged. What emerges is a sense that improvements in occupational health and safety standards were uneven, subject to reversal (in depression and war) and inequalities in experience based on occupation, gender and class persisted (Jones, 1994; Weindling, 1985; McIvor, 1987b). Corporate crime was widespread, a reflection of the power of big corporations and the weakness of legal impediments and government regulation (Jeremy, 1995; Tweedale and Hansen, 1998; Carson, 1970). State intervention was patchy, flawed and its effectiveness was circumscribed, if ultimately ameliorative in effect (Bartrip and Fenn, 1988; Bartrip and Burman, 1983; Bartrip, 1987; Blackburn, 1989; McIvor, 1989; 1997). Trade unions have emerged as significant pressure groups contributing positively to the reform process (Bartrip, 1996; McIvor, 1997), but who could have done more to prioritise occupational health issues (Weindling, 1985; Watterson, 1990; Williams, 1960). The long-run improvement in occupational mortality belies Marxist prognostications of deterioration, though to some extent new hazards and work-related illnesses replaced old ones. There is now wider recognition that British capitalism increasingly adapted to change and exercised authority through consensual (as opposed to 'despotic' and confrontational) strategies, which embraced, by 1950, broader acceptance of the welfarist philosophy that maintaining the health of employees was consistent with efficiency and profit maximisation. The wars played an important part in this transition (Bartrip, 1987; McIvor, 1987a,b; Waldron, 1997), as did the campaigns of the trade unions. Part of the process of what one Marxist (Burawoy, 1985) has termed 'manufacturing consent' to capitalism was the growing acceptance by employers and management of the necessity of reforming grim and unhealthy working conditions. Cumulatively, this amounted to a considerable transformation in the relationship between employment and health.

Occupational Health and Safety before World War One

In the late Victorian period work was invariably risky and dangerous, with almost all occupations having some deleterious impact upon health. Leaving aside the monetary rewards of labour and the relationship wages had to living standards and hence health, there were three main ways in which employment directly affected workers' well-being. Long hours and the pace of work induced fatigue, workers were exposed to the possibility of injury and death by industrial accidents, and contact with materials and fellow-workers opened up the possibility of poisoning and occupational disease.

Overstrain and exhaustion were endemic features of work before World War One in Britain and resulted in a prescribed lifestyle and a premature degeneration in workers' mental and physical health. Worker fatigue derived from long working hours, low pay, the intensity of labour and was exacerbated by the conditions and environment in which people toiled. A female factory worker, Ada Nield Chew, summed up the situation in a graphic comment in 1894:

> To take what may be considered a good week's wage the work has to be so close and unremitting that we cannot be said to live, we merely exist. We eat, we sleep, we work, endlessly work, from Monday morning to Saturday night, without remission. Cultivation of the mind? How is it possible? Reading? Those of us who are determined to live like human beings and require food for the mind as well as the body, are obliged to take time which is necessary for sleep to gratify this desire (Chew, 1982, pp. 75–6).

In the late nineteenth century working hours in Britain were relatively short compared to other countries (Cross, 1989; Bienefeld, 1972), but were still long enough to induce what Meacham termed 'bone-weariness' in many workers. In the 1880s the 10–11-hour (two-break) working day, constituting around a 60-hour, 5½-day working week was common in manufacturing, though very wide divergences in working hours existed across the economy. Working hours were dependent partly on the nature of the work, on custom, on trade union strength, and on the patchy coverage of regulatory legislation, which excluded transport, agriculture, retailing, self-employment and sweatshops (see Table 5.1)

National government employees, building workers, printers, engineers and coal miners were amongst those working the lowest hours, at 45–55 per week. At the other extreme, sweated clothing workers, domestic servants, carters, agricultural labourers, catering and shopworkers commonly toiled for more than 80 hours a week, whilst housewives toiled even longer at unpaid work within the home, aided by few labour-saving devices. Working hours were also frequently irregular, with much cyclical (e.g. shipbuilding), casual and seasonal work (e.g. food processing) involving long spells of inactivity followed by frenetic work. The Glasgow

Table 5.1   Nominal weekly working hours in Britain, early 1890s

Miners	43–55
Construction	50–55
Printers	53–54
Engineering workers	54
Textile workers	56
Railway ticket agents	56–62
Brickmakers	54–69
Chemical workers	53–70
Railway guards	64–70
Paper workers	66–78
Bakers	70
Sailors	72
Foundry labourers	72–84
Retail clerks	82
Tailors	56–96
Restaurant waiters	96

Source: Cross (1989, p. 235).

carters, for example, worked a 98-hour week in season, constituting a 17-hour day, starting at 4.30 a.m., with a shorter stint of 13
hours on a Saturday. Moreover, the work year was also very extensive, with most workers having access to only a few traditional 'holidays', without pay.

Given the length of work time, it is hardly surprising that
serious problems of overstrain and exhaustion occurred. For a
great many workers there simply was no time for the proper rest
necessary for physical and mental regeneration (Sherard, 1897,
p. 32). Even amongst the shorter-hours workers, fatigue existed
as a perennial problem because of the increasing intensity of
labour (discussed in Chapter 3) and because of poor working conditions. In this period, employers invariably refused to accept the
existence of fatigue and exhaustion amongst their workers, nor
the growing evidence that this represented an inefficient use of
labour power (McIvor, 1987a). The old classical economist orthodoxy that output always increased or decreased exactly proportionate to the hours worked remained prevalent. Hence, there
was considerable opposition amongst employers and their organisations to any reduction in work hours. In 1892, William Mather,
a maverick engineering employer, introduced a 48-hour working
week, proving in the process that productivity rose because workers
were less tired (*The Times*, 31 May 1894). Significantly, however,
the Iron Trades Employers' Association and the Engineering
Employers' Federation organised a concerted campaign to denigrate Mather's shorter hours experiment and refused membership to any firm like Mather and Platt who broke ranks. The
48-hour working week did not become common in Britain until
1919/1920.

Overstrain induced by long working hours and intensified
labour was further exacerbated by the kind of environment in
which workers toiled, as Wohl noted. Poor ventilation and lighting,
high temperatures and noise levels and lack of seating provision
could rapidly dissipate workers' energy. The Interdepartmental
Committee on Physical Deterioration placed a portion of the
blame for the poor physique of recruits during the Boer War on
the nature and conditions of work. However, it was probably
amongst the female-dominated sweated trades where low wages
combined with long working hours in overcrowded and cramped
rooms or workshops that the most serious problems of fatigue and

the resultant degeneration of health occurred. As Sidney Webb noted in 1911:

> These industries are exacting more energy than their wages and other conditions suffice to make good, with the result that, after a relatively few years of demoralising toil, the sweated workers are flung, prematurely exhausted, on the social rubbish heap of charity and the Poor Law. It is indeed unfortunately true that the sweated trades literally use up the men, women and children who work at them, as omnibus companies use up their horses (cited in Hutchins and Harrison, 1911, p. xi).

Moreover, the stripping of energy during the work process often had damaging knock-on effects, increasing the risk of injury or death through an accident, whilst lowering a worker's resistance to a whole battery of diseases. The miners' eye disease nystagmus and telegraphists' cramp are two such examples. 'Physical exertion carried to excess', the Victorian industrial hygienist Arlidge noted, 'becomes a cause of disease' (Arlidge, 1982, p. 15). An iron worker provided a similar view based on his direct experience on the shop floor: 'something approximating 50 per cent of us die from lung and heart diseases which may be brought on by the exhaustion due to working in vitiated atmospheres' (cited in Fyrth and Collins, 1959, p. 130).

Whilst the evidence of worker fatigue and overstrain is subjective and impossible to quantify, it is easier to pin down the impact of injuries sustained at work before World War One through figures compiled by the Labour Department of the Board of Trade (Table 5.2). Over the period 1880–1914, around 150 000 workers in the UK were officially recorded as killed by injuries sustained whilst at their work. Deaths are under-represented, moreover, because the official figures only include fatalities occurring within a year of an accident at work, and exclude whole swathes of the labour market not covered by legislation. Much of this carnage, the occupational health specialist, Thomas Oliver, argued, was preventable.

What is evident, however, is that taking into account the increase in total employment over this period, improved reporting and the broadening coverage of the official statistics, Table 5.2 illustrates a declining industrial accident fatality rate over time. Nonetheless, occupation remained a significant factor affecting an

Table 5.2   Persons killed in industrial accidents, UK, 1880–1914 (5-yearly totals)

Years	Factories	Coal mines	Railways	Shipping	Total	Rate
1880–4	2 112	5 394	2 909	n/k	10 832	
1885–9	1 892	5 116	2 303	11 000	20 632	
1890–4	2 200	5 402	2 752	10 960	21 670	0.035
1895–9	2 719	4 821	2 671	9 753	21 750	
1900–4	3 929	5 264	2 626	7 856	22 030	0.028
1905–9	3 903	6 307	2 233	6 622	21 377	
1910–14	4 639	7 288	2 209	7 211	23 616	0.023

Note: The mortality rate is crudely calculated by dividing deaths into total numbers employed according to the decennial Census.
Source: Dept of Employment, *British Labour Statistics: Historical Abstract* (1971, Table 200).

individual's life chances before World War One. This is clearly indicated in the occupational mortality figures compiled by the Registrar of Births, Deaths and Marriages (Table 5.3).

The transport sector included some of the most hazardous jobs in Britain in the late nineteenth century. There were both high fatality and injury rates on the railways, deriving mostly from broken bones, crushed hands and fingers, especially amongst shunters. With 5 killed and 78 injured out of every 1000 railway workers per year, this meant that over a work span of 30 or so years, few left the industry without sustaining an injury. Rising coal costs and inter-line competition led to an all-pervasive speeding-up of work and a rising injury rate. Railway workers at least up to the turn of the nineteenth century also lacked legislative protection and the kind of formal safety inspection that existed for the factories and mines (Bartrip and Burman, 1983, pp. 46–7; 76–7). High accident rates also existed in dockwork, which the Glasgow Factory Inspector (Wilson) put down to fatigue caused by the intensity of work in unloading, loading and turning around ships as quickly as possible (*Accidents Report*, 1911, pp. 471–2). A high accident proneness also existed in shipping and fishing where unpredicable weather took a heavy toll of lives. Obvious difficulties in ensuring legal safety procedures were rigidly enforced, whilst at sea combined with very long shifts and negligent medical inspection and provision, even on the larger lines like Cunard, contributed to the high accident rates in this industry.

Table 5.3 Comparative mortality of males, 25–65 years of age, selected occupations, 1880–2

Clergymen, priests, ministers	100
Farmers, graziers	114
Agricultural labourers	126
Hosiery workers	129
Grocers	139
Carpenters, joiners	148
Coal miners	160
Shoemakers	166
Builders, masons, bricklayers	174
Blacksmiths	175
Wool workers	186
Tailors	189
Printers	193
Cotton workers	196
Stone and slate quarriers	202
Butchers	210
Plumbers, painters, glaziers	216
Cutlers, scissor makers	235
Brewers	245
Cab, omnibus drivers	267
Innkeepers	274
File makers	300
Earthenware workers	313
Cornish metal miners	331
Costermongers, hawkers, street sellers	338

Source: Evidence of Dr W. Ogle, R.C. on Labour, *Digest of Evidence*, June 1893, C7063, 1893, pp. 38–9.

Work in the coal mines was also particularly dangerous. Moreover, the official figures by no means tell the whole story. In 1902, Louis examined the discrepancy between the statistics of the Mines Inspectorate and the Miners' Relief Societies and concluded that government figures under-represented fatalities in the pits by up to 20 per cent and that injuries leading to disability were *more than 20 times* the figures provided by the Mines Inspectorate (Oliver, 1902). However, injury and death rates were declining over 1880–1914. Benson has shown that this was primarily because of extended state regulation of the mines, technological change (better ventilation techniques) and mineworkers' agitation (Benson, 1980). Yet still in 1914 a miner was killed in Britain every six hours and severely injured every two hours. Large disasters intermittently devastated local communities, as at Senghenydd in South Wales in 1913 when 439 lives were lost. However, most deaths in mining occurred from individual accidents: small roof collapses; falls down shafts; tram collisions – what Benson termed 'a steady drip-drip of death'. Moreover, because of widely differing geological conditions some coalfields, such as West Scotland and the Midlands, had a lower accident incidence, whilst South Wales, and especially the Aberdare valley, had the worst safety record (Benson, 1980; Flint, 1910).

By 1880, factory workers were most extensively protected by legislation designed to reduce accidents and worker fatigue. This had been influential in reducing working hours, eliminating women from working nightshifts and curtailing child labour. However, legislation failed even here to prevent a significant harvest of injuries, disabilities and deaths through accidents at work. Technology changed rapidly throughout the 1880–1914 period, creating new unforeseen health hazards, especially as machinery manufacturers were not forced to fit guards and covers – the onus for this lay with the factory owner. Indeed, the most important single source of accidents in factories was unfenced or unguarded steam-driven machinery, especially gearing, shafting, winches, drive bands and vats. There occurred 301 fatalities from this single source of factory accidents alone in 1899, and almost 20 000 injuries. Eye injuries are particularly well documented in cotton factories (flying shuttles) and ironworks (hot splashes). The hazards of power-driven machinery and working with hot metal were exacerbated by uneven, wet and slippery floors and by the inability to cut off power quickly before the widespread adoption of electricity as a prime mover in factories in the 1920s and 1930s. The carrying and manipulating of heavy weights were also particularly hazardous. The cotton finishing unions were swamped by claims for superannuation from claimants in the bleaching and dyeing section who had become permanently disabled due to a hernia or rupture contracted during manipulating vast quantities of heavy, wet cloth through the vats and kiers (boilers). Moreover, there was a close connection between the pace of work and accident rates. The Report of the Departmental Committee on Factory Accidents in 1911 placed payments by results wage systems, speed-up and bad lighting high on their list of causes of industrial accidents. Table 5.4 gives a breakdown of occupational injury and mortality

Table 5.4   Work injuries and fatalities: selected trades, UK, 1910–14

	I Employed	II Injuries	III %	IV Deaths	V %
Mines	1 075 780	177 684	16.52	1 477	0.137
Docks	138 273	15 463	11.18	200	0.144
Quarries	87 466	5 751	6.58	77	0.088
Railways	457 560	24 026	5.25	416	0.091
Shipping	252 980	7 904	3.12	497	0.196
Cotton	598 300	11 818	1.98	44	0.007
Wool/worsted	279 300	3 233	1.16	21	0.008
Other textiles	227 100	3 152	1.39	15	0.006
Total textiles	1 104 700	18 202	1.65	80	0.007
Wood	137 600	5 424	3.94	39	0.028
Metal smelting	414 480	34 320	8.28	168	0.041
Metalworking	801 460	39 865	4.97	155	0.019
Engineering	306 720	29 687	9.68	199	0.065
Paper and printing	313 880	4 470	1.43	23	0.007
Pottery	68 330	1 296	1.90	8	0.012
Miscellaneous	2 005 940	49 838	2.48	342	0.017

Notes:
I = Annual average numbers employed 1910–14.
II = Annual average of injuries for five years, 1910–14.
III = Percentage II to I.
IV = Annual average of fatalities for five years, 1910–14.
V = Percentage IV to I.
Source: Derived from data in the *18th Abstract of Labour Statistics*, 1926, Cmd 2740 (compiled from statistics gathered under the Workmen's Compensation Acts).

rates for a range of the most dangerous trades in the years just prior to World War One. Clearly, manufacturing metal and wood (especially smelting and shipbuilding) was considerably more dangerous than processing textiles and paper.

Workers also suffered fatalities and disabilities caused by a multitude of diseases related directly to particular jobs and to contact with toxic raw materials handled and manufactured. 'There is scarcely any trade or occupation', commented Dr Thomas Oliver in 1908 in his pioneering monograph *The Diseases of Occupations*, 'that is not attended by some risk or other' (p. 14). Recognition of central government responsibility to regulate the most dangerous trades was slowly extending in the 1890s, as Bartrip has shown (Bartrip, 1996). In 1893, the first female factory inspectors were created; in 1895 an inquiry was set up to investigate the 'dangerous trades' and in 1898 a medical inspector of factories was established. The Miscellaneous Dangerous Trades Committee, which included Thomas Oliver amongst its members, went on to produce 5 reports on 22 occupations. In the 1880s and 1890s workers who contracted an industrial disease like lead or phosphorus poisoning rarely obtained any financial compensation from their employers (under the Employers' Liability Act of 1880) because of the long process of litigation necessary to prove employer responsibility for diseases which often had a long gestation period. In 1906 the reforming Liberal government amended the Workmen's Compensation Act of 1897 (which provided for occupational accidents) to include automatic financial compensation for six major industrial diseases: lead, mercury, phosphorus and arsenic poisoning; anthrax and ankylostomiasis. In part, at least, as Bartrip has shown, the 1906 legislation was the product of the pressure group activities of the Women's Trade Union League which had campaigned for a decade from the mid-1890s to attain effective regulation of and compensation for lead poisoning (Bartrip, 1996, pp. 3–26).

Largely due to the widespread use of different types and forms of lead across a range of industries this form of poisoning was the most common in Britain before World War One (Wohl, 1983; Blackburn, 1989; Bartrip, 1996). Entry of lead in powder (carbonate) form to the body could be via the mouth (inhalation or contaminated food), or, more rarely, through the skin. The symptoms were ugly and often led to incapacity to work – sickness, headaches, insomnia, constipation, a sense of weakness and debility. In chronic cases, convulsions and paralysis of the working limbs often set in, whilst loss of sight and brain damage could occur. In pregnant females, the disease induced miscarriage. The worst cases (around 5 per cent of the total) were fatal (Arlidge, 1982, pp. 422–31; Sherard, 1897, pp. 173–206; Chew, 1982, pp. 147–51). The official figures compiled by the Labour Department of the Board of Trade identify in total 15 418 cases of lead poisoning over the period 1900–14. Table 5.5 gives a sense of the wide distribution of occupations where lead poisoning occurred in one industrial town.

Table 5.5   Lead poisoning cases reported in factories and workshops in Glasgow, 1900–14

Industry	Male	Female	Total
White and red lead manufacture, paints, colours and oils	127	8	135
Shipbuilding	58	–	58
Sanitary engineering and enamelling	44	–	44
Mechanical engineering	30	–	30
Painters, plumbers, glazers (including factory painters)	18	4	22
Yarn dyeing	2	14	16
Pottery and earthenware	5	9	14
Printing	8	–	8
Metal mining, smelting and refining	8	–	8
Others	7	–	7
Totals (fatalities = 9)	307	35	342

Source: Board of Trade, *Register of Industrial Diseases*, PRO/LAB 56/1–15.

In 1899 an official government inquiry concluded that the use of lead in paints and glazes should be banned. The state opted, however, to regulate conditions and rely on education, medical inspection, the policing of the Factory Inspectorate and the financial deterrents of compensation to control lead poisoning. This strategy of piecemeal reform in place of banning the use of toxic substances was to be repeated later with phosphorus, carcinogenic mineral oils and asbestos. Bartrip has shown, however, that the lead reforms did have an appreciable impact. Between 1898 and 1913 lead poisoning cases in the UK fell by more than a half. The improvement was even more marked in the pottery sector where new cases reported were below 80 per year by 1910–13, compared to 440 per year over 1896–8 (Bartrip, 1996, p. 26).

Poisoning by contact with phosphorus, mercury or arsenic at work was far less common than lead – indeed fewer than 50 cases were officially reported in the five years 1901–5. Mercury, used in barometer and thermometer manufacture, dyes and felt-hat making, caused sickness, fetid breath, tooth and gum decay, muscular tremors and spasms, occasionally ending fatally. Arsenic compounds were utilised in a whole range of processes, including glass, chalk, colouring, dyeing, printing, wallpaper and artificial flower manufacture. Absorption of the dust or gas resulted in almost immediate vomiting, stomach pain and cramp, vertigo, fainting, convulsions and general debility, whilst chronic cases developed skin rashes, pustular eruptions, permanent headache, emaciation and transient paralysis. Death occurred in extreme cases. White phosphorus was used most extensively in the match-making industry and was usually absorbed through skin contact, inhalation of the vapour or contaminated food. The consequences were appalling. Poisoning usually affected the bone structure of the face, starting with ulceration of the gums, pain and loosening of the teeth, erosion (necrosis) of the jawbone, with fissures and open, fetid and septic holes in the cheeks. Fever and delirium, horrendous pain, and emaciation completed the symptoms, with death occurring in many of the worst cases, usually by sepsis. There was no specific medical treatment. After the exposure of working conditions at the Bryant and May match factory by the socialist Annie Besant in *The Link* in 1889, the government certified white phosphorus as a 'dangerous substance' (1892). However, beyond this the government relied on employers to phase out its use voluntarily, an unrealistic strategy because of the unpopularity in the market place of the alternative 'safety match' made with non-toxic red phosphorus. Only in 1910 did the government finally ban totally the use of white phosphorus in Britain.

Anklyostomiasis and anthrax completed the original six occupational diseases officially incorporated in the Workmen's Compensation Act 1906. Anklyostomiasis was contracted by metal miners, and was most common in the Cornwall tin mining industry. The disease consisted of internal absorption of the eggs of an intestinal worm, which hatched in the warm temperature of the digestive tract. Reinfection occurred from contact with the faeces of carriers down the pit. The symptoms were dizziness, multiple skin boils, fatigue and anaemia. The disease rarely killed but did often result in complete and permanent disability from carrying on any heavy physical labour (Burke, 1985). Anthrax was a disease commonly associated with cattle, especially in Asia. However, the infection could lie dormant in dried animal blood on wool, hair, hides and skins and could infect workers handling, transporting or manufacturing such imported materials through absorption by inhalation, or, more commonly, through an abrasion on the skin. There were 920 cases of anthrax reported in the UK between 1900 and 1914, 167 (or almost 20 per cent) of which ended fatally, usually after only a few days of contracting the infection. There was no cure prior to effective treatment with anti-biotics after 1945. The majority of cases occurred in Bradford, where the affliction was known as 'woolsorters' disease'.

The six diseases included in the 1906 amendment of the Work-men's Compensation Act were, however, just the tip of the ice-berg. A document produced by the American Bureau of Labor in 1912, for example, listed 54 common industrial poisons being handled by workers. Indeed, the rationale for the inclusion of the six diseases in 1906 was simply that the linkages between occupa-tion and disease in these cases were virtually irrefutable. Workers in *most* other occupations, as Oliver noted, were susceptible to diseases and disabilities which could seriously impair health. Domestic servants suffered from anaemia and knee joint inflam-mation ('housemaid's knee'). Cotton spinners were exposed to carcinogenic mineral oils used on the mule and contracted scrotal cancer (the connection here between oil and cancer was not made until 1922). Weavers transmitted all kinds of diseases via the process of 'shuttle kissing' – sucking the yarn through the shuttle eye preparatory to weaving. Rheumatism, sciatica and lumbago also resulted directly from the nature of work in pottery, coal min-ing and textile bleaching and finishing. Nicotine poisoning afflicted women engaged in biting cigar ends and licking tobacco leaf with their tongues. Over 10 000 miners in Britain were inca-pacitated by 1914 with the eye disease nystagmus. Dermatitis, skin damage, teeth and bone rot were also common complaints of those working with various chemicals and gases across a wide range of processes (Hardie, 1899; Sherard, 1897; Oliver, 1908). In 1897 Sherard recalled meeting chemical workers with teeth so damaged from their employment that they paid colleagues five shillings a week to masticate their food for them.

However, respiratory diseases caused by inhalation of fine par-ticles of dust within the factory, workshop or mine environment were probably the most prevalent of all occupational health hazards. Industrial processes which generated dust were placed at the top of a 'Classification of Occupations by Health Hazards' drawn up by the industrial hygienist Arlidge in 1892 (Arlidge, 1892, pp. 70–1). Dust inhalation damaged the throat, bronchial and lung tissue causing the pneumoconioses. Silicosis, caused by the inhalation of inorganic dusts – stone, flint, clay and metal –

afflicted many workers, including stone masons, coal and metal miners, and was endemic amongst the Sheffield cutlery grinders and the Staffordshire potters. The Staffordshire potters' life expectancy was seven years less on average than non-pottery workers primarily because of the higher incidence of respiratory disease. Byssinosis, contracted by inhaling cotton fibres, was especially prevalent in the preparatory departments and the cardroom, where death rates from respiratory disease were three times higher than the average of all cotton workers. Moreover, the significance of dust inhalation at work goes far beyond this because the damage caused reduced resistance to a whole battery of other respiratory diseases, not directly associated with employment, including bronchitis, emphysema and tuberculosis (Ransome, 1890; Arlidge, 1892; Burke, 1985). However, because of the difficulty of medically determining the difference between respiratory disease caused by dust or the tubercule bacillus, pneumoconiosis was not included in the list of occupational diseases for which compensation was automatic until 1918 (initially silicosis). Nonetheless, data compiled by the Registrar General of Births and Deaths indicated a clear relationship between occupation and mortality from respiratory disease (Table 5.6).

Table 5.6 Comparative mortality from lung and respiratory disease, males in selected occupations, 1880–2

Agriculture, fishing	100
Grocers	130
Coal miners	148
Carpenters, joiners	155
Bakers, confectioners	183
Drapers	197
Masons, builders, bricklayers	208
Wool workers	213
Tailors	217
Cotton workers	250
Quarrymen	268
Printers	288
Cutlers	350
File makers	360
Earthenware workers	514
Cornish miners	528

Source: Evidence of Dr W. Ogle, R.C. on Labour, *Digest of Evidence*, June 1893, C7063, 1893, pp. 38–9.

The evidence therefore indicates clearly that work was a very significant source of ill health and mortality. Of fundamental importance in any attempt to explain why this was so must be the attitudes and strategies of employers towards the utilisation of their labour power. Such attitudes and strategies varied considerably, as we discussed in Chapter 4. However, what appears evident is that most employers utilised labour inefficiently and unscientifically, and despite the propaganda efforts of a small group of 'welfarist' employers (like Seebohm Rowntree and Edward Cadbury), most employers had a deep-rooted disregard for the biological limitations of workers. Employers largely remained unimpressed by the arguments that improving the welfare and health of workers produced dividends in improved worker productivity. Workers worth their salt had to be seen to be grafting. This was partly a consequence of ignorance and the lack of scientific training of most managers brought up in the 'rule of thumb' school of management. Moreover, improving safety standards and workers' health cost money. In the face of growing foreign competition and a squeeze on profits few employers operating in unprotected markets were willing to spend scarce cash resources to raise health standards at work above the bare minimum required by law. Hence few firms created formal works medical services, or even employed a nurse before World War One, and thus the potential for discovering health problems at work at a remedial stage rarely existed. One respondent to the Accidents Committee of 1911 noted how inadequate provision of washing facilities, basic first aid (including antiseptic dressings) and trained workers resulted in many minor abrasions and wounds turning to serious blood poisoning (Q12953). Dr Scott, a Glasgow certifying surgeon, commented on the high incidence of eye injuries to Clydeside metal-workers and the *ad hoc* treatment administered to victims:

Hardly an hour passes during the working day in which some dresser does not receive injury through small particles of iron flying from his chisel and lodging in his eyeball. First aid is rendered by his fellow workmen, who are ready to fix the injured party's head against the wall, and, with a pin or pocket knife, extract the offending chip. Should this somewhat heroic treatment be ineffective, the patient is sent to the Eye Infirmary (*Clydebank Press*, 13 July 1906).

The route to the eye infirmaries from the industrial districts of the major cities must have been a very well worn one.

Employers justified their position by arguing that those furthest down the social scale did not require the same standards, or environmental conditions, or need the degree of regenerative recreation and rest necessary for those in the privileged, upper reaches of society (Lady Bell, 1911). Each to their place. Moreover, there was a long tradition of blaming the victim – of ascribing responsibility for health at work to the individual concerned. This can be picked up throughout the Minutes of Evidence to the Dangerous Trades Committees of the 1890s and the Diseases Inquiry of 1907. Accidents at work were thus the result of reckless behaviour, stupidity or oversight, and industrial disease contracted because of hereditary weaknesses, personal habits, manners and lack of cleanliness. Often establishment medicine could be relied on to back up and legitimise such assertions, medical evidence being used in litigation, for example, to prove the victim was to blame for their own misfortune, or to suggest that factors outside the employment environment (like diet and housing) had a critical influence (Oliver, 1902, 1908; Arlidge, 1892). Furthermore, in the employment contract workers were deemed to have explicitly accepted work under prevailing conditions of risk. It has also been argued that because most employers insured themselves against claims for accident or disease compensation with an annual premium, the incentive to introduce preventive safety standards in the workplace was significantly diluted (Wilson, in *Accidents Committee*, 1911, p. 472, Q12979–81). The historians of workmen's compensation have argued that as preventive measures designed to improve safety standards the Workmen's Compensation Acts of 1897 and 1906 were a failure (Bartrip and Burman, 1983). In some industries, such as cotton spinning, weaving and finishing, employers organised themselves to subvert the legislation at the implementation stage, engaging accident inspectors of their own to contest claims and prove 'wilful misconduct' (McIvor, 1996, pp. 79–81).

State intervention in many areas of the labour market and working conditions increased over 1880–1914. The initial patriarchal stimulus – evident in the 1842 banning of child and female employment underground in coal mining – was superseded by the 1890s with a broader concern to regulate unhealthy and excessively exploitative working conditions. The state was stung by humanitarian criticisms of work conditions and influenced by the national efficiency movement and pressure groups such as the Trades Union Congress and the Women's Trade Union League. With the widening of the franchise the government was subject to popular pressure. Moreover, the growing capacity of the unions to sustain national strikes sharpened the state's concern to maintain social stability through a programme of limited reforms. Hence Factory Acts were extended and special powers were conferred on the Secretary of State to declare any occupation a 'dangerous trade' and impose a legally binding code of safety regulations upon the employers (e.g. lead, 1894). Working hours were further reduced in factories and workshops (to a 55 ½ hour week by 1914), controls extended over the factory environment (ventilation, temperature and sanitation standards) and the fencing of machinery was more rigidly enforced. Automatic employer liability was introduced in the workmen's compensation legislation and the state established a minimum wage norm in some of the worst, sweated trades with the Trade Boards Act in 1909. The factory, mines and Trade Board inspectors played important roles as social investigators, data collectors, mediators, advisers and teachers, as well as law enforcers (Jones, 1985).

However, whilst recent research has tended to confirm the ameliorative impact of such legislation, what has also been demonstrated is that right up to 1914, and indeed beyond, industrial legislation remained uneven, full of loopholes and difficult to police and enforce (Bartrip and Fenn, 1988; McIvor, 1989, 1997; Blackburn, 1989). The protective legislation developed in response to particular evils and had many gaps in coverage. Cotton textiles and coal mines were well covered; railways less so, and areas like general labouring and domestic service were almost completely overlooked. Moreover, many workers and employers remained ignorant of the regulations; it was noted, for example, that the Shops Act of 1886 was virtually unknown and almost totally inoperative for a decade. Anyone examining the *Factory Inspectors Reports* cannot fail to be struck by the widespread evasion of the legislation. Factory crime remained endemic, as Carson has shown. Breaches of regulations in cotton relating to mealtime cleaning of machinery, humidity levels (steaming) and time cribbing were commonplace, and the four-week exclusion rule after pregnancy was said to be completely inoperative (McIvor, 1997; Clark, 1899; Hutchins and Harrison, 1911). This was partly because the size of fines meted out in the courts for factory crime were paltry and failed to provide a deterrent. The Factory Inspectorate was also under-resourced. The 217 factory inspectors in 1913 had 275 000 workplaces under their jurisdiction. Visits were infrequent. One ironworker commented in 1906: 'I have not known or heard tell of a single visit from any one of these gentlemen during my 17 years experience of foundry life' (Fyrth and Collins, 1959, p. 130). On the other hand, the courts failed to adequately recompense workers for injuries sustained in the course of their employment (Bartrip and Burman, 1983). Family employment remained virtually unregulated and a wife and children could still be grossly overworked by a husband within the law. Moreover, the Trade Board Act of 1909 was ineffective before 1914: in a survey of tailoring workers in London and Colchester Tawney found over 50 per cent paid under the minimum. Blackburn has shown how strikes were necessary to force compliance and how evasion of the minimum wages was commonplace because of a miniscule inspectorate of 12 persons policing around 12 000 firms employing around half a million workers (Blackburn, 1989, pp. 65–6).

Therefore, whilst undoubtably legislation provided a significant matrix of protection which ameliorated the adverse interaction between work and ill health across some sectors of the economy, its impact should not be exaggerated. In reality its coverage was patchy, its enforcement often ineffective and its service to the community was consequently limited.

Workers did try to protect themselves. Much contemporary testimony refers to self-help techniques, ranging from stuffing cotton waste into the mouth to act as a filter to taking alcohol to dull the pain and swigging laudanum to help keep up with the pace of the machines. However, what is striking is the degree to which workers were inured to very high levels of risk and quietly accepted the prevailing hazards of work. In mining, on the docks, in shipbuilding and the railways this was partly bound up with prevailing notions of masculinity. The more powerful and well-established trade unions – including the coal and cotton unions, the TUC and the WTUL and NFWW – did increasingly campaign on occupational health and safety issues and were a force in the broader reform network (Bartrip, 1996; McIvor, 1997; Blackburn,

:nded to strike activity in some cases over 1910–14.
ıch activity was prescribed before 1914 by the rela-
f the union movement and by a tendency to prior-
l organisational survival over occupational health
ındling, 1985).

The interaction between work and ill health thus remained pervasive before World War One, with many thousands of workers continuing to be killed at work and many tens of thousands maimed and disabled each year. Long work hours, fatigue and overstrain seriously circumscribed workers' lifestyle, restricted opportunities and diluted the quality of life, leaving little free time or energy for enjoyment of leisure, recreation, education or family life – as Owen bitterly reflected in *The Ragged Trousered Philanthropists*. Moreover, a fatal accident or serious disability meant for many families a downwardly spiralling experience of diminished earnings, credit, the pawnshop, immiseration, poverty, malnutrition, deficiency-related illness and incarceration in the dreaded workhouse. As Constance Smith commented in 1905:

> We have only to consider what a loss of an arm, a hand or even a finger, means to a young working man or girl – much more to the breadwinner of a family; how fatally it handicaps such combatants in the hard battle of life; how inevitably it entails upon them descent to a lower place of living, if not to actual penury and dependence upon the community for subsistence (Smith 1905, pp. 435–6).

The Impact of Economic Recession and War, 1914–50

World War One had important implications for occupational health and safety in Britain. The demands of war necessitated maximising productivity and this had to be achieved amidst massive upheaval in the labour market as workers (predominantly male) left their jobs and flooded into the armed forces. They were replaced by what were often new, inexperienced 'dilutees', drafted into the munitions and war-related work factories. By 1916, 1.4 million male workers and 400 000 female workers were employed in munitions factories (Winter, 1985, p. 206). Initially, little thought was given to work organisation and occupational health, largely because of the widespread belief that hostilities would be over in a few months. Within a year, the war effort was being threatened by declining productivity. This was the consequence of workers toiling in 70–85-hour working weeks, with few breaks, resulting in accumulated and in many cases quite chronic fatigue. This emerging crisis led the government to establish the Health of Munitions Committee (HMWC) with a remit to investigate and report on the conditions most conducive to both industrial health and efficiency.

The HMWC carried out a series of pioneering works studies over 1915–17, commissioning psychologists, physiologists, statisticians, medical researchers and industrial hygiene specialists to undertake a series of scientific experiments into aspects of industrial medicine, health, efficiency and fatigue. In its findings, published in a series of interim memoranda and a comprehensive Final Report in 1918, the Committee pinpointed a clear relationship between excessive working hours and a worker's fatigue threshold and declining productivity levels. It went on to elaborate on the correlation between environmental conditions of work – issues such as illumination, ventilation, seating, washing, sanitary and safety arrangements – and efficiency and to develop awareness of the influence of other factors external to the workplace (such as diet and housing). A number of the HMWC recommendations were incorporated into state wartime labour policy, including the reduction of working hours, rest breaks, the abolition of Sunday working and the provision of works canteens (McIvor, 1987b; Braybon and Summerfield, 1987; Ineson and Thom, 1985).

The primary motive behind such activity remained, however, the maximisation of productivity for the war effort. The agenda of the HMWC was not occupational health *per se*, but was narrowly confined to the munitions sector and represented the continuation of the pre-war concerns of a patriarchal state, exemplified, for example, in the factory legal code. Little attention was paid to the most injury-prone male-dominated occupations, such as mining, the railways, metalworking and construction. Therefore, the intense pace of productive activity during the war kept occupational injury and mortality levels high. Indeed, the average rate of industrial deaths at 4545 per annum over the years 1915–18 slightly exceeded that of the average death rate over the pre-war decade (at 4499 per year). There is also some evidence to suggest that such official figures may well have underestimated actual deaths in production during wartime to maintain morale on the 'home front'. The dangers of working with TNT, for example, which led to a number of fatal industrial injuries during World War One, was kept closely under wraps by the government (Ineson and Thom, 1985).

From World War One to the mid-twentieth century, the Home Office data for occupational injuries and mortality rates suggest considerable improvement in industrial safety standards in Britain (Table 5.7). Between 1914 and 1950 the chances of a worker sustaining a fatal injury at work fell by more than a half. On the positive side a number of ameliorative influences were at work. In part, the figures reflect the changing nature of the labour force (see Chapter 2). By 1950 a much larger proportion of the labour force were employed in safer employment in offices and shops than in more dangerous workplaces, in extraction and 'traditional' sectors of manufacturing, such as cotton mills, timber yards, ship-building and iron and steel. Moreover, the application of science and technology to the labour process and the workplace could raise health and safety standards, making work less physically demanding (for example mechanisation in agriculture; cranes and conveyors in the docks). Technology removed some specific hazards. Important here was improved illumination with the transition from gas to electric lighting and the reduction in drive-band injuries due to the replacement of steam motive power by the machine-specific electric motor. This was not, however, a one-way process, and new materials and processes could create new

Table 5.7   Persons killed in industrial accidents, UK, 1915–49

	Factories	Building	Coal	Railways	Shipping	Total	Rate
1915–19	6 159	496	6 499	2 020	5 073	21 942	0.023
1920–4	4 081	458	5 462	1 442	3 566	16 020	0.017
1925–9	3 558	705	4 959	1 282	3 052	17 819	0.019
1930–4	2 898	584	4 626	1 100	1 964	11 954	0.012
1935–9	3 420	1 005	4 151	1 195	2 193	13 052	0.013
1940–4	4 768	1 359	4 063	1 526	1 661	14 463	0.014
1945–9	3 095	1 101	2 639	1 218	1 282	9 782	0.009

Source: Department of Employment, British Labour Statistics, Historical Abstract (1971, Table 200). See note, Table 5.2.

hazards (including the use of electricity). Furthermore, given the interconnections between general standards of health and occupational problems, the general improvement in real wages and living standards (housing quality, diet, reduced working hours, increased leisure time) undoubtedly had an ameliorative impact. In this respect, the extension of a state National Insurance system from 1911, the passage of the Holidays with Pay Act (1937: not enforced until after World War Two) and the creation of the 'Welfare State' towards the end of our period were vital contributory factors.

Indeed, more extensive state regulation of the workplace helped to protect workers from the worst excesses of competitive, free-market capitalism. In this respect the workmen's compensation legislation, rationalised by the Industrial Injuries Act of 1948, played an important role. So too did the extension of the factory and mines legislation and the passage of an increasing number of multifarious 'special regulations' by the Home Office designed to regulate specific dangerous working practices, such as the use of carcinogenic mineral-based lubricating oils or the inhalation of insidious airborne fibres within the workplace. The latter represented an attempt to control what was perhaps the most serious of occupational diseases – the pneumonicoses (e.g. silicosis, asbestosis, byssinosis). The first regulations to control asbestos dust and monitor those exposed were introduced in 1931. As Bartrip has shown, these new rules did have an ameliorative impact upon asbestosis rates (Bartrip, 1998). However, their impact was circumscribed by a number of flaws and by the conservative attitude of the Medical Boards who inspected victims of the disease (Tweedale and Hansen, 1998). The establishment of statutory medical inspection in the most dangerous trades and the extension of this practice in the 1937 Factory Act to any workplace where the Secretary of State deemed illness might be due to the nature of work were also considerable strides forward. However, many workers were suspicious, sceptical and evasive, fearing loss of employment and the use of such mechanisms to victimise labour activists (as occurred in shipping).

What is also evident is that workers, managers and employers became more aware of the interrelationship between occupation and health and from such consciousness evolved self-help and collective strategies to minimise risk. The spread of trade unionism

proved important in this respect, at two levels. The unions operated as effective parliamentary pressure groups, campaigning for
extension of legislative protection, as, for example, with the
Factory Act of 1937 and the Industrial Injuries Act of 1948. More
importantly, perhaps, the growth of workplace representation
and the power of the shop stewards, especially in manufacturing
and mining, added in another tier to the protective matrix offered
by collective organisation. By the 1940s many stewards were operating as unofficial health and safety officers, acting as a conduit
through which information was passed on to the Mines and Factories Inspectorate. The Inspectorate policed the legislation, but
Helen Jones' research has shown how important their educative
role was, not least in facilitating the formation of joint committees
between employers and unions to promote health and safety. The
formation of works safety committees in some of the larger companies helped to spread awareness of the work–health interface
(Mass Observation, 1942) as did the wartime joint production
committees (Hinton, 1994; Price, 1986).

The development of occupational medicine and state-sponsored
research also played key roles in changing attitudes and influencing policy, though the gap between identification of a specific
hazard and effective action to address it remained a wide one. The
influence of individual doctors and industrial hygiene pioneers
like Sir Thomas Legge continued to be significant in exposing
work practices insidious to health. Periodically, the *British Medical
Journal* publicised occupational health problems, as, for example,
the discovery by two Manchester physicians of the link between
cotton spinners' cancer and the oil used to lubricate the spinning
mule machine in 1922. More important, however, was the work of
several organisations created during the inter-war period specifically to promote industrial health, including the Industrial
Welfare Society, the National Institute of Industrial Psychology
(founded 1921) and the Industrial Fatigue (1918–28) and Industrial Health (1928–48) Research Boards. The latter organisations
significantly extended the theoretical knowledge of the 'human
factor' in industry, broadening out the work initiated by the
HMWC during World War One. The IFRB and the IHRB alone
produced 84 special research monographs and numerous articles
in the academic and medical press publicising their findings on
methods of work, job design, the work environment, vocational

psychology, occupational disease and monotony at work. These were amongst the first British initiated systematic work studies. Such ideas filtered through to industry via the influential Management Research Groups, Rowntree's Oxford Management Conferences, the British Science Guild, the Industrial Health Education Council and the Industrial Welfare Society (founded in 1918 as the professional body of the growing number of welfare officers in British industry).

'Welfarist' employers improved conditions, whilst legislation tended to lag behind much of the 'best practice' of the most progressive employers and to provide a basic minimum standard for the majority. The long-delayed Factory Act of 1937 (first mooted in 1922) legalised the maximum 48-hour working week, regulated permissible overtime to a maximum of six hours per week, introduced rest pauses and guidelines on weight carrying, extended medical inspection and made the provision of washing, seating and cloakroom facilities compulsory in all factories. This significantly extended the 1901 Factory Act and increased somewhat the role of preventative medicine in industry. Basic, minimum standards across industry rose as a result of such state initiatives.

The point needs to be made, however, that it was predominantly the expanding, relatively prosperous, modern sector of the economy based largely on the Midlands, South and South-East and London that registered the greatest gains in improving occupational health and safety standards. The new factories embodied the latest innovations in design and construction and were generally much better illuminated (larger windows and the use of the sodium discharge lamp), heated and ventilated, and had the most modern sanitary arrangements (*Factory Inspectors Report* – hereafter *FIR* – 1933, pp. 13–14, 49). In a comment on the benefits of migrating south for employment, the Chief Factory Inspector D. R. Wilson noted in 1937:

Another advantage gained by such transfers is that light and airy modern single-storey factories, scientifically planned to economise labour, and situated in open and healthy surroundings, take the place of the old, many storeyed buildings, with their restricted supply of fresh air and daylight. Work is consequently carried on under far more advantageous conditions both as regards the health of the worker and economy of labour and overhead charges (*FIR*, 1937, p. 13).

Electric power substituted for steam and gas and facilitated a cleaner, brighter and less accident-prone work environment. Moreover, as Waldron has noted, it was in the newer, more progressive plants, such as ICI, Boots, Lyons, the Chloride Company and Pilkingtons, where medical and welfare departments were established (Waldron, 1997, p. 198). Whilst there were relatively few company doctors employed, there were 1500 nurses and 1800 welfare officers employed in industry by 1939 (Stevenson, 1984, p. 191).

Recognition of significant changes and ameliorative tendencies needs to be balanced against evidence of much continuity in experience. Webster has shown how the economic depression impacted adversely on general health indices in those regions worse hit, such as Clydeside, Tyneside and South Wales. Gollan has also pointed out that the rising number of army recruits rejected on health grounds as the Depression deepened shows the impact of economic deprivation on workers' health. Forty per cent were rejected in 1933, 52 per cent in 1934 and 68 per cent in 1935 (Gollan, 1937, p. 192). It was in the older, depressed, staple sectors of the economy that industrial health standards stagnated and in some cases worsened in the inter-war years. The Factory Inspectorate identified mining, textile manufacture, ironworking, heavy engineering, shipping and shipbuilding as providing the least healthy working environment, the result partly of older factory architecture, design, space utilisation, technology, habits and entrenched attitudes (*FIR*, 1933, p. 41). Underemployment and short-time working took its toll, as one factory inspector commented:

Workers are returning to employment often after long periods of enforced unemployment. Many of them are suffering from lack of nourishment, and physically and mentally are less alert and more liable to mishap than in normal times. Again there is evidence that in restarting work after a long spell of illness more workers tend to over-exert their strength and energy, while others take time to get accustomed to working conditions again (*FIR*, 1933, p. 23).

Bryder and Burke have also argued that in two declining sectors –
slate quarrying in North Wales and metal mining in Cornwall –
standards of health at work deteriorated over *c*. 1900–39. Workers'
health was further undermined by the mental strain and anxiety
of recurrent short-time working, underemployment and unemployment, and by the intensification of workload ('speeding-up')
and increased monitoring and direct discipline that characterised
the inter-war period (see Chapter 3). Moreover, improving health
and welfare was an expensive proposition. In a cut-throat market
place such hard-pressed employers were wary of adding to their
costs. Hence the employment of works doctors, nurses and
welfare officers was rare, and technological renewal and electri-
fication quite sluggish in these industries.

Deteriorating working conditions were clearly evident in the
inter-war coal and iron industries. To cut costs, necessary repair
and maintenance work was ignored, so machinery became more
dangerous. A steelworker, James Stirling, commented on how
'Board of Trade regulations were infringed with impunity'
(Stirling, 1938, p. 82) and how the penny-pinching regime of a
new manager jeopardised safety standards in the works in the
1930s:

> Nasty things happened.... Chain tackle began to break. On
> one occasion a huge block, hook and chain fell some thirty
> feet from a roof beam to the floor and injured a man. He was
> lucky. The chain struck him. The block would have pulped
> him. The workers were scared and took risks rather than lose
> their jobs. Things happened that were not in the book; that
> would have been 'contributory negligence' had anything
> serious resulted. The accident rate did not fall proportionately
> to the reduced numbers employed or to the reduced volume of
> output (Stirling, 1938, pp. 86–7).

In the older factories, safety methods could still be extremely
primitive and negligence of safety was widespread. One worker at
the North British Locomotive Works in Springburn, Glasgow
recalled:

> The furnace men were protected with bags around their
> heads...and bags down their legs. The brickies used to wear

covers like hoods when they went into the boilers to do the
work, for the boiler was still hot.... We didn't wear glasses to
protect our eyes ... nobody bothered. It was the same with protection in guillotines. It was only when the factory inspectors
came in to complain that we had to do something with the
guards. But the men didn't want to use the guards, because it
was restricting them ... if you went down the shop, the guard(s)
was tied up (Hutchison and O'Neill, 1989, pp. 59–60).

Many coalowners exploited the markedly changed power relationship in the inter-war recession to skimp on safety and health,
as B. L. Coombes graphically recalled in his autobiographical
account, *These Poor Hands*, in 1939. Supple's research has shown
how occupational health and safety standards in British mining
stagnated between the wars, and, after a long trend of decline, the
incidence of accidental deaths in the pits increased in the 1920s
and 1930s (Supple, 1987, pp. 426–8). In mining it was estimated
that in the 1920s five miners were killed in Britain every working
day, and 850 were injured. Around one in 20 British workers
were engaged in mining, yet the industry accounted for around a
quarter of all occupational accidents. As before World War One,
mining remained plagued by a high incidence of injuries and
deaths in numerous small occurrences in pits up and down the
country. Mcintyre has argued that this was the product of mine-
owners intensifying the exploitation of labour, using the
depressed conditions to excessively speed up work. Big explosions were well publicised (such as the disaster at the Gresford pit
in Wales where 265 miners were killed in 1934), but it remained
this constant flow of accidents that accounted for most of the major
disability and death in the industry. Coombes' autobiography
evocatively captures the powerlessness of miners in this period
and the machismo milieux of the miners' workplace (Coombes,
1939, pp. 249–52). The miners' work environment also continued
to influence health and safety. Standards of ventilation and temperature were particularly important. Research by the Industrial
Health Research Board undertaken in the 1920s demonstrated
that miners working on hot pits at temperatures of 80°F and
above experienced 65 per cent more days off through sickness
and four times more minor accidents than those working in relatively
cool pits (defined as under 70°F). These conditions inevitably took

their toll on miners' health. By the late 1930s, medical reports were showing a very high incidence of sickness within mining communities and an increase in psychological problems (Morris, 1974, pp. 341–6).

Mechanisation through the introduction of coal cutters and conveyors also brought new hazards. Miners commented on how the noise of the new power-driven machinery at the coalface meant that they could no longer hear advance warning (by creaks, tears and 'splits') of a fall of rock face or ceiling:

> As we re-start to throw into the tram, we hear a sound like calico being ripped high above our heads, then a shower of small stones falls. We jump back, listen awhile, dash in again and fill until more falls again, then leap back to the safety of the standing timber. We work that way until the tram is level full.... We are always watching and listening, and always afraid that we might not jump quick enough. We do not fear the small stones so much, for their little 'taps' are part of our working life, and a small cut or a large swelling is not considered worth mentioning; but when these small ones drop, they are usually a warning that bigger ones are moving above (Coombes, 1939, p. 273).

Moreover, the new machinery, at least in the early stages (before dust dampening became commonplace after World War Two), generated higher quantities of dust, which exacerbated what was perhaps the most prevalent of miners' occupational health problems – 'black lung', or pneumoconiosis (Black, 1953, p. 105). After a long campaign the miners' union had succeeded in 1929 in getting pneumoconiosis added to the list of certified diseases and subject to compensation. Thereafter, the official statistics show that around 20 000 miners were declared 'pneumos' and dismissed from their work between 1931 and 1945. The disease was widespread, though particularly prevalent in the coalfield of South Wales, where the nature of the anthracite coal created particularly dry and dusty working conditions. In one post-war survey of around 3 000 miners in the Rhondda valley in 1952, half of all adult miners X-rayed had pneumoconiosis, many with the advanced form of progressive fibroid fibrosis that usually ended fatally. This created a dilemma. Working in the pits incubated the disease, but the government's policy of forcing pneumoconiotic miners out of work in the 1930s and 1940s through the Medical Panels, created massive hardship, as Francis and Smith have shown, in mining communities where there was little alternative employment (Francis and Smith, 1980, pp. 438–41).

Textile manufacturing provides another good illustration of stagnating occupational health and safety standards during the inter-war economic recession. In northern England the conditions in the cotton and wool factories deteriorated. Workers had to try to work with older machines and cheaper, shorter staple fibres, as employers sought to cut costs to stay competitive. Production was speeded up, worsening customary problems of noise, leading to a high incidence of minor accidents and overstrain. One spinner noted this propensity towards speed-up:

They put a little thing in the wheels at the end, which speeded the machine up. So we were having to work twice as fast, and they weren't giving us any extra money. We were running about like scalded hens! (Howarth, 1989, p. 31).

Similarly, a female weaver reflected back in the mid-1920s over 30 years of employment:

Whether spinner or weaver, the textile operatives are on their feet from the first turn of the wheel in the morning till the last turn in the evening. Their feet are never still, their hands always full of tasks, and their eyes always on the watch. For 48 hours a week year in and year out one is expected to keep up with the machine monsters. While the machinery runs the workers must stand; it cares nothing for fatigue or weakness or worry... (Pollock, 1926, pp. 234–5).

Whilst standards of safety were undermined by competitive pressures, the work environment became dirtier and dustier, incubating serious health problems, as Jones has noted, especially of the respiratory system (Jones, 1994, p. 71). In 1922 the connection between the lubricating oil used on the spinning mule and scrotal cancer was proven by two Manchester Royal Infirmary physicians. This was made a registered industrial disease and almost a thousand cases were reported between 1923 and 1939, around a third of which resulted in death. Periodical medical examination was the obvious preventative measure. However, this was rejected as an option by the mill-owners on the grounds of cost. Nor did mill-owners step up significantly the transition to the safer ring spinning technology. Long overdue, a simple anti-splash device using an oil-soaked pad was first utilised by a large spinning firm in 1938, 16 years after the *BMJ* article exposed spinners' cancer. Neither the addition of this device, nor provision for regular medical supervision specifically for mule spinners was incorporated in the 1937 Factory Act. As Wyke (1987) has shown, the regulations that were created, based upon a safer 'diluted' carcinogenic oil, were of only limited effectiveness.

In the weaving sheds the critical issues were the practice of artificial 'steaming', the volume of noise and the standard of illumination. The issue of humidity had long been a controversial one, with the unions campaigning from the 1880s to ban all forms of steaming. However, a comprehensive survey of the sickness records of some 20 000 cotton workers in the 1920s by the Industrial Health Research Board indicated that there were no significant differences in morbidity between those working in wet and dry sheds. In response, the state introduced revised regulations governing humidity levels, but did not outlaw the practice of steaming. Another IHRB investigation in 1935 showed that the clatter of the weaving shed (with noise levels in the 90–100 decibel range) seriously impaired hearing and had adverse effects upon weavers' productivity. To cope, weavers mastered the art of lip reading. In the mid-1930s the cotton trade unions complained of serious eyestrain and fatigue and a Factory Inspectorate survey of eight weaving sheds substantiated such claims. Again the employers' association rebuffed this agitation on the grounds of additional cost. 'Few of the cotton manufacturing firms', the Chief Factory Inspector noted in 1937, can at present afford the expert survey and the cost of a reorganised and rearranged lighting system' (*FIR*, 1937, p. 24).

The record for reducing work-related deaths and serious injuries was better than that of industrial diseases, a reflection, perhaps, of the later commitment of the state to regulating occupational health, as distinct from safety. As one dangerous practice or toxic substance was discovered, investigated, regulated and controlled,

Table 5.8   Reported cases of industrial diseases (deaths and injuries), 1901–39

	1901–5	*1921–5*	*1935–9*
Lead poisoning	2 093	1 083	677
Phosphorus poisoning	6	–	–
Arsenic poisoning	9	12	18
Mercury poisoning	32	13	20
Anthrax	129	125	144
Epitheliomatus ulceration*	–	324	821
Aniline poisoning	–	31[†]	47
Chrome ulceration	–	142	526
Total	2 239	1 730	2 253

* Mostly spinners' cancer.
[†] Just 1925.
Source: *Factory Inspectors Reports*, 1901–1939.

so links between other materials and ill health were discovered. New hazards replaced old ones as the economy developed. Between the early 1900s and the late 1930s, for example, the numbers of recorded cases of industrial disease (itself a significant underestimation of this problem) hardly changed, but industrial cancers took over from lead poisoning as the worst problem (Table 5.8).

The failure to control industrial disease was to be indicated later with the discovery of dust-related disease of epidemic proportions, especially in relation to miners' emphysema, asbestosis and industry-related cancers (such as asbestos mesothelioma). This was the product of several related factors. Because of the insidious, longer-term nature of many industrial diseases (where gestation periods of decades are not uncommon, as with asbestosis) the effects were not as immediately apparent as traumatic injuries sustained at work. Secondly, policy-making tended to emphasise financial compensation over really effective preventative measures. The state bowed to industrialists' views (for example in delaying the passage of a new Factory Act from 1922 to 1937 – see Rodgers, 1988), invariably regulating the use of dangerous substances (e.g. carcinogenic mineral oils; asbestos, 1931 regulations) rather than banning them altogether. Concomitantly, the economistic orientation of the British trade unions and their failure to prioritise occupational health issues played a part.

World War Two saw similar errors occurring in labour utilisation as over 1914–18: massive extension of working hours; intensification of labour and dislocation in labour markets, resulting in accumulating fatigue, growing absenteeism and a declining capacity to perform normal work tasks adequately. Again, the Factory Acts were suspended to facilitate production. Mass Observation in their 1942 study and an official government inquiry in 1947 lamented the slow diffusion of the 'human factor' research findings between the wars and the failure of such to achieve the critical mass capable of influencing early state wartime labour policies. Again, fatigue became a serious problem because of long work shifts and inexperience (Croucher, 1982, p. 261; Hartley, 1994, p. 147; Mass Observation, 1942, pp. 31–2). Some employers resorted to providing milk and vitamin supplements in workers' pay packets to help maintain their strength (Brown, 1998). Enforcing the blackout made matters worse, reducing factory ventilation, making for a hotter, more wearisome, vitiated atmosphere in which it was difficult to work. The position of married women with a family was particularly difficult, where they were occupied in war work and carried a double burden. Waldron has shown how the intensity of work and exhaustion of munitions workers led directly to higher accident rates: fatalities rose from 944 in 1938 to 1372 in 1940 and a peak of 1646 in 1941; whilst total recorded accidents rose from 180 103 in 1938 to a peak of 314 630 in 1942 (Waldron, 1997, pp. 203–5). Injury rates of female workers rose particularly dramatically during the war, with the numbers injured in the worst year, 1942, five times higher than 1938 (Braybon and Summerfield, 1987, p. 224). In response to such problems, working hours were reduced in munitions in 1942 to a maximum 55-hour week.

The resulting alienation helped to fuel rising trade union membership and political radicalisation. There were a series of wartime strikes and protests against grim working conditions (and unequal treatment). Croucher has argued that women were less willing to tolerate poor working conditions in wartime than male workers who were long accustomed to such standards (Croucher, 1982, pp. 262–3). In reality, as Penny Summerfield's recent seminal reconstruction of women's wartime lives shows, gender identities varied significantly, and it is difficult to 'pigeonhole' women's attitudes and reactions. Summerfield demonstrates this point by reference to the different reactions of two 'types' – the stoic and the heroic – to the increased dangers of wartime employment. Some women articulated fear, distaste and trepidation, though stoically accepting the necessity for such working conditions during the war emergency. Others positively welcomed the opportunity to engage in different work, relishing the heightened risks and dangers involved in their wartime careers (Summerfield, 1998, pp. 102–4).

Nevertheless, the pressures of wartime were to again prove ultimately ameliorative in their impact upon occupational health and safety standards. Accident rates fell after 1942 and even in that year Mass Observation could optimistically report that 'there is certainly no sign of a universal decline in industrial health. . . . Mostly it is those working long hours who are less healthy' (p. 203). What appears evident is that improvement in occupational health and safety standards was more widespread and less uneven across the labour force during the 1940s. This was partly the result of rising workers' bargaining power within the older 'staple' sectors of the economy as wartime pressures raised demand for labour and unionisation increased. A key factor, however, was the more pro-active wartime and post-war state. Ernest Bevin, as Minister of Labour, used coercion and the threat of removal of employers' privileges under Order 1305 to force companies to radically extend company welfare facilities and improve sanitary and safety provisions. The factory inspectors could force employers to employ a works nurse or doctor, and during the course of the war the number of works doctors rose from 60 to about 1000 (Braybon and Summerfield, 1987, p. 225). Such provision was much more extensive within the large factories, however, and most smaller employers continued to barely comply with the minimum provision of a first aid box.

Managerial and employer attitudes towards occupational health and safety continued to vary widely, though it is possible to detect change in a more progressive direction through the course of the first half of the twentieth century, and especially in the 1940s. In part, this represented the absorption, albeit in a slow and uneven way, of the lessons learnt by World War One and the drip-feed diffusion of the ideas of the occupational physiologists and psychologists. More of those in authority – employers and managers – came to realise the validity of the welfarist maxim that maintaining the morale and looking after the health and welfare of their labour force reaped rewards in terms of increased productivity. Such developments fed through into a marked fall in occupational mortality in the post-war years when the average fell below 2000 persons killed per year for the first time since official records began. In relative terms (and taking into account the rising total numbers employed in the economy), this meant that a British worker was, on average, almost three times less likely to meet his or her death through sustaining an injury at work in 1950 compared to the 1880s. The changing nature of the labour force, medical research, the wars, growing union power, changing employers' attitudes and state intervention were all significant factors in explaining such a transformation in experience. A further important variable was the reduction of exposure time as the period spent in employment shrank due to the raising of the school leaving age (11 in 1893 to 15 by 1950), the reduction in work hours (from 60 to average 44–5 by 1950), more holidays (one week with payment) and the increasing tendency to retire from work at age 60 (females) or 65 (males).

Conclusions

The evidence clearly indicates then that working conditions were much improved and the hazards of work considerably reduced between 1880 and 1950. Statistically, the risk of death through a work-related injury had been three times higher in 1880 than it was in 1950. It is more difficult to be definitive about occupational health, but controls over poisonous substances, such as lead and phosphorus, and the reduction of dust inhalation at work indicate marked amelioration in 'traditional' hazards, though to some extent this was offset by new diseases (e.g. cancers) and exposure to toxic substances (such as asbestos). The control of dangerous work practices that was achieved by 1950 was the product of several factors: growing awareness of the connections between work and health (the outcome of medical knowledge, research and intervention); changing employers' attitudes (embracing welfarist notions that improving health raised productivity and efficiency); public opinion within a more democratic state; labour and trade union pressure in the workplace, in national collective bargaining and in politics; and a more active, interventionist state which

extended regulatory mechanisms widely across industry to reform
the worst excesses of predatory, exploitative capitalism. Moreover,
occupational health cannot be divorced from public health. In the
late nineteenth century, poor and physically weak workers were
more susceptible to injury and disease at work. The massive
improvements in living standards, the attack on absolute poverty
and creation of the Welfare State all impacted positively on workers'
well-being and occupational health by 1950. This amounted to
quite a transformation in experience, though wide gaps in health
indices, as Jones has shown, still persisted between social classes.

   Nonetheless, work still impacted adversely upon health in 1950,
albeit to a markedly lesser degree than the Victorian period. As
late as the 1960s, engineering, construction, transport and foundry
workers suffered twice the incidence of bronchitis of professional
employees; labourers more than three times and miners and
quarrymen almost four times (Kinnersly, 1973, p. 147). Grim conditions in the past also cast a long shadow. Zweig was struck in his
1948 survey of coal miners by the prevalence of eye disease and
blindness, bow-shaped legs, blue-scarred faces and bodies, and
lost limbs: 'nowhere else can you see the same relative number of
disabled men as in a colliery village' (Zweig, 1948b, pp. 5–6).
Because of slow and relatively negligible change in patriarchal
attitudes, moreover, female workers continued to face the debilitating dual burden of paid work and sole responsibility for what
were still very labour-intensive tasks within the home. The comment made by Sybil Horner, one of the female factory inspectors,
in 1933 was still valid: 'women's work often begins where it
nominally ends. The house and dependants make their claims
upon the woman worker. Her work is never done' (*FIR*, 1933,
pp. 50–1). There was also a growing awareness of the adverse
impact of deskilling and monotony upon the workers' psyche, as
well as work-related stress, which increasingly cut across the man-
ual/non-manual work divide. In the 1930s the Senior Medical
Inspector of Factories noted:

   It is true that the pleasure of the craftsman is being crushed by
   the steady increase in mechanised processes, the result of which
   is seen in the tendency to rise of sickness rates for 'nervous
   disabilities'. . . . Repetition processes undoubtedly create a weariness not expressed in physical terms but in a desire by the

worker for temporary relief from the enforced boredom of occupation in which the mind is left partially or entirely unoc-cupied.... Vastly more days are lost from vague, ill-defined, but no doubt very real, disability due to *ennui* than from all the recog-nised industrial diseases put together.... The uninterested worker is an industrial invalid. Interest in work leads to indus-trial good health (*FIR*, 1931, p. 75).

With the changing nature of work a clutch of new hazards – such as occupational cancers – and stress-related problems, linked to the monotony, the pace and pressures of work, were emerging and replacing older recognised problems (such as lead poisoning, mine explosions and machinery-induced injuries). Despite much amelioration, occupational health and safety standards in Britain in 1950 diverged widely along a broad spectrum, much as in 1880. Working-class, blue-collar and blue-blouse workers were more adversely affected than middle-class professionals and office workers, who had always enjoyed cleaner and less dangerous work environments, shorter hours and more holiday entitlement. Occupational health provision in the 1940s was confined to the larger factories and was minimal in small firms, leading to wide disparities in standards across the labour force (Mass Observa-tion, 1942, p. 204). Such wide inequalities reflected, in part, a fundamental weakness within Britain's voluntary occupational health system.

At mid-twentieth century in Britain there was still a discernible tendency not to prioritise occupational health and well-being. This can be seen within the workplace, the unions and politics. As Mass Observation noted in 1942: 'In view of its evident impor-tance to production, the extent to which industries and unions concern themselves with the health of their workers is noticeably slight' (p. 203). The failure to recognise the importance of occupa-tional health was exemplified in the decision (criticised in two government committee reports in the later 1940s) not to create an occupational health service as an integral part of the National Health Service (Johnston and McIvor, 2000). This represented a major lost opportunity to reduce the wide gap between social classes and between best and worst practice, and thus radically improve occupational health and safety standards in the British workplace.

6

REGULATING WORK: THE ROLE
OF THE STATE

Between 1880 and 1950 one of the major changes which impacted on the nature of work in Britain was the encroaching intervention of the state, which extended its influence and regulatory activity deep into the heart of the workplace. 'The state' might be defined as the national and local government institutions within society in which power lay. Such developments were linked closely to a series of quite fundamental political, economic and social changes. As the franchise expanded, in 1884, 1918 and 1928, to provide working-class people with the vote, government needed to adapt to a broader constituency – indeed was forced to do so by the realignment of politics created by the rise of Labour to political power. The Labour Party was itself committed to a broader ideal of social justice, to be achieved through the mechanisms of higher levels of state intervention in social welfare and the economy, which impinged upon employment and the workplace. Growing awareness and the pressure imposed by public opinion and organised labour drew the state in to regulate the worse excesses of competitive, free market capitalism. Intensifying economic pressures, as British industry faltered in the face of foreign competition, also prompted state involvement in an attempt to maintain efficiency and international status. The state also reacted to the implantation and expansion of trade unions and the growing breadth and depth of strike activity and other popular protest, in both the economic and public interest, to maintain social stability. Two world wars also drew the state into unprecedented levels of

involvement and regulation of economic and social affairs, including significant engagement in the direction and organisation of
labour power and industrial relations. This chapter examines the
role played by the state in this sphere from c. 1880 to the middle
of the twentieth century, analysing the causes, extent, the impact
and the limitations of government intervention.

As we have reviewed in Chapter 1, there are several ways of conceptualising the role of the state in the workplace. Views conflict.
To briefly reiterate, Marxist historians utilising a materialist
model argue that the state in essence represented the dominant
economic interests within British society – the industrial bourgeoisie by the late Victorian period. Thus the state – at local and
national levels – provided a mechanism through which the power
and dominance of the bourgeoisie could be exercised over the
subordinate working classes. State control was initially coercive
and authoritarian but evolved as circumstances changed with the
growing power of organised labour in economic and political
spheres. The survival of capitalism came to depend upon making
concessions, upon flexibility and pragmatic reform as trade
unions grew in strength and the Labour Party achieved political
power (Reid, 1992). Maintaining power became, as Gramsci
argued, a more complex exercise, necessitating the extension of
control from the economic base to the political superstructure,
including influencing ideas and inculcating consent and commitment to capitalism within what he termed 'civil society' – the
neighbourhood, schools, churches and the clubs and institutions
of popular culture and leisure. Hence state intervention to legitimise the legal position of trade unions, ameliorate grim working
conditions, provide for workers' welfare in the event of unemployment and old age and provide minimum wages in the worst
'sweated trades' were designed to ensure capitalist hegemony.
According to Hay, these were elements within a 'social control'
strategy (Hay, 1978). Meanwhile, employers successfully resisted
any significant encroachment into what they regarded as the
fundamental right of private property: the power to manage
their own labour as they deemed fit.

There are now many historians who baulk at the oversimplicity
and teleological nature of such conceptualisations of state power.
The critique has been based upon the view that in reality the state
operates autonomously, policy varies according to the parties in

power, individual politicians have had a major influence and that power operates at numerous levels, sometimes pulling in different directions – local–national; different ministries; politicians and civil servants (Lowe, 1987; Wrigley, 1982, 1987). Political power is diffuse, partly because the competing interests are themselves divided internally; neither the elites nor labour were a monolithic entity. Fragmentation and heterogeneity – the incomplete nature of class formation – make it erroneous to read off from government the pursuit solely of capitalist interests, or, for that matter, the interests of any one class (Reid, 1992; R. Davidson, 1982; Tolliday and Zeitlin, 1991). After World War One, as Fraser has commented, the state was concerned to balance the interests of capital and labour (Fraser, 1999, p. 170).

It will be argued here that economic power was an important determining influence but that political outcomes – in this respect in relation to the reform of the labour market, work conditions and capital–labour relations – were the product of struggle and the interplay of competing ideologies and interests. The capacity of both capital and labour to influence policy-making ebbed and flowed with economic, political and social circumstances and could be radically affected by external events, such as war. However, a fundamental point is that labour were a powerful agency in this process over the period 1880–1950. This was partly the product of the extension of the franchise and the related development of a specific political presence for workers, in the rise of the Labour Party.

The outcomes were significant. Whilst the nature of industrial capitalism survived intact in Britain, it was markedly different – modified, liberalised and regulated from above – by 1950. With extensive state intervention in the working of the labour market and the workplace, nationalisation and a comprehensive Welfare State by 1950, much of the uncertainty and insecurity that characterised work in the past was removed. Workers also benefited in purely material terms with rising real incomes and reduced work time. Working conditions were considerably less exploitative and much of this transformation was the product of the protective matrix of state regulation, which had eliminated many of the worst excesses of the repressive capitalist work regimes of the Victorian era.

Nonetheless, the system survived virtually intact. The state was not a panacea for all ills. There were limitations to the penetration of the state into people's working lives, such intervention was not always in an ameliorative direction, and not always welcome. A wide gulf could exist between legislative provision and actual workplace practice. Fundamentally, the survival of capitalism as the dominant partner within the 'mixed economy' left intact the traditional system of production relations based upon exploitation of labour for profit rather than for the needs of society. Workers may well have organised themselves and enhanced their political power to the extent that they were more effectively cushioned from market forces, but they were still subjected to them nonetheless, as the depredations of the 1930s economic slump demonstrated. Moreover, the British state did little to encourage real democracy at work, even in the nationalised industries, in contrast to a number of other countries, and failed to fundamentally address the problems of occupational health. Initiative in this area was left largely to the private sector, deemed a prerogative of management. A critical failure, as argued in Chapter 5, lay in not incorporating an occupational health tier within the National Health Service. Despite considerable extension of state intervention in the workplace, capitalist control remained very real. Inequalities based on class and gender were blatantly apparent, and workers remained subject to the vagaries of a fragile economy and labour market, as well as the inexorable force of deindustrialisation in the middle of the twentieth century.

The State and the Workplace, c. 1880

The notion of the Victorian state imbued with a non-interventionist ideology of *laissez-faire* is now widely accepted as a myth. There was considerable government involvement, in a number of significant areas, including employment. However, it remains reasonable to describe the engagement of the state in this area by 1880 as severely prescribed, although this intervention did impact significantly upon some workers' experience in the labour market, notably child and female labour.

The motivating ideology in the nineteenth century was not the need to protect workers *per se* from the predatory tendencies of exploitative capitalism, but rather such legislation reflected patriarchal values (see Harrison and Mockett, 1990; Walby, 1986).

Initially, and up until the 1870s, the body of employment-related legislation only regulated the engagement of children and women in the labour market. The working hours of children were restricted by the early legislation and the first government inspectors and certifying surgeons (who checked the age and physical fitness of child workers) were introduced in 1833 to police these laws. Subsequent factory legislation further restricted the employment of children in various designated 'dangerous occupations' (e.g. chimney sweeping, 1875; white lead working, 1878). From the 1840s, some female workers were drawn into this state protective matrix, with women (and children under 13) being banned from employment underground in mines (1842) and the working day of female textile workers being confined to ten hours (1847). Later, women were banned from nightwork in factories. The Victorian conscience was clearly pricked by the graphic and lurid drawings in the 1842 Mines Inquiry which portrayed scantily clad female miners engaged in gruelling physical labour in close contact with male workers.

Behind such policy-making lay the patriarchal 'domestic ideology' of the Victorian period, which perceived women as of subordinate status to that of men and saw their 'proper sphere' to be the private domain of the home. Such views gained ground at all levels, within the state, employers and workers' trade societies of the mid-Victorian era, supporting the exclusion of women from the formal economy, by legal means if necessary. The hypocrisy of this, however, was that the intensely exploitative conditions of female employment in other smaller-scale and hence less noticeable, occupations, such as the clothing 'sweatshops', went unregulated. It did mean, however, that unequal treatment of women in legislation, as Alexander has noted, 'placed women in a different relationship to the state than men' (Alexander, 1984, p. 146).

The narrow basis of such employment legislation was broadened somewhat by 1880. The legislation was extended to incorporate some basic safety regulations (including a ban on children cleaning machinery whilst in motion), was made applicable to all factories employing over 50 workers and, in 1874, the normal working week was reduced to 56½ hours for all factory workers, male and female. Other notable legislation impinging on working conditions by 1880 included legal controls on unseaworthy and overloaded ships (Merchant Shipping Act 1876) and the Employers'

Liability Act of 1880. The latter admitted the culpability of employers for injuries and death sustained at work, though a court case was necessary to prove such liability (negligence or breach of statutory duty) and win damages by way of compensation for loss of earnings (Bartrip and Burman, 1983).

The other main area of state intervention which impinged on the nature of work was in the passage of labour law. Legislation passed between 1871 and 1876 (influenced by the extension of the franchise in 1867 and the growth of union membership and power in the early 1870s) not only legalised unions' very existence but clearly defined their rights at law regarding the protection of members' funds from damages and the right to picket during strikes at the place of employment. The legislation allowed unions to register as friendly societies, removed criminal liability in cases where workers breached their employment contracts and removed the possibility of prosecution of unions simply for conspiracy in restraint of trade, leaving unions with apparent legal immunity to strike in pursuit of a legitimate trade dispute. One historian of labour law summed up the impact of such changes thus: 'Certainly it was now the case that while a trade union's actions might be challenged, its very right to exist was now beyond question' (Brown, 1982, p. 119). This put British trade unions in an enviable position compared to their continental and North American counterparts.

This proved to be just about the limit of state intervention in the workplace up to 1880. The factory and mines code played an important role in consolidating gender inequalities within the Victorian workplace, adding legitimacy to concepts of separate spheres and the lesser value of female labour power. However, the protective matrix of the state was very uneven and selective, with most workplaces in 1880 completely unregulated, untouched by the arm of the state. Exemptions from the factory and liability legislation were commonly negotiated: 'contracting out' of the Employers' Liability Act was frequent; whilst the 1878 Factory Act had a longer section of exemptions and qualifications than the text of the Act itself. Employers could also delay special regulations (such as those on lead), as Bartrip has shown, through the arbitration clauses in the legislation (Bartrip, 1996). Evasion of workplace law was also commonplace (see Chapter 5). Moreover, apart from providing troops and police to maintain law and order during strikes and lockouts, the state kept out of industrial relations. It was deemed to be the sacrosanct prerogative of employers to strike an individual contract with a worker, paying whatever the market would bear.

Work, Industrial Relations and the Labour Market, c. 1880–1914

The extent of state involvement in working conditions and the labour market increased markedly from the 1880s as governments responded to accumulating pressures from a more hostile product market, the expansion of the franchise, the germination of a mass labour movement and war. The influence of the state expanded at three levels: as an exemplar, as policy-maker and law enforcer, and as a mediator in industrial relations between capital and labour.

The state, at the national and local level, was the largest single employer of labour throughout our period. On the eve of World War One something like a million workers were employed in the armed forces, the civil service, the Post Office, royal munitions factories and dockyards, and in local government services: roads and building maintenance, transport and the utilities. Conditions across such occupational categories varied markedly and belie any attempt to generalise. What appears to be the case, however, is that in the 1880s the state operated much like other private employers. Indeed an anti-trade union culture pervaded national and local government (Daunton, 1985; Lunn and Day, 1999; Lummis, 1994). In the main, wages were somewhat lower than equivalent private sector employees, but the compensation for state employees came in the forms of a wider package of non-wage benefits (such as pensions) and more job security, as Lummis has recently argued for the Post Office workers. By World War One the state was taking its responsibilities towards its directly employed workers more seriously and government became 'model' employers, at least in terms of working hours and contractual conditions. Local authorities, for example, were increasingly adhering to 'fair wages' clauses in their contracts of employment which matched local trade union rates and conditions (much to the annoyance of private sector building contractors). Royal munitions and dockyards were amongst the first to switch to a shorter 48-hour working week in the 1890s.

Union recognition, moreover, was granted relatively early for state employees (Clegg, 1985), a process Daunton associates with a conscious attempt to incorporate the growing and more militant unions in this sector. Unions were recognised for the 200 000 or so post office workers, for example, in 1906. By 1910, employees in national government were amongst the most well unionised of British workers. At a time when about one-fifth of the entire labour force were union members, 43 per cent in national government were unionised, almost on a par with cotton spinners (44 per cent) and not so far short of the coal miners (at 60 per cent).

The role of the state as an exemplar in labour markets was weakened somewhat during the interwar depression, though the increase in Labour-controlled local authorities after 1914 spread 'model rules', including formal union recognition and acceptance of the closed shop. By 1950 the state's presence and influence as an exemplar was even more significant with the massive expansion of public employment due to the nationalisation and Welfare State programmes. In local labour markets dominated by disproportionate state employment such a role undoubtedly had a significant upgrading impact on wages and working conditions.

In policy terms, several important new initiatives were taken pre-World War One, suggesting a critical shift by the state into new areas of intervention in the workplace. The passage of the Workmen's Compensation Acts of 1897 and 1906 have been interpreted as a revolutionary extension of state involvement in work which made compensation for injury, death and some prescribed industrial diseases at work automatic (see Hunt, 1981; Bartrip and Burman, 1983). The Trade Boards Act 1909 also set an important precedent, effectively breaching the free market mechanism and establishing minimum wages in some (initially six) of the lowest paid, 'sweated' trades. The Act created Wages Boards, comprising representatives of employers and workers, in four scheduled occupations (chain-making; box-making; ready-made clothing; lace-making), which established minimum wage rates. In some cases earnings doubled as a result. The number of scheduled occupations was widened progressively and the 1918 Trade Board Act laid down that minimum wages could be applied to any seriously underpaid workers. The factory and mines codes were also massively extended during this period (discussed in Chapter 5). Meanwhile state provision was also extended, notably by the radical Liberal administrations of 1906–14, to more effectively regulate the labour market and to insure workers for loss of employment and for old-age retirement. Designed primarily to alleviate poverty, such measures had a significant knock-on effect on employment: easing frictional unemployment (via the labour exchanges); laying a floor on wage undercutting; helping to maintain physical efficiency (and hence subsequent employability); and taking some older workers out of the labour market altogether. By introducing the minimum wage through the Trades Boards and the social wage through National Insurance (extended and made applicable to most workers in the early 1920s – though excluding domestic servants and agricultural labourers), the state had a major impact in the labour market. Local authority commitment to 'fair wages' clauses for their directly employed labour provided a further progressive influence in pre-Depression labour markets.

Views on the overall impact of ameliorative legislation, however, vary considerably. Much of this was welcomed by workers, though some changes were unpopular because of their intrusive nature and adverse effects. Lower-paid workers, including apprentices, opposed the contributions they had to make to National Insurance, whilst others felt threatened by loss of work after medical inspections under the special regulations (Young, 1979; Knox, 1990). The patchy coverage of legislation and *ad hoc* half-hearted nature of policy-making continued to characterise such initiatives. Evidently, the state continued to respond to specific pressure points, as and when they were forced to intervene or react (Wrigley, 1982; R. Davidson, 1982). Lack of collective organisation, or the absence of a specific public campaign, pressure group or reform network left considerable chunks of the labour force without any significant protection. Domestic servants, agricultural labourers and clerical workers would be good examples. Elsewhere, pressure groups such as the Anti-Sweating League, the Women's Trades Councils and the Women's Trade Union League had notable successes (for example in getting the Factory Acts extended to cover laundries, and the Trades Boards legislation). At the other extreme, the state intervened strategically to placate the well-organised and militant coal miners, which were the only group of workers in Britain to achieve both a maximum eight-hour working day (1908) and a minimum wage (1911) by legislation. This was a reflection of the collective power of the MFGB, the pivotal importance of coal to the economy and the growing concern of the state to mediate in industrial concerns in the public interest.

One contemporary talked of the 'chaos of legislative regulation' (Proud, 1920) on the eve of World War One, which he put down to the piecemeal process of employment legislation as the state reacted to particular exposed 'evils'. Apart from its uneven coverage, the legislation was notoriously difficult to enforce. Perhaps less visible but by no means intangible hazards to health – dust, temperature in spinning rooms, shuttle-kissing, fining systems, lighting and noise – were regulated very late in the day or simply ignored. Moreover, as we discussed in Chapter 5, the response of the British state to workplace dangers was invariably to regulate and control, rather than ban practices proven to be insidious to health. Some elements of the factory code (e.g. child labour) were easier to enforce than others, which were ignored or widely subverted. The latter applied to the ban on cleaning machinery in motion, lack of machine guards, time-cribbing, employment after childbirth, reading hygrometers (measuring humidity) and the system of certifying surgeons approving young workers as fit for employment (Bolin-Hort, 1989, pp. 67–100; Joyce, 1980, pp. 69–70; McIvor, 1997). A cotton overlooker admitted in 1910 that his mill had a bell-push warning system connected from the gate house to the mill to give warning of the arrival of the inspector (*Cotton Factory Times*, 30 Dec. 1910; see also *FIR*, 1911, p. 97). A dearth of inspectors appointed from the working class, combined with fear of victimisation, hampered successful prosecution of law-breakers so that the Factory Inspectorate pre-1914 were only 'sporadically effective . . . non-compliance was evident everywhere' (McFeely, 1988; Jones, 1994, p. 17).

The involvement of the state, and its influence, was also clearly felt in one other area impinging upon the workplace – industrial relations and labour law. Wrigley has persuasively argued how even prior to World War One the notion of industrial relations being the 'private affair' of employers was breaking down. The state was drawn in, though initially this was *ad hoc* and hesitant. Direct government mediation in an industrial dispute first occurred in the 1893 coal lockout. A strike was averted in the national rail dispute in 1907 by the intervention of Lloyd George,

President of the Board of Trade. The Conciliation (Trade Disputes) Act of 1896 and the formation of the Labour Department of the Board of Trade – both recommendations from the Royal Commission on Labour 1891–4 – were significant indicators of an extension of state responsibility at the end of the nineteenth century. Public opinion was becoming more favourable towards the unions and a firm legal framework was re-established with the Trades Disputes Act of 1906, after reverses in the law courts culminating in the infamous Taff Vale decision. During the 1910–14 labour unrest, moreover, the state was drawn inexorably into capital–labour relations. The Cabinet discussed most of the major confrontations of this immediate pre-war period, with the Labour Department of the Board of Trade (especially George Askwith and Winston Churchill) playing a major role as conciliator and industrial relations troubleshooter. The aims were twofold: to minimise disruption to a fragile economy under increasing threat from overseas competition, and to stabilise fracturing industrial relations (Wrigley, 1982; R. Davidson, 1982).

Countervailing Tendencies: the Wars and the Depression

From 1914 to 1950 state intervention in the workplace and in industrial relations increased massively, influenced by political contingencies, the strategies of political parties, external factors, including economic pressures and public opinion. However, the two world wars were critical catalysts. World War One drew the state into unprecedented levels of intervention in the workplace. The government took vast swathes of industry into direct control – comprising some 3.5 million workers by the end of the war – and formulated a strategy of labour utilisation which would achieve its main wartime objectives: maximum output for the war effort whilst balancing the demands of the armed forces for personnel. The Emergency Powers Act and the Munitions Act of 1915 enshrined government policy, constituting what Rubin has defined as 'a more coercive, legally backed industrial relations strategy' (Rubin, 1987). It laid down that unions were to accept the dilution of labour – the importation of unskilled male and female labour into the munitions and war-related work factories. Regional dilution 'commissioners' were subsequently appointed to oversee such a transference of labour (Lord Weir was the most controversial appointee on the Clyde). A new disciplinary code was introduced, with legal backing, allowing the removal of all restrictive practices, including ca'canny (going slow) for the duration of the war. Labour mobility in war work was stopped, by the introduction of a leaving certificate system (which was later extended to the private sector). Strikes and lockouts were declared illegal and arbitration in disputes compulsory. To enforce such policy a network of munitions tribunals were established throughout the country. In one of the first cases, three shipwrights from Fairfields shipyard on the Clyde were imprisoned for taking illegal strike action in October 1915. Emergency powers were used to push through the dilution campaign in the face of labour opposition, notably on the Clyde and in northern England.

In James Hinton's classic thesis this demonstrated the dominance of capitalist interests in the wartime Cabinet and epitomised the pro-employer state, creating a 'servile' labour force, subjugated and coerced to the whim of capital during the war. Others, however, see the policies of the state as reflecting a range of sectional and competing departmental interests, with tactics varying from region to region (Wrigley, 1982, 1987) from which it is difficult to generalise. Middlemas has developed the theory that state wartime policy represented a push towards a more corporatist state in which the government played a key role as the manager of industrial relations. Rubin's history of the munitions tribunals argues that the state was moving more to a corporate approach, stressing the reciprocity of wartime state policy and the even-handed treatment of employers and workers. Reid (1985) goes further to argue that wartime policy by the state favoured labour, a result of the strategic growth of trade unions and wartime demand for workers. At the extremes, the wartime state is portrayed alternatively as the coercive messiah of capitalist interests or the altruistic, benevolent champion of workers' aspirations.

In reality, state policy developed in an *ad hoc*, experimental fashion, characterised by sectional infighting but, in the main, a preoccupation with maximising productivity which in practice meant encroaching upon the entrenched interests of both capital and labour, and attempting to reconcile the interests of both. Compensations to dominant groups within the labour force during the war were, on paper at least, quite significant. The government was forced to create an excess profits tax to control profiteering, to promise legislation to return to the pre-war status quo and to maintain piecework wage levels during the war. The creation of a Ministry of Labour in 1916 constituted an acceptance by Liberal politicians that labour's interests merited institutional recognition (Melling, 1989). By the end of the war the state was directly intervening to improve welfare provision in munitions factories and was actively promoting the extension of collective bargaining through the formation of Whitley Committees in poorly organised trades. Some labour and trade union leaders were also offered Cabinet positions and became members of vital wartime government committees, suggesting a conscious attempt to co-opt or incorporate organised labour into the corridors of power.

The impact of state policy, however, was uneven. The maintenance of morale and the muzzling of strikes and lockouts undoubtedly contributed to a marked fall in working days lost during strikes in the war years in contrast to 1910–14. Nevertheless, strikes continued and, indeed, roughly doubled in intensity in the final two years of the war compared to the first two years. At the heart of such militancy was a shop stewards' movement with syndicalist aims. The strikes and the germination of radical workshop organisation were partly a protest reaction to the ongoing process of dilution and a reflection of disillusionment with the failure of state policies, especially relating to price controls (inflation ate severely into wage levels) and the failure to prevent wartime profiteering. In reality, the excess profit tax was largely a dead letter – and Burgess has persuasively argued that there was an inequality of sacrifice during hostilities. War weariness also played a part. Moreover, state intervention promoted scientific management schemes and the more intensive exploitation of labour, further extending the division of labour. Much depended upon the pre-war context upon which such changes were impinging. The extension of workplace organisation and resistance was most marked, Hinton has demonstrated, where dilution was most unusual prior to the war – areas such as Sheffield and the Clyde. Whereas in other regions where engineering and metalworking was already deskilled, or where there was a weaker craft tradition (such as in the Midlands), wartime state regulation went virtually unchallenged.

What is clear is that by the end of World War One, the state was much more intimately involved in the workplace, the labour market and industrial relations, indeed to an unprecedented degree. Policy, however, proceeded off the cuff. Wrigley has identified a 'mosaic of ad hoc state controls and interventions' (Wrigley, 1987, p. 65), and a recent historian of the period has suggested that the government's labour power policy was chaotic and ineffective until the final year of the war (Grieves, 1988). Be that as it may, the evidence still strongly supports the view that on balance, state policy was detrimental to the interests of large sections of labour during wartime, fundamentally stripping power from workers, shackling the trade unions and undermining workers' independence and autonomy. One Scots labour leader, Robert Smillie, aptly termed the Munitions Act 'the workers' slavery bill' and even the right-wing *Glasgow Herald* admitted that it ushered in a return to despotic, arbitrary management. As one Glasgow shop steward (David Kirkwood) spat out to Lloyd George: 'I am as much a slave to Sir William Beardmore [his employer] as if I had the letter "B" branded on my brow' (Rubin, 1987, p. 255).

Between the wars, the state continued to have a significant influence upon employment and the workplace, through legislation, industrial relations policy and its economic and social welfare strategies. As before the war, this was influenced by electoral reform, by the state of the economy and labour markets. The brief post-war boom gave way to a deep and sustained recession, characterised by mass unemployment throughout the 1920s and 1930s. Shifting public opinion was also important, as was the relative power of capital and labour.

Again, interpretations of state involvement during this period differ markedly. Recent research has been severely critical of earlier Marxist-driven accounts which perceived inter-war state policy as a direct reflection of capitalist interests, functioning to contain and neutralise the emerging workplace and trade union movements by strike-breaking activities, maintaining high levels of unemployment and passing draconian anti-labour legislation, notably the Trade Disputes and Trade Union Act of 1927. On the contrary, 'revisionist' writers such as Lowe, Crowther and Whiteside stress the high commitment of inter-war governments to social welfare and the extension of social expenditure during the recession, especially the maintenance of unemployment pay in the 1920s, which impacted positively in the workplace through the 'social wage'. Furthermore, the working out of government industrial relations policy, such commentators argue, was neither one-sided nor cynically constructed to discipline labour. Rather, Lowe has argued, 'the principal objective of successive governments was always to force industry, in the absence of any spontaneous consensus, to confront and then to resolve its own problems' (Lowe, 1987, p. 189), and both organised capital and labour supported a return to 'voluntarism' in industrial relations. The state, in short, was not a bludgeon manipulated by the industrial bourgeoisie to destroy workshop organisation, undermine the trade unions and resurrect employer hegemony after the dislocation of the 'radical decade', 1910–20.

There is much of value in such a reappraisal, especially in relation to the expansion of state social welfare provision, which had major implications, as Whiteside has pointed out, for trade unionism and collective bargaining. Clearly there is a need for a more balanced evaluation of state policy as it impinged on the workplace. Nevertheless, what fails to be brought out clearly from such revisionism is that state policy reflected changing power relationships between the wars. State industrial relations policies both reflected and contributed to the declining power of labour at the point of production, as unemployment deepened, the shop stewards' movement atrophied and union membership collapsed. Whilst political capacities emanating from the workplace were castrated, as Price has demonstrated, the power of labour in national politics was enhanced as government reacted to the radical extensions of the franchise, adapted to the electoral rise of the Labour Party and became even more aware of the need to govern through co-operation and consent.

The argument for a state-supported drive to cut labour costs and stabilise volatile labour relations over 1918–27 *largely upon the employers' terms* remains convincing. Decontrol of wartime industries left workers in the staple sectors virtually unprotected to face the vicious vagaries of market forces during the recession as union membership spiralled downward. This led the way to deep wage cuts and a growing divergence in social experience between the 'depressed areas' and the more prosperous growth areas of the economy. Money wages fell by a half in coal mining and iron and by over a third in heavy engineering, cotton and shipbuilding, bucking a national trend of relative wage growth (Peden, 1985, p. 69). In the main, the state supported the employers' inter-war

counter-attack against labour in so far as it pursued the dismantling of syndicalist-influenced workshop power, the undermining
of the strike weapon and endorsement of peaceful collective
bargaining and moderate trade union policies, controlled by a
more centralised union structure headed by the TUC. The strategies utilised to facilitate a revival of managerial control and
authority on the shop floor varied with the state treading a thin
line between coercion and incorporation: the carrot and the stick.
After World War One the government developed a quite sophisticated strike-breaking mechanism, which led Morgan to the
conclusion that by 1921 'an anti-labour front was what the government closely resembled' (Morgan, 1979, p. 280). This was
brought into full play during the General Strike of 1926, when the
state's preparation for such a struggle was extensive, decisive and
suggests that the government at the end of the day welcomed an
opportunity to demonstrate the futility of direct action, thus critically undermining the key weapon of labour during the 1910s.
The anti-labour legislation passed in 1927, the failure to pass new
ameliorative factory legislation until 1937 (first mooted during
the minority Labour government in 1922) and the sidelining of
trade union influence in the corridors of political power in Westminster demonstrate further the hegemony of capital over labour
in inter-war industrial politics. As Price noted, none of the governments of the 1930s were interested in according a consultative
role to the trade unions. MacDonald kept the unions at arm's
length in his concern to demonstrate that Labour could govern in
the 'national' interest; Baldwin temperamentally preferred to do
nothing; and Chamberlain was wary of the concessions that would
be necessary in return for Labour's co-operation over rearmament. Thus even during the rearmament period, the trade union
presence at Whitehall was shadowy. There was no consultation
over conscription, for example, and Chamberlain was unwilling
to win Labour support by repealing the Trade Disputes Act
(Price, 1986, p. 185).

It is important to stress, however, that the primary target was
the socialist, syndicalist and revolutionary left, and their power
base within the workplace, not the trade union movement *per se*.
Mass unemployment largely took care of the latter, at least until
the later 1930s. Moreover, many policy-makers, including Baldwin, recognised the role that a weakened but significant union

movement could play as a bulwark against the spread of communist ideas and militant tactics. There had to be legitimate channels
for workers to express grievances otherwise they were liable to
take unofficial action, creating space for the proliferation and
growing influence of 'rank and file' movements. Hence, the
Trades Disputes and Trade Union Act of 1927 represented both
a draconian anti-labour policy, severely restricting union rights –
a 'charter for blackleg labour' as a Transport and General Workers' Union official put it – and was remarkable, as Anderson and
Lowe have shown, for what it omitted (including demands for
strike ballots and compulsory arbitration). Thereafter, the state
swung its weight behind a corporatist approach, epitomised in the
Mond–Turner talks, recognising on the one hand the legitimate
rights of organised labour to strike and bargain collectively, as
well as the freedom of trade unionists from victimisation, and, on
the other hand, supporting a progressive strand of employers in
their attempts to remove restrictive practices, raise efficiency and
modernise industry. In the 1930s, the state largely left business
interests to their own devices: as Peden has argued: 'Under the
National Government, business confidence was not to be disturbed
by departing from the "rules of the game" whereby government
confined itself to establishing conditions in which private enterprise
could flourish. . . . Fiscal orthodoxy, and a reluctance to intervene
directly in business decisions, remained as relics of *laissez-faire*'
(Peden, 1985, p. 119). Thus, judicious utilisation of coercion and
corporatism by the state facilitated the restabilisation of capitalist
hegemony in the workplace after the challenges of wartime. This
process of stabilisation, however, involved concession and reform,
as well as elements of coercion, not least through extended state
social expenditure and social provision between the wars which
had significant and lasting implications for work and industrial
relations.

   The traditional notion of the inter-war years as a barren period
in terms of state social policy has now been substantially revised
(see Crowther, 1988; Peden, 1985; Whiteside, 1996). Social service
expenditure significantly increased over the inter-war period. The
largest expenditure was on unemployment benefit, introduced in
1911 and massively extended in scope after World War One with
the Unemployment Act (1920) and the introduction of 'uncoven-
anted benefit' in 1921 (that is, benefit not covered by workers'

National Insurance contributions). Undoubtedly, the provision of such benefit helped to alleviate hardship, neutralise labour unrest and maintain social stability. It also had a number of direct effects on those in work. Firstly, the social wage consolidated the floor below which wages would rarely fall. This helped to reduce the number and attractiveness of casual jobs within the economy, the resort of many unemployed workers pre-1914. Secondly, it helped workers to maintain their physical efficiency, thus enhancing their potential re-entry into the labour market. The anomalies within the legislation, however, impacted adversely upon particular groups, notably married women and agricultural workers, who were largely prohibited from benefit. In practice, it favoured those willing to take on any work, whilst discriminating against those made unemployed as a consequence of industrial action, for example through involvement in a strike. State intervention was limited, moreover, to the outpayment of the dole in the event of loss of work. There was no concerted effort to alleviate unemployment by providing work through economic management strategies or public works programmes, as, for example, in the 'New Deal' in the USA. It has been suggested, further, that high levels of state benefits between the wars actually increased unemployment levels, because the social wage reduced the incentive to take on low-paid work and corroded the work ethic (Peden, 1985, p. 110). The evidence for the latter assertion, however, is extremely tenuous.

In a seminal study, Whiteside has demonstrated how the extension of social welfare by the state in the inter-war period impacted upon the workplace and had important implications for industrial relations. In this respect state policy was diametrically opposed to employers' interests. The dominant employers' organisations between the wars bitterly objected to the additional costs that such state welfare provision meant. Moreover, by the end of the 1930s, the assumption that wages from employment were the basis of workers' subsistence and living standards was seriously eroded by the extension of state welfare benefits. The role of the unions in providing welfare benefits had atrophied sharply and workers had come to rely directly upon state provision. After much initial opposition the unions adjusted to such a heightened state role. There was widespread support for the Beveridge Report of 1942. As Whiteside argued: 'By the outbreak of the Second World War, a much weaker movement was generally placing far less emphasis on the extension of union autonomy and control through the bargaining process and far more on the benefits to be gained from cooperation with central government. This was chiefly evident in labour policies promoting a centrally planned economy and state services' (Whiteside, 1987, p. 212).

World War Two and the landslide Labour victory of 1945 brought state intervention in the workplace to new levels. This was partly the product of the severity of the wartime emergency and the post-war reconstruction, which necessitated the mobilisation of all the productive forces of the country under the direction of the government. The process was facilitated, though, by a shift in both public opinion and the policies of the major parties between the wars towards a heightened state role and by the prior experience of the 1914–18 conflict. Between 1939 and 1945 political views were pushed further to the left, with a change in ethos even detectable within progressive segments of the industrial bourgeoisie towards the 'encroaching' state. As Sir Cecil Weir, head of the British Employers' Confederation, noted after the war:

> Public ownership was not of itself the bogey which it had been. We had to ask whether a particular enterprise would work better under public or private ownership and it was clear there were cases where the former could not be avoided. Where it was in the interests of the community, certain services should be publicly owned (in Middlemas, 1979, p. 296).

We lack the space here for a detailed treatment of government policies during the 1940s. But it is possible to highlight several areas that particularly impinged upon employment and the workplace. The mobilisation of labour power in prosecution of the war was both more extensive and more successful than during World War One. The dilution of labour created less antagonism and days lost through industrial disputes during wartime were around half the average of 1914–18. This was partly the consequence of experience and fortuitous external factors – not least the deep-rooted commitment of the dominant organisation on the revolutionary left – the CP – to the war effort after Hitler invaded the Soviet Union in 1941. However, the critical factor was the state's handling of labour during wartime. In Churchill's newly formed coalition government of May 1940 a number of Labour leaders were given prominent Cabinet posts. However, the truly inspired appointment was that of Ernest Bevin, general secretary of the TGWU (and not even an MP) as the Minister of Labour. Through the Essential Works Orders, the Emergency Powers Act and Order 1305 Bevin used the law to tightly control labour. This regime reintroduced the sorts of controls that existed in 1917–18, including bans on industrial action and labour mobility, and a draconian fining system to punish recalcitrant behaviour. Voluntary dilution was replaced from December 1941 with the compulsory conscription of female workers, bringing an extra 2 million into paid employment. Bevin assumed what were virtually dictatorial powers – even more extensive than during World War One. There were, however, two crucial differences in the operation of state labour management during World War One and Two. Firstly, workers' commitment to the 1939–45 war was cemented by the fact that it was predominantly their own representatives in the coalition government that were directing the workplace. At the pinnacle was Ernest Bevin, Minister of Labour, cajoling workers to maximise effort to ensure the defeat of fascism.

Secondly, Bevin and the wartime Labour ministers ensured that in contrast to World War One there would be much more of an equality of sacrifice within society. Hence, despite vociferous employer complaints, profiteering was effectively controlled, as was wartime price inflation (by rent controls and subsidising foodstuffs). Taxation was heavily redistributive upon the high income brackets (the top tax rate reached 98 per cent in 1949). Moreover, wartime wages were allowed to rise in line with, and earnings to surpass, the rate of price inflation. The result was a period of sharply narrowing wealth inequalities. Fox has estimated that over 1938–47 the real value of wage incomes rose by some 18 per cent, salaries fell by some 21 per cent and property income fell by 15 per cent (Fox, 1985). Bevin also made a special case for raising the wages of the poorest paid male workers, including agricultural labourers, railwaymen and miners. The extension of company welfarism also helped cement worker consent to the war effort. Here, again, Bevin played a critical role, cajoling and forcing employers, under threat of removal of their Essential Works Order, to improve company medical and welfare provision. Hence nurses, doctors and welfare officers multiplied on the shop floor and the provision of works canteens increased threefold.

Almost 5000 canteens were directly created by Bevin in controlled establishments and a further 6800 by private employers by 1944.

Industrial stability was further enhanced by the integration of the trade unions into joint consultation at all levels of government and industry. At the peak level, the TUC was drawn in from the wilderness to represent labour on the National Joint Advisory Council (1939) and the Joint Consultative Committee (1940). The employers' organisations were conceded similar status, leading Middlemas to argue that organised labour and capital had become 'governing institutions' within a tripartite industrial relations system with the state at the fulcrum. This corporatist conceptualisation may well be an exaggeration, but there is something in the idea that wartime circumstances raised the status of organised labour to one of parity with capital in Whitehall. As Bevin's biographer noted: 'The organised working class represented by the trade unions was for the first time brought into a position of partnership in the national enterprise of war – a partnership on equal not inferior terms, as in the First World War' (Bullock, 1960). Bevin further extended collective bargaining by radically extending both the Whitley Committees and the Wages Boards (as the Trades Boards were renamed) – 46 new Whitley Commitees were formed during World War Two and by the end of hostilities a colossal 15.5 million workers were covered by the minimum wage provisions of the Wages Boards. On the shop floor, moreover, Bevin directly encouraged the formation of joint production committees to extend workers' participation. At their peak in June 1944 there were almost 4500 such committees, covering 3.5 million workers (Price, 1986; Hinton, 1994). By the end of the war, the JPCs were seriously encroaching into managerial prerogative, with issues previously regarded as the sacrosanct domain of management being regulated, including wage payment systems, piece rate fixing, technology, machine staffing, transfers of labour, health and welfare. These were quite profound changes: A Mass Observation survey in 1942 noted how 'the quick sack and the unexplained instability' of the 1930s had virtually disappeared and how the war brought 'reduced scope for crude discipline by threat' (Mass Observation, 1942, p. 106).

In many respects these fundamental changes in workplace relations forged by an interventionist wartime state persisted and were adapted and extended further in peacetime by a Labour administration with a massive majority, a mandate to radically reconstruct society and a commitment to extend further the responsibility of the state in the well-being of people's lives. Employment in the public sector was massively extended as a large chunk of the economy was nationalised (coal, electricity, gas, civil aviation, iron and steel, transport, the Bank of England) in line with manifesto pledges. Legislation impinged directly upon the workplace in several important respects: legislation in 1946 resurrected the immunities the trade unions enjoyed prior to the vindictive Trades Disputes Act of 1927. This laid a firm foundation in law on which further trade union expansion occurred post-war. The Industrial Injuries Act of 1948 replaced the workmen's compensation legislation, easing workers' ability to gain financial recompense for occupational injuries and disease, and significantly raising such benefits. The latter were set at £2.25 a week in response to concerted trade union pressure, considerably above the rates of £1.30 for sickness and unemployment benefit. The implementation of the Holidays with Pay Act (1937) meant that the post-war generation of workers were the first to enjoy one week's remunerated holiday. The Welfare State itself, based upon the 1942 Beveridge Report, extended the 'social wage' with all the ramifications for workers and industrial relations that Whiteside noted for the 1930s. Pensions and the raising of the school leaving age exorcised two of the most injury-prone segments of the late nineteenth-century labour force from employment, whilst the extension of the policing mechanisms (regarding Wages Boards, mines legislation, Factory Acts and Home Office special regulations for dangerous trades) raised occupational health and safety standards. The new Labour government was also firmly committed to economic management, and used controls over the economy to maintain full employment (at less than 3 per cent) in the post-war years.

These were radical changes, but need to be kept in perspective. There were limits to the encroachments made by the state into the post-war workplace. Managerial prerogative may well have been eroded, but market forces continued to determine wages and conditions across some 80 per cent of the economy still in private hands, perpetuating massive inequalities in incomes and job security, across the manual/non-manual divide, by gender and skill. Moreover, the public corporation made no specific provision for direct workers' participation, hence a real opportunity to extend worker democracy and control in industry was squandered (see Chapter 8). Furthermore, the chance to radically overhaul occupational health and safety, bringing it within the orbit of the NHS, was rejected by the Labour government in the later 1940s (see Chapter 5). Finally, the state continued to pursue what were orthodox, patriarchal strategies in relation to female participation in the labour market. Wartime crèches and nurseries were allowed to lapse at the end of hostilities and married women were again expected to return to the home. Moreover the state continued to legitimise the undervaluation of female labour, for example in supporting two separate minimum wages based on gender for the same work and in their failure to implement the Royal Commission on Equal Pay (1946). These policies of the post-war 'socialist' state helped to mould attitudes, perpetuate gender apartheid at work and consolidate the prevailing view that – in peacetime at least – paid work and all that impinged upon it were not the proper domain of married women.

These caveats apart, it was clearly the case that nationalisation, labour law, the welfare reforms and full employment extended the reach of the state much deeper into the workplace by 1950. This had important consequences. Such developments facilitated a consolidation of trade union power and authority, both on the shop floor and at the national level, where the trade unions enjoyed a close working relationship with the Attlee administrations. State labour policies also helped to stabilise industrial relations, with working days lost running at about half the level of World War One. Workers' rights and working conditions were transformed through this mediation in the labour market, at a number of levels, by the state. This may not have been quite the 'new Jerusalem' promised by Labour's mandarins, but the outcome was a radical change, involving a sharpened sense of citizenship in the workplace which imbued workers with a sense of optimism, hope and confidence for the future.

Conclusions

By 1950, then, the protective matrix provided by a 'grandmotherly' government was impressive enough. Indeed, the British workplace was probably more extensively regulated by the middle of the twentieth century than any other developed nation. Nevertheless, we should not be blinded by the catalogue of ameliorative legislation into exaggerating the impact this had upon the lives of ordinary workers. Several caveats are worth emphasising which help to place state intervention in the workplace in this period in perspective. Firstly, Young and Whiteside have reminded us that it would be erroneous to argue that all workers welcomed such state paternalism – indeed, opposition to unwarranted 'interference' in people's lives and to the social control aspects of such legislation was widespread. Secondly, the legislation could enhance or diminish employers' power and authority – it did not necessarily reflect dominant economic interests. For example, Savage has demonstrated how the labour exchanges were exploited by employers prior to World War One to provide non-unionist, 'blackleg' replacement labour during disputes. Thus the exchanges helped to bureaucratise recruitment mechanisms and reduce employers' dependence upon pivotal craft and supervisory workers (such as the cotton spinners). Medical inspections under the special regulations governing dangerous trades were treated with suspicion; justifiably so, as it turns out, because some unscrupulous employers (e.g. shipping companies) used such mechanisms to sack older, less efficient workers (deemed a safety risk) and, in some cases, to surreptitiously weed out labour activists.

Over time, however, with the growing political power of the organised labour movement, the balance shifted and state intervention, by the 1940s, was more evidently reflecting the interests of the working class. This was no uniform or linear process: policy varied across local governments and from ministry to ministry (see conflicts between Munitions and Reconstruction during 1914–18) and was subject to variation according to different administrations at Westminster, as well as being influenced by economic circumstances and, intimately, by the pressures of war. The evidence suggests that there also remained a wide (if diminishing) gap between legislation passed and actual workplace practice, because of ignorance, evasion, poor policing and inadequate sanctions for workplace crime.

The generalisation that the role of the government in the workplace was a much more pervasive one by 1950 needs to be qualified in the light of these caveats. Nonetheless, this was an area where the scenario had fundamentally changed. By 1950, the

state's role had extended into maintaining social stability and
enhancing economic efficiency and such aims drew the state
inexorably deeper into the workplace and industrial relations.
Whether this worked in the employers' interests is a moot point
and the subject of much debate in the literature. The evidence still
seems to me to strongly support such a view for the period from
the 1900s to the General Strike in 1926. However, to argue a 'conspiracy' by the state to subjugate labour to the economic interests
of the dominant industrial bourgeoisie is too crude. Three elements
of the Marxist model which appear untenable are the emphasis on
economic determinism, the notions of coercive control from
above, and, related to this, the impotency of labour to significantly
resist, modify and shape policy. On the other hand, the revisionist
perspective which at its extreme perceives the state operating in
an even-handed manner as a neutral arbiter between the conflicting
interests of capital and labour can also be found to be wanting.
Much depended upon circumstances, contingency and the working out of what were often countervailing and contradictory
tendencies. In reality, both the independence and discretion of
management and labour were curtailed with the extension of
state intervention. Having said this, however, I would argue that
there remains much of relevance in a reformulated and more
flexible 'social control' thesis, positing that state policy was influenced by dominant economic groups. Over 1880–1950 such
policy played a vital function in reforming and regulating the
most exploitative aspects of free market capitalism and, hence,
in helping to ensure its very survival. The actions of a more interventionist state helped to divert labour from an oppositional,
syndicalist/socialist stance, where the moral economy of the workplace was in many respects anti-capitalist, to a reformist position,
where organised labour was incorporated and integrated by 1950
firmly into the body politic. The state played its part, in other
words, in manufacturing co-operation and consent within the
workplace, producing, by 1950, a considerably more contented
labour force than a generation earlier.

Taken together, the regulatory and protective matrix of
employment law, the role of the state as exemplar as the largest
single employer of labour, the passage of more liberal labour and
industrial relations legislation, and the function of the state as
mediator in capital/labour relations all critically transformed the

context in which work was performed in Britain between 1880 and 1950. The importance of this for workers in a strictly material sense in Britain was amply demonstrated when much of this framework was dismantled in the deregulation mania of the 1980s and 1990s. Whereas in 1880 the interests of workers in employment were fought over within the workplace, by 1950 Whitehall was a pivotal location for such conflict, and increasingly both trade unions and employers' organisations exerted influence at this level. As Price has pointed out, this very transformation in state responsibility, incorporating the maintenance of full employment, provided the context in which a revived stratum of workplace organisation was to flourish in subsequent years, as shop stewards 'warrened' the British workplace in the 1950s, 1960s and 1970s.

7
WOMEN, GENDER RELATIONS AND INEQUALITIES AT WORK

Recent research has massively extended our knowledge and understanding of gender relations and inequalities within the workplace. The development of feminist history, women's history and gender history over the past three decades has produced a proliferation of studies focusing upon the nature of patriarchal society, structural subalternation of women at the point of production, gender relations at work and the differing identities of female workers. Early feminist and women's historians emphasised the deep roots of patriarchal ideologies and the structural nature of sexual discrimination in employment, whilst resurrecting the neglected participation of women in paid work, trade unions, pressure groups and political organisations (see Liddington and Norris, 1978; Lewenhak, 1980; Boston, 1980; Walby, 1986; Lewis, 1984; John, 1986; Reynolds, 1989). Latterly, the emphasis has swung towards focus upon the range of different identities women developed through engagement in work – influenced by class, age, culture and religion – and upon the importance of gender as an explanatory framework, with notions such as masculinity coming under scrutiny (see especially Braybon and Summerfield, 1987; Summerfield, 1998; Glucksmann, 1990; Gordon, 1991; Clarke, 1997; Tosh, 1999; Simonton, 1998). Interpretations vary within an eclectic range of perspectives. Such work unequivocally demonstrates, however, the importance of interactions between home, family and work, and the necessity of discussing the relationships and inequalities between the genders that characterised the British workplace in the nineteenth and twentieth centuries. Much of the work has prompted a serious questioning of the commonly held view that a 'quiet revolution' occurred in women's social, economic and political status in the first half of the twentieth century, as expounded, for example, by Myrdal and Klein (1956), Marwick (1991) and Marshall (1983). Moreover, women were *active* players in the workplace and recent work encourages us to reconsider prevailing notions of women as passive victims.

This chapter draws upon such recent research to provide an examination of the nature of patriarchy in the British workplace, assessing the evidence for continuity and change in women's experience of employment over the period 1880–1950. It will be argued that these years did not witness any fundamental transformation in the sexual division of labour and that discrimination and inequality based upon sex persisted in the workplace tenaciously through to the mid-twentieth century (and beyond), transferring over from 'traditional' sectors of employment, such as domestic service and textiles, into the new growth areas of office and shopwork. The world wars brought significant change, but the transformative impact of war should not be exaggerated: in many respects, as Rex Pope (1991) has suggested, society returned to the 'old grooves' thereafter. To adequately assess continuities and change over time, however, a benchmark is needed, so I start by discussing the position of women within the late Victorian workplace.

Gender Relations at Work in Late Victorian Britain

In the late nineteenth century Britain was an intensely patriarchal society, where women lived acutely prescribed lives and were commonly regarded as inferior, second-class citizens. A regime of gender apartheid prevailed, both inside and outside the workplace. The notion of 'separate spheres' was deeply entrenched – with women confined largely to the private sphere and men occupying the public sphere. In almost all areas of life in Victorian Britain, women were subordinate to men. They were less free, more dependent, less valued and more constrained due to the prevailing patriarchal legal system and the dominant chauvinist values and attitudes of the day. There were, however, important differences in women's experience depending upon social class and locality.

Gender discrimination operated acutely within the workplace, education, training and the trade unions in the mid-Victorian period. Helen Corr has shown how school curricula continued to emphasise a domestic training – 'housewifery' – for girls and technical skills for boys (Corr, 1983a). In working-class families, daughters were usually removed from school before sons and, not surprisingly, literacy levels were lower amongst women than men. Higher education remained strictly a male-only domain, at least until the late nineteenth century, when some courses in some universities were opened up to women. Access remained severely restricted, however, until after World War One. Similarly, working-class women found it difficult to get entry to and training for skilled craftwork. Simonton noted: 'skill is regularly described as something which belongs to men, and is part of male essence' (Simonton, 1998, p. 265). This was partly the product of patri-archal prejudice by employers of labour who rationalised that women would leave employment on marriage and hence were not worth the trouble and expense of training. However, as Lewenhak, Boston, Gordon and others have shown, trade unions also played a key role through their exclusionary tactics, their stranglehold over recruitment into some skilled occupations and their rules forbidding the employment of women in their trades. Thus, 'trade union practices reproduced and reinforced the sexual divisions of labour in both the home and the workplace' (Gordon, 1991, p. 101). As trade unions became more powerful, gender discriminatory tactics could become more effective, as the example of the Edinburgh printing trade demonstrates (Reynolds, 1989).

A well-defined sexual division of labour characterised society in the Victorian period, with men occupying the public arena of paid work, politics and trade unions whilst women were confined predominantly to the domestic sphere – to home and family. Social convention within the middle and upper classes dictated that daughters and wives should remain at home, servicing the husbands' needs, and not engage in paid work. Some sought relief from such a prescribed, ornamental existence through engagement in philanthrophic endeavours – such as workhouse, hospital and prison work, or aid through the Magdalene institu-tions to the burgeoning prostitutes of the major cities (Mahood, 1992, pp. 42–64). There was less sexual constraint further down the social scale, more illegitimate births and irregular marriages (including cohabitation). Nevertheless, middle-class ideals permeated downwards as the Victorian period progressed, reforming elements of plebeian, rough culture. Robert Gray (1976) has demonstrated how a non-working wife was deemed a vital element of the lifestyle of the Edinburgh craft artisans. Domesticity may have been limiting, but within the world view of Victorian society it denoted respectability and status. Critically, for working-class women in Victorian Britain, marriage invariably meant a reorientation of their lives, from paid employment in the formal economy, in factories, sweatshops and in domestic service – to unpaid labour located within the confined isolation of the home and family.

Around this prevailing pattern, there were significant local and regional variations. The textile manufacturing towns of Lancashire (cotton) and Dundee (jute), for example, had much higher than average participation rates by married women in paid fulltime employment. Gender relations in such towns were thus somewhat different, with women enjoying more economic independence and developing a distinctive and quite radical factory culture. In Dundee, according to popular mythology, men were the 'kettle-boilers' (Gordon, 1991, pp. 137–211). Matriarchal power was also evident in some of the fishing communities in the north-east of Scotland where many women were involved in the industry as equal partners with men, owning property with the right to sell fish from a creel being passed down the female line (Livingstone, 1994, p. 15). Such examples suggest that the prevailing and somewhat abstract notion of patriarchal dominance needs to be qualified with a recognition of the rich mosaic of experience across a variety of different communities, labour markets and traditions. According to the decennial Census (see Table 2.9), moreover, significantly fewer married Scottish women before World War One were engaged in paid work outside the home (5 per cent) compared with their English counterparts (14 per cent). Whilst this may simply reflect the greater job opportunities for women in England compared to Scotland, it seems probable that this signifies the more intensely patriarchal nature of Scottish culture (McIvor, 1992). Wider gender differentials in wages, union activity, education and political involvement support this hypothesis, though more systematic research is necessary before a definitive conclusion can be reached.

Cyclical and seasonal unemployment and underemployment, as well as low male earnings (notably amongst unskilled rural and urban labourers) invariably drew married women into the formal economy to maintain family income and ensure survival. Much of this, on the fringes of the 'black economy' – for example child-minding, washing, mending, sewing, knitting and the taking in of lodgers – remained unrecorded. It is important to re-emphasise (see Chapter 2) that the main primary source used to evaluate occupational structure and change – the decennial Census – significantly underestimated female involvement in paid employment, due very largely to the gender bias which saturated its recording methodology. Much of the activity women did within the home had economic value anyway, so it would be quite wrong to postulate that married Victorian women did not work.

The unpaid work of a married working-class woman within the home in the Victorian period was extremely labour-intensive and invariably exhausting. Such work included a wide range of phys-ically gruelling tasks, performed seven days a week: nursing, caring, feeding and minding children; washing and ironing laundry; frequent shopping; food preparation, cooking and washing-up; scrubbing, sweeping and polishing the house and blackleading the kitchen range; sewing, knitting, making and mending clothes; as well as responsibility for financial budgeting and management. Most of this was done without the aid of any sophisticated equip-ment, and hence was extremely debilitating, hard physical graft. Laundry in itself usually took up a full day. Moreover, once married there was little relief for working-class Victorian women from the drudgery of such domestic toil. Given the size of families and female life expectancy (at birth) of around 45 years in the late Victorian period few women would have experienced life without dependent children under the age of 12 within the home. Indeed, more than half of the total duration of women's lives were taken up in producing, nursing and nurturing children. Furthermore, Victorian notions of the sexual division of labour dictated that child rearing and household tasks were unequivocally defined as 'women's work'. Daughters were expected to contribute help with household chores and childminding very early on in life, whilst sons and fathers were usually exempt from all but a few specialised tasks, such as decorating and shoe repair (Roberts, 1984; Jamie-son, 1986). For daughters, housework invariably continued even after entering full-time employment. All this was bound up with deeply entrenched notions of masculinity and femininity.

The sanctity of marriage and family was reinforced by the existence of formal and informal marriage bars operating across the economy. It was customary to leave work on marriage. Such discrimination meant that full-time paid employment in the Victorian period was largely, though not completely, undertaken by younger women (see Table 2.7). Occupational choice, moreover, was severely constrained, with the Census clearly showing quite stark segmentation in labour markets according to gender (discussed in Chapter 2, see Table 2.3). Gender segregation – both horizontal (across the economy) and vertical (within occupations) was probably at its height in the mid to late Victorian period. At this point, the work women did (with only a few exceptions) was synonymous with poor earnings, low status and monotony.

The value attached to women's labour power provides a clear expression of the subalternation of women within Victorian society. The first systematic government wages' survey in 1906 shows that the average weekly earnings of adult women were 69 pence in England and 65 pence in Scotland compared to £1.51 pence and £1.43 pence respectively for adult men. On average, in other words, women's earnings were some 45 per cent of men's. This average, however, masked a range of experience. In textile manufacture, one of the most highly paid female occupations, women earnt almost 55 per cent of the male average, whilst 'sweated' work, for example seamstressing, was amongst the lowest paid. Moreover, evidence suggests that in the relatively rare cases where women did the same work as men, they were invariably paid considerably less than their male counterparts (Busfield, 1988). Skill could be socially deconstructed.

Gender wage differentials reflected the prevalent chauvinist attitudes of Victorian employers and the state, the ghettoisation of women into lesser skilled occupations and the social exclusion of women from much craft artisanal work. Work performed by women was invariably labelled as unskilled, irrespective of objective elements, such as task range, discretionary content and training period. The Victorian period also saw the linked notions of the 'family wage' and 'supplementary earnings' become firmly entrenched. It was almost universally accepted (including by the trade unions) that the male wage should reflect the idea that he was supporting a family, whilst the female wage duly reflected economic dependence. This custom had serious implications for women in general and independent unmarried adult working women in particular. As we have seen, the government also played a role in legitimising such undervaluation in discriminatory employment legislation, such as the Factory Acts and the Trade Boards Acts.

The dominance of domestic ideology and the structural subordination of women in Victorian Britain did not, however, go unchallenged. Recent work has shown how working-class women were actively involved in strikes and other forms of collective action, including rent strikes, food riots and political activity (Clarke, 1997; Gordon, 1990, 1991; Boston, 1980; Liddington and Norris, 1978; Young, 1985). This threw up some strong female leaders and role models, such as Mary MacArthur, Ada Nield Chew, Selina Cooper and Helen Crawford. Such challenges to patriarchy intensified as the Victorian period progressed and there were some limited successes, such as the (albeit restricted) extension of the local/municipal franchise to women and the (albeit limited) opening up of higher education and a few of the trade unions. Textile factory workers were amongst those who demonstrated a sharp sense of collective consciousness and a willingness to actively resist the worse excesses of exploitative capitalism, expressed through a high strike rate in the late Victorian and Edwardian years. Significantly, however, such activities tended to be spontaneous, arising organically from below, invariably taking place outside the formal channels of the male-dominated trade union movement, which continued to neglect women's interests and ignore them as potential members (Gordon, 1991). Separate, gender-specific organisations emerged to represent women's political aspirations and trade union concerns, such as the Women's Social and Political Union, the Women's Freedom League, the Women's Trade Union League and the National Federation of Women Workers. Recent research has demonstrated how women were an active agency in the workplace, rather than passive recipients of a male-centred culture and patriarchal control.

However, it remained difficult to break down generations of socialisation and acculturation. Sporadic and periodic evidence of female activity, resistance and organisation thus needs to be kept in perspective. Getting into the mentalities of folk is one of the hardest tasks of the historian. However, many women in the Victorian period internalised and rarely, if ever, questioned their inferiority and second-class citizenship – the lack of rights, job segregation, undervaluation and structural subordination which characterised this intensely patriarchal society. By the same token, few men would have questioned their superiority in gender relations (or working-class men their subordinate 'place' in society's hierarchy in the late nineteenth century). The notions of separate gender spheres and male superiority even applied to most within the growing trade unions and socialist movements pre-World War One, as the Clydeside socialist Harry McShane noted in his memoirs, *No Mean Fighter*: 'Most of the socialists were just like other men in their attitudes in the home. Many of them had big families and lived in appalling conditions, and it was the women who carried the burden' (McShane and Smith, 1978, p. 34). Gender apartheid was part of the 'natural' order of things in Victorian Britain. Autobiographical and oral evidence for the late nineteenth and early twentieth centuries, tends to support such a conclusion (see Burnett, 1974; Thompson, 1975; Jamieson, 1986; Braybon, 1981; Roberts, 1984). How then did this scenario change during the course of the twentieth century? Why and to what degree did gender inequalities within the British workplace erode over *c*. 1880–1950?

Unpaid Work: Home and Family

Women's lives were intimately bound up within the family and the household and this 'private sphere', in turn, impacted critically upon women's involvement in the 'public sphere' of paid work and politics. Significant changes took place within the unpaid work of the home and the family, though commentators who focus upon such matters are divided as to how much emphasis to place upon them and to what extent this really affected the everyday experience of women's lives. The critical change was probably the control women achieved over their fertility. From the 1870s to the turn of the century there was already a modest fall in fertility rates, notably amongst the middle classes. The trend continued downwards until World War Two. In 1880 women averaged nine pregnancies and in 1950 just three. Average family size more than

halved over this period. The consequence was that the maternal
care period – producing and nurturing children – contracted
from around 50 per cent of an average woman's total life span in
the 1870s to constitute only around 25 per cent of a woman's life
span by the 1950s.

The decline in the practice of live-in relatives, less children, the
diffusion down the social scale of electricity and labour-saving
household gadgets, rising housing standards and improved health
and longevity combined to have positive effects upon women's
lives. Such substantive changes went some way to emancipate
women from the stultifying drudgery that characterised housework and family responsibilities at the end of the nineteenth
century, and provided women with more freedom and autonomy.
However, such changes came slowly and their impact can easily be
overemphasised. The evidence suggests that neither the distribution of resources within families nor the sexual division of labour
within the home underwent any radical transformation between
1880 and 1950.

Oral testimony for the first half of the twentieth century suggests
a relatively unchanging pattern of activity and experience within
the private sphere of the home and family (Thompson, 1975;
Roberts, 1984; Jamieson, 1986, pp. 66–7; Stirling Women's Oral
History Transcripts). Changes in citizenship – political emancipation via the franchise – had little direct impact upon the everyday
socio-economic experience of women prior to World War Two.
Within the family, girls continued to be prepared carefully for
a life of servicing, one way or another, the male 'breadwinner'. In
response to the question 'did your father help your mother with
any jobs in the house?' (referring to the 1930s) one Stirlingshire
woman commented: 'No. No. No, my father was very well looked
after in the house, even to the fact that his tea was poured out for
him, and everything was just there for him to sit down. He was the
worker o' the house' (Stirling Transcript, G1). Long habituation
and socialisation meant that such sex stereotyping of roles within
the working-class family continued to be accepted without question. An Edinburgh woman recalled life for her mother before
World War Two thus: 'She was always working, she never got out
anywhere. That was her life.' She continued: 'I had six brothers
and four sisters. As we got older we did more work. My brothers
were treated like gentlemen. That was general. I was second

youngest but the ones before me got a lot to do. We didn't mind; that was our life' (Pentland and Calton, 1987, p. 10; see also Faley, 1990, pp. 58–60). Domestic tasks continued to be performed with the minimum of mechanical aids – the domestic technological revolution was an incremental process, but few working-class families even had access to electricity before the 1930s. Thus the domestic labour process remained physically debilitating up to World War Two – doubly so where women in poorer families engaged in paid work to increase family income.

Whilst oral testimonies have begun to redress a serious gap in our knowledge, the internal life of the family in the twentieth century still remains relatively mysterious and badly in need of more systematic research. We know very little about how, when and to what degree relationships, resource distribution and the sexual division of labour within families changed. A recurrent theme that emerges in the literature, however, is domestic violence. Hughes, Young and McIntyre have unearthed evidence of wife-beating within working-class homes (Hughes, 1996; Young, 1985; Mcintyre, 1980). One historian has recently argued – using oral evidence – that relatively high levels of domestic violence on Clydeside between the wars was intimately linked to a crisis of male identity brought on by the collapse of male employment in the traditional heavy industries and resultant changing patterns of recreation (Hughes, 1996, pp. 9–19, 46–7).

Moreover, it has been persuasively argued that despite the so-called 'revolution' in domestic technology there was little, if any, fall in the number of working hours spent by full-time house-wives on housework and child-rearing before the mid-twentieth century (Hardyment, 1988; C. Davidson, 1982; Cowan, 1989). This apparent paradox has been explained by the fact that standards in all areas of the domestic labour process – childcare, cleaning, cooking, laundry, etc. – have increased commensurately. Nevertheless, labour-saving domestic technology has been emancipatory in its impact in the sense of providing more choice over the allocation of time within the general context of household and childcare work. What appears to have happened is that childcare and socialisation became more important within the family (Davidoff, 1976, p. 147). Moreover, these continued to be the responsibility of women. The uneven progress of technological change also needs to be recognised. By 1950, the domestic revolution had brought hot water, electric light, vacuums and electric or gas-powered stoves into the working-class home. Washing machines and fridges, however, were still rare and so the laundry and shopping tasks still remained very labour-intensive. Most importantly, all the evidence points towards no significant change in the distribution of unpaid work within the home. Zweig's post-war survey (1952b), Gershuny's work (going back to 1961) and Oakley's 1974 study indicated very limited involvement of men in domestic work, with only around 10–15 per cent of routine domestic tasks being performed by husbands (Thane, 1994, p. 401; Oakley, 1974a). There was a wide gap even where both wife and husband were working full-time. As Lewis has commented, this was 'one of the most unchanging aspects of post-war life' (1992, p. 88).

Furthermore, evidence suggests that unequal distribution of resources within the home continued through the first half of the twentieth century. Oral and other evidence indicates that married men typically kept a portion of their income as personal pocket money (for booze, tobacco, newspapers, etc.), thus enhancing their access to regenerative and diversionary recreational activities such as football, betting and the pub (Jamieson, 1986, pp. 66–7). This practice remained common in the 1940s (Zweig, 1948a, 1952b, p. 155). Moreover, economic dependence on the husband's higher wage increased women's vulnerability to future poverty in cases of marital breakdown. This was part of a vicious circle. The undervaluation of female labour in the formal economy could be used to rationalise an unequal sexual division of labour within the home, with women designated the lion's share of housework and child-rearing, on the strategic grounds of maximising family income. Then the time spent on such unpaid work in the home in turn disadvantaged women (in the sense of loss of accrued employment experience) in the formal labour market. This conundrum demonstrates the continued strength of patriarchal values, which remained deeply embedded within the British family at mid-twentieth century.

Paid Employment

After a long struggle, women achieved equality of citizenship, gaining the franchise on equal terms with men in 1928, whilst trade unions were also opened up to women and significant changes occurred in women's experience of waged work. Important developments through the period have been the increasing movement of married women from the home into paid employment, some erosion in occupational segregation by gender, rising real wages and declining gender wage differentials and the erosion of gender-specific discriminatory employment practices, such as the marriage bar. However, at the same time, regional and class differences in experience have remained quite significant and gender inequalities in the workplace clearly continued, indeed remained blatantly evident at mid-twentieth century, despite the wars, the vote and a socialist government. Ameliorative change was slow, patriarchal attitudes doggedly persisted and the workplace remained a site of segregation, undervaluation and discrimination based on gender.

World War One was an emancipating experience and a consciousness-raising episode for many of the working-class women who flooded into the munitions factories, the railways, the trams and other jobs replacing male labour drawn into the armed forces. In their own memories of this period women articulated mixed feelings of strain and fatigue, of release, freedom, pride and satisfaction – what Braybon and Summerfield (1987) termed 'a new sense of self-worth' (p. 131). Changes in women's experience of work played an important part in this process. Through wartime 'dilution', large numbers of women suddenly became exposed to a wide range of skills and tasks previously denied to them, to the camaraderie of large factories, to higher wages, to more mechanised production, and to trade unionism. The demystification of cherished male-dominated crafts, as women came into closer contact with such work, had an important, liberating effect, as did the physical transition from stultifying domestic service – characterised by uniformed servitude and relative isolation – to large-scale factory production. Women also found themselves at the sharp end of escalating wartime price inflation – running at around 25 per cent per year during the war – which seriously eroded the higher earnings on war work. Frustration with restricted mobility, job fragmentation, petty discrimination and the failure of wartime equal pay policies bred bitterness and encouraged militancy. The pressures and circumstances of wartime thus strengthened independence, confidence, morale and class and gender consciousness amongst working women. At one level, this

advanced awareness was illustrated in rapidly rising female membership of trade unions (see Table 8.1). Perhaps the most tangible
expressions of this heightened class awareness amongst working
women occurred on Clydeside. Witness, for example, the spate of
female workers' strikes and spiralling demands for inflation-
matching wage rises and for recognition of unions recruiting
women (especially the National Federation of Women Workers
and the Workers Union) over 1910–14, the Clyde rent strikes of
1915, the clothing industry strikes of 1917, the active female participation in the massive 100 000-strong 1917 May Day demonstration
in Glasgow and in the anti-war movement (Gordon, 1991; Young,
1985, pp. 146–8; Melling, 1983).

Whether World War One constituted a major watershed in the
position of women within British society has been the subject of
much debate. On closer scrutiny, however, the war appears to
have had little but a marginal, transitory impact on gender
relations in the workplace. The gains that accrued were largely in
the political (women over 30 gained the vote in 1918), rather than
the socio-economic sphere. Post-war legislation did open up new
opportunities in the law and professions for middle-class women.
However, working women were rapidly displaced in 1919–20 by
demobilised soldiers. Domestic ideology proved to have been only
suspended for the duration of hostilities and the pre-war employment situation was rapidly restored, including time-honoured
sexual divisions of labour. The wartime agreements on dilution
between the trade unions and the government enshrined in the
Treasury Agreement and Munitions Act of 1915 meant that the
withdrawal of women from specific areas of the labour market was
inevitable once peace was restored. The pre-1914 patterns were
quickly re-created, hence the occupational profile provided by
the 1911 and 1921 Censuses are remarkably similar. There is
nothing here to suggest a cataclysmic discontinuity. In the event,
the emancipating experience of wartime proved to be a transient
one, raising expectations only to be brutally frustrated in the
immediate aftermath of hostilities (Braybon and Summerfield,
1987).

It was only really in clerical work and distribution that some
working-class women managed to maintain the ground penetrated
during World War One. The reality for most working class women
after the war was a continuation of or a return to traditional roles

within the home, or to domestic service or the customary female-dominated sectors of textiles and clothing manufacture. In other words a return to less interesting, lower status, poorer paid work. From 1920, the emergence of structural unemployment in the male-dominated staple industries indirectly affected the female labour market in an adverse fashion during the inter-war years. This created an undynamic consumer market in the depressed areas – in marked contrast to south-east England – and meant that the new consumer-orientated industries which drew very largely upon female labour were under-represented in the industrial regions of Scotland and northern England (Glucksmann, 1990).

The largest single sector of female employment between the wars remained indoor domestic service. After 1918, women were herded back into traditional areas of female employment, such as domestic service, partly because unemployment benefit would be withheld from those women who refused to take such jobs when offered at the Labour Exchanges. In service, predominantly young women under 25 toiled for a 12–13-hour day, six or six and a half days a week, in virtual bondage to their masters and mistresses. As one housemaid in the Scottish Highlands (Jean Rennie) bitterly noted in her memoirs: 'My greatest horror was the knowledge that I would now have to submit to the badge of servitude – a cap and apron' (Burnett, 1974, p. 235). Domestic service was a heterogeneous occupation where conditions and work relationships varied considerably between employers, and this makes valid generalisation difficult. Some oral testimonies indicate that women could gain much intrinsic satisfaction, pride and enjoyment from their role as a servant (Harrison, 1988, pp. 48–54). However, enough evidence exists to suggest that the 'upstairs downstairs' image of a large and robust group of uniformed servants operating under a fine division of labour and elaborate hierarchical structure is an erroneous one, such households being unusual by the 1920s (Burnett, 1974). Most servants worked alone; a solitary existence with a monotonous and physically demanding daily routine of cleaning, washing, serving, caring. One general servant in Stirling described her work in the 1930s thus:

You were up in the morning – about the back of seven. You would be shouted to and you would be at their beck and call 'til about eight or nine at night.... It was hard work there was no

hoovers in those days, it was the wee brush and the pan, down
on your knees and scrubbing. Scrubbing, blackleading the big
ranges and cleaning the flues (Stirling, Transcript X3.1).

Despite the compensations of relative security and, taking food
and lodgings into account, reasonable levels of remuneration
(often paid only yearly or half yearly) there is much evidence to
suggest that domestic service was becoming more and more
unpopular. Increasingly, domestic service became a stepping
stone to other work in factories, shops and offices. One of the most
significant changes in the occupational profile of women workers
in Britain over 1880–1950 has been the decline of indoor domestic
service. From employing 36 per cent of all working women in the
late nineteenth century, indoor service accounted for just 11 per
cent of all female workers in 1951 (Lewis, 1984, p. 156).

Manufacturing remained a significant employer of female labour
between the wars, with declining opportunities in sectors like textiles and clothing being compensated somewhat by growing job
vacancies in the newer light and electrical engineering, consumer
goods industries (see Chapter 2). The labour process in the latter
sections, where conveyor belt techniques and detailed division of
labour were increasingly being employed, could be repetitive,
monotonous and soul-destroying. According to a government
inquiry in 1929 such work was well suited to women because, they
argued, 'females were apparently unaffected by the monotony of
the work' (A Study of the Factors, Cmd 3508, 1930). However, evidence from Lancashire and from Dundee suggests that employment
in the textile mills was comparatively well remunerated, work
conditions were well regulated, and job satisfaction higher than
most other female jobs. Pride in the work and an identity with
one's machine was expressed in the oral recollections of many
female textile workers, who invariably recalled intricate details of
the work and rarely articulated a feeling of boredom or monotony. The repetitive labour process and close monitoring by
predominantly male supervisors could be mediated in what were
relatively large factories, by female companionship, camaraderie,
and, as Jayne Stephenson has noted, by chatting, joking and singing.
'We had a great time, we had', one textile factory worker recalled
(Stirling Transcript A1; see also Stephenson, 1988, p. 5). Wage
payments by piecework placed some women on a par with male

workers, whilst a relatively high level of trade unionism amongst female textile workers helped to improve wages, conditions and standards of health and safety at work. On the negative side, insecurity of employment and work intensification (see Chapter 3) savaged the clothing and textile industries through the 1920s and 1930s and the constant fear of unemployment undoubtedly had a disciplining effect at the point of production in such sectors.

The main growth areas for female labour were working in offices and shops. Women employed in distribution increased almost threefold over 1881–1931, when one in four employed women worked in the distribution, food and drink sectors. Employment in a shop, especially a large store, appears to have been regarded by many working-class women as rather higher status, 'posher' work than a factory. 'I've got you a job . . . it's a nice one, not a factory' one Edinburgh woman indicated to her daughter in the 1920s (Pentland and Calton, 1987, pp. 19–20). However, higher status needed to be weighed against a series of unsavoury aspects of such employment. Shopwork was notorious for its 'blind alley' employment, lack of security, blatant age discrimination, petty rivalries and snobbery between grades, poor wages and lack of trade union penetration. Working hours in distribution were long, varying between 60 (food) and 80 (confectionery) per week, and the sector was poorly regulated and marginally protected. Up to the late 1930s, legislation only enforced definite meal-times, a weekly half-day holiday and a 74-hour maximum working week for workers under 18 years of age. Moreover, these rules, and the minimum wages set by Trade Boards, were often ineffective, argued Miss I. Davidson of the Shop Assistants' Union in 1932, because of lack of inspection and policing which had been cut back in the economy drive of 1921–2. The one notable exception to this scenario was employment in the Co-operative Wholesale Society, where a trade union closed shop operated.

The first half of the twentieth century saw the feminisation of office work: in 1911, 18 per cent of clerks were female; by 1951, this had reached 60 per cent (Lockwood, 1958 (1989 edn.), p. 36; Anderson, 1988). Important here was the invention and diffusion of the typewriter, the operation of which came to be regarded as 'women's work'. Working conditions, however, varied enormously, as Davy (1986) and Sanderson (1986) have shown, with major differences between large and small offices and the private and public sector. Nevertheless, several salient features are discernible. Working-class female clerks tended to be clustered at the bottom end of the employment hierarchy, doing the routine clerical work as typists and filing clerks. Upward promotion, as Lewis has shown, was rare within such work. Middle-class women moved further up the ladder dominating the secretarial grades, whilst male office workers tended to monopolise the top jobs, as managers, accountants, commercial travellers, administrators, etc. Job opportunities for women also grew in teaching and nursing, though again few women made it through to headships or into the higher grades of the medical profession as doctors or consultants. Sexual segregation and discrimination at work – with unequal pay, poor promotion prospects, opposition to female unionisation and rigid defence of the marriage bar – was particularly prevalent in the growing non-manual occupations, more so, Lewis has argued, than amongst those in manual work in the traditional sectors.

Before World War Two strong social and institutional pressures existed to ensure that married women's involvement in the formal economy was severely constrained (though casual and part-time work by married women, especially undertaken within the home, remained common, and continued to be under-represented in the Census). A barrage of propaganda after 1918 was directed at women to remind them of their primary responsibilities as mothers and homemakers. Such 'masculine madness', as one Scottish feminist (Eleanor Stewart) called it, meant that discrimination, especially against married and older women in the labour market, abounded in the inter-war period (Young, 1985, pp. 181, 183–4). The marriage bar remained firmly in place in teaching and the civil service and many other occupations exercised an informal bar and, indeed, preference for younger, unmarried workers. Working after marriage still brought with it a stigma. One Edinburgh shop assistant recalled:

If you were allowed back to work after marriage they would have said 'what a shame she's got to go and work'. So even if you were hard up, the last thing was to go back to work. It was not the done thing – Oh no! In those days the man was supposed to be the provider (Pentland and Calton, 1987, pp. 19–20).

Oral testimony suggests that this was an accepted and rarely challenged norm before World War Two. One woman (born 1919) from Springburn in Glasgow noted: 'My mother didn't work at all. No way. Women just didn't work in those days. It took ye to keep a house' (Margaret Burniston, in Faley, 1990, p. 53).

From 1880 to 1950, then, there were significant changes in the type of work undertaken by female employees and some, albeit limited, erosion in occupational segregation by gender. At the very broadest level, there was a marked shift from manual, industrial, primary employment towards tertiary, clerical, service and distributive work. In 1950 only about a third of all working women were engaged in the traditional sectors of domestic service, textile and clothing. The major employment growth area for women was the non-manual, services sector – insurance, banking, business services, public administration, local government, teaching, nursing and shopwork. A wider range of job opportunities were opening up to women. Nevertheless, it remains the case that gender inequalities persisted and a distinct sexual division of labour continued to characterise the employment market, passing over into the new industries. In 1951 around half of all women workers were clustered in just 3 out of 16 broadly classified occupational orders (distribution, professional and scientific, 'other' services). Moreover, segregation operated at another level. It was predominantly women who performed the part-time jobs – defined loosely as 15 hours a week or less. In the 1950s, around 90 per cent of all such jobs were undertaken by female workers. The position of part-time female workers perhaps best reflects the continuing undervaluation, degradation and discrimination exercised against women in the labour market in Britain at the mid-twentieth century. Part-time workers remained amongst the least organised and most exploited sections of the post-war labour force – low paid; low status; often working unsocial hours; with few of the employment rights enjoyed by full-timers.

Gender segregation in employment was undoubtedly less prevalent by 1950 compared to the mid-Victorian period, but it remained pervasive nonetheless, as the work of Hakim, Lewis and Kendrick has shown. Many areas of manual employment continued to be monopolised by male workers, women patently failing, for example, to penetrate in any significant numbers the traditional bastions of heavy metalworking, mining, construction and shipbuilding (see Table 2.4). Formal training beyond that obtained by observation and practice on the job was rare for women. The declining number of apprenticeships remained monopolised by men – a policy tacitly supported by male-dominated trade unions. Male apprentices and articled clerks outnumbered females by a ratio of more than 10 to 1. Hence women were denied access to skills outwith the 'female trades' (e.g. needlework), whilst chances of promotion and upward mobility were much more constrained. Women constituted 65 per cent of the labour force in the clothing industry, but male employers, managers, overlookers and foremen outstripped females by a ratio of more than 4 to 1. As late as 1951, male managers outnumbered women in a ratio of almost 6 to 1 (see Table 2.12). Such structural subordination had important implications, not least facilitating the continuation of sexual harassment in the workplace. One important reason for this subalternation in the labour market has been the characteristic degradation in job status experienced by women on re-entering employment after an absence rearing children, exacerbated by the fact that married women were more geographically immobile (Joshi, 1989, pp. 169–70).

Part of the ameliorationist or 'quiet revolution' thesis is premised upon the notion of growing economic independence through the twentieth century for women as real earnings and the real value of state welfare benefits rose. However, the undervaluation of female labour remained an enduring feature of British society over the period 1880–1950. The differential between female and male earnings changed little over 1880–1930s, with female average earnings rising from 44 per cent of the male rate in 1906 to 48 per cent by 1935 (Lewis, 1984, p. 164). By 1950, women were earning, on average, around 55 per cent of male earnings. The ghettoisation of women to the bottom of the employment hierarchy, deeply entrenched beliefs in the concepts of the male 'family wage' and female earnings as supplementary 'pin money', combined with the proliferation of part-time employment limited the erosion of gender wage differentials. Moreover, the gender wage differential was even greater if earnings over a lifetime are considered. A major cause of this persistent gender wage differential has been (and continues to be) the economic penalty women pay for withdrawal from the labour market to have and rear children. Joshi has calculated that women taking eight to ten years out of employment potentially reduced their lifetime earnings by almost 50 per cent in comparison to a woman who remained childless.

Moreover, by accepting the majority recommendations of the Royal Commission on Equal Pay (1946), the state continued to legitimise the undervaluation of female labour. On top of that, the state-initiated formal incomes policies over 1948–50 restrained wage rises which particularly penalised clerical and shopworkers (where female labour predominated and where overtime and bonus payments were rare) compared to blue-collar workers. Employers proved to be persistently reluctant to promote women or to train women for skilled and responsible positions pre-1950. This was recognised during the equal pay debates in the 1970s as a crucial issue: 'Without equal opportunities, equal pay is only a partial success', commented the Scottish Schoolmasters' Association. Gender differentials in educational attainment were also a pivotal cause of undervaluation in the labour market. Sex-typing in education eroded painfully slowly, thus contributing to sustaining inequalities and constraining women's chances of upward social mobility. Double standards in educational provision for girls and boys persisted into the post-World War Two period, including a markedly greater chance of young men gaining qualifications through higher education than women. In Scotland, for example, of those born in the 1930s and 1940s, men were three times more likely than women to be educated to degree level (McIvor, 1996, p. 203).

It is argued in Chapter 8 that trade unions played a vital role in protecting workers' interests against rapacious employers and the vagaries of volatile labour markets. There exists a positive correlation between high wage industries and levels of trade union density. It follows, therefore, that participation in such collective organisations by women would enhance their living standards, contribute to economic independence as well as having spin-offs in terms of better contractual conditions and a more conducive work environment. However, whilst collective protest and industrial action by women were not unknown before World War One, in common with other areas of public life women were largely excluded from the male-dominated world of the trade unions (John, 1986; Gordon, 1991; Reynolds, 1989; Knox, 1995; McIvor, 1992). For much of the twentieth century trade unions continued to absorb and reflect the dominant sexist values of the day, rather than championing the cause of gender equality. Female union member-ship levels were substantially lower (proportionately) than males and whilst there were a number of actively involved women, female representation in executive, decision-making positions within union hierarchies was marginal (Lewenhak, 1980; Boston, 1980). For example, in 12 Scottish unions in 1938, with a com-bined density of more than 20 per cent female membership, only 68 women held positions of branch chair, secretary and treasurer out of a total of 1281 such positions (McIvor, 1992, p. 155). From the 1930s women were drawn more systematically into the institu-tions of the labour movement and, as members, reaped some of the benefits of collective organisation for mutual protection. By 1950 the 1.7 million female union members constituted 19 per cent of total union membership. There remained, however, a considerable gap between the genders, with 55 per cent of male workers unionised in 1950 (7.5 million) compared to 25 per cent of female workers (see Table 8.1).

Male chauvinism within the trade unions undoubtedly declined through the period 1880–1950, reflected in the gradual opening up of the male-dominated trade unions to female membership. Walby has shown that there was a time lag of roughly 40 years before the craft unions allowed female membership. Even the general, so-called 'new unions' of the 1880s and 1890s – which recruited more widely amongst unskilled workers – had an average time lag of some 20 years before they admitted women. The oft-quoted example is that of the Amalgamated Society of Engineers (ASE). The ASE initially encouraged women in engineering to join the National Federation of Women Workers so that they did not have to open up their union to them. The renamed Amalgam-ated Engineering Union allowed membership to unskilled male workers in 1926, but did not admit women until 1943. Slowly, however, unions were becoming more sensitive to the needs and aspirations of the female segment of their membership. This was partly in response to the revived civil rights and feminist move-ments, to the impact of the wars and to the crisis trade unionism suffered as a result of the erosion of their traditional membership base as coal and heavy industry contracted after World War One. Nevertheless, the evidence strongly supports the view that issues pertinent to women workers continued *not* to be prioritised on the trade unions' policy agendas up to 1950, as Zweig recognised

(1952b, p. 154). In her study of women in the trade union movement Lewenhak notes growing frustration among women activists
that the Trades Union Congress would not tackle 'women's issues'.
Significantly, there was little campaigning within the trade union
movement to achieve equal pay, to remove discrimination at work
(including the marriage bar and discriminatory social services
legislation), nor to oppose the dismantling of wartime nurseries.
At mid-twentieth century, trade unionism was still widely regarded
as a man's world.

World War Two did change many things, though what really
stands out is the extent to which gender inequalities in the workplace persisted and were reformulated through the 1940s.
A number of new areas of work were opened up to women as
a consequence of the extraordinary demand for female labour.
By 1944, women constituted 39 per cent of the total labour force
in Britain, compared to 27 per cent in 1939. As with World War
One, many women expressed a sense of heightened job satisfaction and greater self-worth in their wartime jobs compared to the
drudgery, isolation and 'trivial' nature of home life and domestic
toil. However, Summerfield has shown how the patterns of
pre-war employment tended to be reproduced during wartime,
with women largely channelled into subordinate level manual
and non-manual jobs and men promoted upwards (Summerfield,
1998; Braybon and Summerfield, 1987). War work was also
invariably reorganised and fragmented, so few women got access
to the level of skilled work previously performed by male artisans.
After interviewing hundreds for their 1942 'People in Production'
project the Mass Observation team noted that they failed to
'encounter a single woman anywhere in the higher grades of industry' (Mass Observation, 1942, p. 106). As with World War One, the
experience was, nonetheless, confidence building for women,
who often expressed in their oral testimonies a great sense of
pride, achievement and identity in their wartime work.

The gains, however, mostly appear to have been fairly short-
lived. Braybon and Summerfield have argued this case persuasively, and neither Lewis nor Roberts conceptualise World War
Two as a major watershed. Indeed, some historians have argued
that war led to a sharpening of gender divisions rather than any
erosion (see Smith, 1986). Whilst a larger number of women
retained their jobs after 1945 (especially older women) compared

to World War One, the common experience was a loss of employment and a drift back to former occupations, or to the home. From a peak of 7.8 million women employed in 1943, numbers employed dropped back to 6 million by 1947. Thane has noted how younger women withdrew from the economy voluntarily to marry and have children after the war (Thane, 1994, p. 394). By 1947, however, labour shortages led the government into officially encouraging married women *without children* to re-enter full-time paid employment and mothers to consider part-time work. The introduction of paid maternity leave in 1946 facilitated this, whilst family allowances (1946) did something to aid economic independence. By 1950, there were almost a million more women in paid employment than in 1947. The really notable jump was in the participation of the 35–49-year age group. In 1901, 24 per cent of all working women were aged 35–49, whereas by 1951 this figure has increased to 45 per cent (Lewis, 1984, p. 154). A number of factors combined to raise the capacity of women to take on such paid employment, including smaller families, shorter working hours, changing attitudes, rising expectations linked with 'consumerism' and domestic technology.

Nonetheless, neither the patterns of female employment nor the conditions of work were profoundly transformed by 1950. In the final analysis, it is the continuities in experience that stand out. There remained strong social pressures against mothers working. This was not considered 'respectable' and was widely regarded as harmful to the children. Sexual segregation in the labour market remained a marked feature of work in 1950. Indeed, Hakim's detailed research suggests little change in the extent of sex-typing in British employment through the first half of the twentieth century, with 84 per cent of women located in jobs dominated by women in 1951, compared to 86 per cent in 1901 (Lewis, 1992, p. 81). The subalternation of women into the lowest status and lowest paid occupations in 1951 was noted in Chapter 2 (see Table 2.12). There were only 24 female MPs after 1945 out of a total of 640, and very few women doctors, barristers, engineers, managers or university lecturers. Undervaluation also persisted. Whilst some female professionals had achieved a marked narrowing in wage differentials (notably teachers, with 80 per cent of the male rate), the agitation for equal pay for comparable work failed, with the majority recommendation of the Royal Commission on Equal

Pay (1946) being accepted by the Labour government and the unions. Participation in paid work also continued to be difficult because of the lack of nursery and crèche provision and the back-breaking nature of domestic work. 'The workplace', as Simonton has observed, 'was a gendered context in which women often encountered a hostile environment' (Simonton, 1998, p. 269).

It should be emphasised again though that women were active rather than passive players on this historical scene. Examining the cold, objective reality of working women's lives with the benefit of hindsight gives the impression that women calmly and deferentially accepted their lot and that the female experience of work – either in the formal economy or the home – was a distinctively negative one. This was not entirely the case. Workers of both sexes interacted with their environment, responded vigorously and spontaneously to exploitative, discriminatory working conditions and enjoyed their work. As Zweig noted in his 1952 study of women at work: 'Most women like their jobs in industry.... They regard this as a change, an escape from the four walls, the basis of their independence and dignity, a symbol of their higher status' (1952b, p. 153). Though little systematic research has yet been undertaken on female strike propensity and other modes of protest, there is enough evidence to indicate that the prevailing image of a quiescent female labour force is a mythical one (Clarke, 1997; Gordon, 1991). Degradation in relative terms may well have been a marked feature of women's work and home life, but working women rarely articulated a perception of such alienation. Rather, many women expressed a great deal of satisfaction, pride and status from their employment, their changed roles during wartime and indeed from their domestic activities, as effective, responsible, caring mothers, carefully and efficiently managing the home and a tight household budget. Given limited resources, the latter key task often involved a very high degree of skill and ingenuity. Summerfield's recent work has emphasised how important it is to draw a distinction between what can be identified as structural elements of subordination, discrimination, segregation and gender inequalities and just how ordinary women perceived their existence, expressed their identity and related to their work (Summerfield, 1998). Oral evidence, in particular (though not without its pitfalls for the historian), provides strong support for the hypothesis that work was a source of identity, camaraderie, job satisfaction, pride and self-respect for women as well as men. Female shop assistants, clerical workers, domestic servants, seamstresses, teachers, nurses, print and textile workers have all articulated an intense commitment to their paid jobs. In this sense, the differences in orientation to work between male and female employees may be more apparent than real. Stephenson and Brown's (1990) extensive analysis of women's work in Stirling, based on oral testimony, makes this point persuasively: 'The vast majority of working-class women respondents *enjoyed* their working lives, finding it a positive and rewarding experience combining pride in work and skill, and participation in the collective culture of working-class women' (p. 24). Summerfield has shown how gender identities in the workplace varied considerably across a wide range of views, incorporating both the positive and the negative, during World War Two. Given the nature of female employment in this period – the immobility, inequalities, ghettoisation, undervaluation – this is a most remarkable illustration of the character and resilience of working-class women.

Conclusions

The main conclusion I would draw from the evidence about gender relations at work is that the notion of a 'quiet revolution' in women's lives over the period 1880–1950 is unhelpful. At the very least such a concept should not be employed without hedging it significantly with caveats and qualifications. The latter would include more sensitive recognition of the varied pace of such transformations, dependent upon variables such as region and class. A degree of economic independence came soonest to urban middle-class and professional women and latest to poorer urban and rural women. That is not to deny that women in Britain by mid-twentieth century did have a higher status and more respect as citizens, and enjoy more autonomy, more choices and a less prescribed existence than their Victorian counterparts. In this respect political and legal reforms have contributed, as well as widening job opportunities and limited access for a growing minority of female workers to the protective matrix offered by the trade unions. Declining family size was a critical ameliorative influence. It should also be stressed that women themselves – through collective organisation and protest movements – have been a very active agency in this process. Patterns were changing and more women were choosing longer periods in paid employment.

The key point to be emphasised, however, is that whilst gender inequalities within society, like class divisions, eroded, they were still a fundamental feature of the British workplace and society in 1950. The limits of change need to be clearly recognised. What did *not* happen was any significant shift in labour distribution within the sphere of unpaid work within the home, nor were women valued equally within the labour market, whilst women's access to positions of power and decision-making within society remained sharply circumscribed. The ability to vote and open access to the institutions of power (e.g. local and national government) were not translated into anything like equal representation of women. Despite the provision of a more level playing field, women continued to be massively disadvantaged in the labour market. Indeed, occupational segregation, the undervaluation of female labour and a distinctive sexual division of labour within the home and family remained three persistent features of women's lives over *c*. 1880–1950. Improving general living standards have masked the disparity and inequality of opportunities, disguising the fact that the economic dependency of women upon men continued, albeit in somewhat modified forms. The enduring structures of family and home life are of particular importance in this respect because a basic prerequisite for real equality of opportunity and full participation by women within the public sphere on equal terms with men was (and remains) a more equitable distribution of domestic work and family responsibilities within the private sphere of the home.

8

TRADE UNIONS, WORK AND POLITICS

The changing nature of work was a pivotal factor in the germination of a strong trade union movement in Britain and, in turn, workers and their trade unions were influential agents in the organisation and regulation of wages, working conditions and, to an increasing extent, the labour process itself. This has been alluded to at several points in the text so far. This final chapter explores in more depth the incubation and the role of the trade unions in the workplace over 1880–1950. Whilst recognising the limits of trade union penetration, especially within the non-manual occupations, the argument developed here stresses the transformation in labour's power and authority *vis-à-vis* capital by mid-twentieth century that mass unionisation achieved. In this respect, the contrast between 1950 and 1880 is very stark. By focusing attention at three levels, political, industry and workplace, it is possible to argue a case that the influence of the trade unions extended considerably beyond their numerical membership. This is evident, for example, in the passage of employment legislation that regulated the work situations of all workers, organised and unorganised. In Britain, trade unionism became entwined within labour politics, and much of the literature stresses the importance of work in explaining the emergence of both the political and the industrial strands of the labour movement. The final section of this chapter briefly examines the arguments for and against the view that the experience of work had an impact upon workers' consciousness, attitudes and politics, which led to the rising popularity of socialist and labourist ideas, and culminated in the ascension to power of the Labour Party in Britain.

The Incubation, Development and Limits of Trade Unionism

Within the capitalist enterprise of the mid-late Victorian period individual workers (with the exception of many artisans) lacked effective power, especially in the overstocked urban labour markets. They came to learn, however, especially when demand for labour was high, that through acting collectively and in unison they could exert influence which might mediate grim working conditions and dilute employers' unilateral control over production. Informal, workplace collaboration, through peer pressure and the 'customs of the trade', had a long history amongst the artisans and miners, and even extended, as Price has shown, to some groups of unskilled workers, such as the dockers. Other modes of collective organisation and action developed rapidly, however, from the 1880s, notably mass unionisation and increasing strike activity. The growth of trade unionism and strike propensity was uneven, however, with major differences in experience based on occupation and gender, and fluctuated with external circumstances. The Depression years of 1920–33 witnessed a sharp fall in

Table 8.1 Trade union membership (in millions) and density (%), by gender in the UK, 1892–1950

	Union membership (millions)	Union density (%)		
		Total	Male	Female
1892	1.6	10.6		
1896	1.6	10.5	13.8	3.0
1900	2.0	12.7	16.7	3.2
1910	2.6	14.6	18.6	5.3
1914	4.1	23.0	29.5	8.0
1920	8.3	45.2	54.5	23.9
1930	4.8	25.4	30.8	13.4
1939	6.3	31.6	38.9	16.0
1945	7.9	38.6	45.1	25.0
1950	9.3	44.1	54.6	23.7

Source: Bain and Price (1980, pp. 37–8).

Table 8.2 Manual and non-manual trade union membership, GB, 1900–51

	Manual (density)	Non-manual (density)
1900	1830000	78300
1911	2730900 (20%)	398000 (12%)
1921	5519300 (40%)	992700 (24%)
1931	3544000 (24%)	1025400 (21%)
1941	5435600	1612600
1951	7090700 (49%)	2174900 (31%)

Source: Bain and Price (1980, pp. 41–2).

union membership, and the period after the General Strike of 1926 a steep decline in working days lost through strike activity. Tables 8.1–8.4 illustrate such patterns.

Table 8.3 Trade union density by industry, 1892, 1939 and 1950 (expressed as % of potential membership)

	1892	1939	1950
Agriculture, horticulture, forestry	3.6	6.8	20.9
Fishing	9.8	19.5	45.3
Distribution	1.0	11.8	15.0
Insurance, banking, finance	1.8	19.5	28.0
Food and drink	6.4	23.7	37.9
Tobacco	20.5	18.1	61.1
Chemicals	11.2	20.4	33.3
Pottery	9.2	33.5	55.7
Clothing	6.2	23.6	34.9
Construction	7.7	21.3	44.9
Bricks and building material	11.6	21.2	30.8
Timber and furniture	16.3	21.6	45.0
Local government and education	5.1	62.5	65.5
Post and telecommunications	19.8	77.8	77.9
Cotton, flax and man-made fibres	23.8	54.4	74.3
Other textiles	10.0	26.8	37.0
Metals and engineering	31.9	35.5	51.8
Footwear	25.4	63.4	71.8
Printing	27.7	51.4	76.0
Paper and board	5.4	33.3	34.7
Sea transport	26.9	55.9	76.2
Coal mining	59.5	81.1	88.4

Other mining and quarrying	18.4	27.2	51.8
Port and inland water transport	61.3	84.2	93.1
Gas	23.9		75.9
Electricity			66.4

Source: Bain and Price (1980, pp. 43–76).

Table 8.4   Working days lost through industrial disputes in Britain, 1893–1951

	Approximate annual average (millions)
1893–1902	8.75
1903–12	8.56
1913–22	20.58
1923–32	20.83
1933–42	2.48
1943–51	1.89

Source: Clegg (1994, p. 421).

   Recent work on the patterns of trade union development has defined more clearly the limits as well as the extent of growth. In an important revisionist piece, Benson (1989) has argued that prior to 1939 the labour movement meant very little to vast swathes of ordinary working folk outside the union heartlands of coal mining, cotton and the metals and engineering industries. To some extent, the figures in Tables 8.1–8.3 support such a view. A marked gender differential continued to characterise union membership, though clearly, over time, the capacity of female workers to organise collectively was improving. The same was true for non-manual workers, where anti-union attitudes amongst employers persisted and smaller-scale employment was less conducive to collective organisation before the 1930s. Still something like four out of every five clerical workers, servants, shopworkers and agricultural workers were not members of trade unions at the outbreak of World War Two.
   Statistics and accumulated averages do have a tendency to obscure as much as they illuminate, hiding local, regional, occupational, gender and other variations and differentials. The recent proliferation of local and regional histories have pointed to a much broader range of experience, of varying trajectories, of uneven

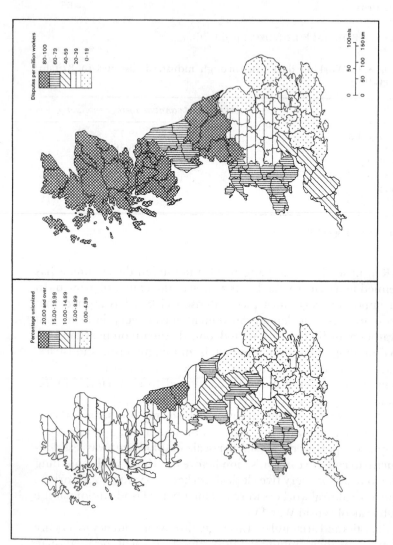

Figure 8.1 Trade union density and strike activity by region, 1892
Source: L. Southall, in J. Langton and R. J. Morris (eds), *Atlas of Industrialising Britain, 1780–1914* (1986), by permission of Routledge

development across Britain, with a major divide between the urban and rural experience (see Figure 8.1). The Webbs' survey of 1892 found levels of trade unionism in Scotland 20 per cent lower than in England and Wales, and in their recent work on labour in Scotland, Fraser, Knox and Foster have explored (from very different perspectives) the ramifications of this. Such work contrasts sharply with, and indeed revises, the orthodox interpretation of the inevitable and unilinear rise of the labour movement. The process, in reality, was much more disparate, subject to sharp reversals as well as surges forward at the troughs and peaks of the trade cycle.

So, it is important to keep the growth of trade unions in perspective. Nonetheless, there is something here that requires explaining. British trade unionism expanded from a narrow base amongst the skilled craft artisan elite (with an organised proportion in the region of around 5–10 per cent of the total workforce in the mid-1880s) to embrace a substantial slice of semi-skilled, unskilled, non-manual and female workers. The skilled unions that dominated the movement before 1914 were joined and eventually displaced by the omnibus general unions who recruited semi-skilled and unskilled workers (see Table 8.5). This changed the shape and the nature of trade unionism. By 1920, craft unionism had been replaced by mass unionism. Benson's view, therefore, seems to me to be a necessary but somewhat negative corrective which underestimates the importance of trade unions in British society and, in particular, the difference unionisation made to workers' lives. But why did union membership expand to embrace almost half the entire labour force by 1920? How has recent research influenced our understanding of the growth of trade unions?

The orthodox Marxist interpretation of the rise of unions and strike action from the 1870s stresses underlying socio-economic changes creating a more homogeneous working class with a growing awareness of itself as a group with mutual interests diametrically opposed to those who employed their labour power. The engine of growth was firmly located at the point of production. Marxists placed primacy on developments in the labour process: the increase in external competition in the late nineteenth century prompted many employers, as we have discussed, to intensify workloads and deskill work, which in turn radicalised and alienated workers. This process fractured traditions of deference and loyalty to the company and led workers to organise

Table 8.5   Membership of the ten largest unions, 1910 and 1951

1910 (000s)		1951 (000s)	
Miners Federation	597	Transport and General	1242
Weavers	112	General and Municipal	785
Engineers	100	Engineers	716
Railway Servants	75	Mineworkers	602
Teachers	69	Railwaymen	392
Boilermakers	49	Shop and Distributive Workers	342
Cardroom Workers (cotton)	45	Woodworkers	192
Carpenters	43	Electricians	192
Postmen	38	Teachers	190
Gasworkers	32	Public Employees	175
Total	1160	Total	4833

Source: Clegg (1985, Table 9; 1994, Table 2).

collectively to protect themselves against exploitation. The increasing size of companies depersonalised industrial relations, eroding paternalist relationships and thus diluting workers' loyalty to the company. Marxist historiography also stressed the key role of individual socialists in helping to form and sustain trade unions, particularly of the lesser skilled (Hobsbawm, 1964).

Other commentators emphasised the relationship between the economic cycle and union implantation and expansion, which came in surges – 1870–2; 1888–90; 1910–20; 1933–50 – and played down the catalytic influence of socialists and labour process changes in union formation and growth (Lovell, 1977; Clegg *et al.*, 1964; Pelling, 1987; Laybourn, 1992; Matthews, 1991). In such interpretations, growing unionisation largely represented an economistic response by relatively conservative workers reacting to eroding real wage levels (from around 1900) when the opportunity of tight labour markets raised workers' bargaining power. The preconditions for growth were also laid by a more liberal state, through periodic legislative initiatives (1871–5, 1906) providing basic rights to organise, strike and picket (Fraser, 1999, pp. 97–127). Relative ease of communication, rising levels of literacy, the radical press, the rising scale of production units, growing awareness of poverty and inequalities and the knock-on effects of successful unionisation and strike action are all significant supplementary variables contributing to collective organisation. The wars had a further catalytic effect and were both marked by particularly fast growth in membership.

Many of these elements within Marxist and more traditional approaches remain intact and unchallenged. However, with the dramatic shift away from institutional developments towards the social history of the working class, new evidence has emerged which challenges, modifies and extends previous interpretations of the emergence and growth of organised labour.

Firstly, some studies have developed and refined earlier Marxist perspectives, locating and explaining the implantation and growth of trade unions by reference to the evolution of capitalism and adverse changes at the point of production of a more intensely exploitative nature (Price, 1980, 1986; Burawoy, 1985; and, in the Scottish context, Holford, 1988; Knox, 1999; Kenefick and McIvor, 1996). Whilst the pace of deskilling, work intensification and related changes in work organisation, as well as the applicability of such developments across the economy, have been debated (as discussed in Chapter 3), this research has persuasively identified the years from $c.$ 1880 to the 1930s as a period of speed-up and work intensification as employers responded aggressively to declining profitability. Technological and organisational innovations, task reallocation, the spread of piecework wage payment systems and more systematised direct modes of supervision were part of a more general process whereby employers were applying pressure upon labour to achieve more from the wage for effort exchange. These developments, in turn, helped to incubate trade unionism and ignite industrial militancy. Hobsbawm and Price have shown this to be the case with the 'new unionism' of transport and gas workers from the late 1880s. Work intensification was also a key factor in the union growth and 'labour unrest' of 1910–14 (Holton, 1985; Cronin, 1979; Kenefick and McIvor, 1996). What occurred at the Singer factory in Clydebank provides a concrete example. Here, reduction of squad sizes, increasing pressure of work and experimentation with American-inspired ideas of scientific management over 1908–11 prompted a rapid expansion of union membership into the unorganised semi-skilled segment of the Singer labour force followed by a major strike to reduce workloads and attain union recognition in 1911.

Historians such as Gospel, Zeitlin, Tolliday, Price, Joyce and Melling have helped to reinstate employers as significant players on this particular scene. Research here has been multi-faceted but on a number of counts has contributed to our understanding of the dynamics of trade union growth and development. Whilst there exists considerable debate on the degree of power and cohesion of British employers, most commentators agree that Britain had a long tradition of associational activity amongst employers as well as workers. One argument has been that British employers in general have been weak and disunited and have thus lacked the power of their US counterparts to smash trade unions (Tolliday and Zeitlin, 1991; Phelps Brown, 1983). Thus British employers contributed to trade union growth and the fossilisation of 'restrictive practices' through their own organisational impotence. My own work on north-west England suggests a rather different scenario: much more powerful and effective employers' organisations championing class interests as a defensive response to trade unionism (McIvor, 1996). The relationship, I would argue, was more of a symbiotic one, with an incremental cranking-up of employers' organisation at the local, industry and national levels (stimulated by market pressures and state intervention, as well as the threat from organised labour and strikes) prompting counter-initiatives within the ranks of labour (and vice versa) in an attempt to maintain the balance of power. This thesis of powerful, class-conscious employers' organisations is supported elsewhere in the literature, notably in the work of Gospel, Johnston (on Clydeside) and Magrath (on Yorkshire) and is discussed in more detail in Chapter 4. Early employers' associations may well have tried to root trade unions out, following the American model. However, increasingly from the 1870s violent strike-breaking declined and employers came to recognise and work with unions, developing progressively more sophisticated collective bargaining procedures, thus legitimising their presence and removing much of the fear of victimisation for union activities. This process of accommodation to trade unionism took place slowly and unevenly across the economy, and could be subject to reversals when economic circumstances allowed a more militant employer stance (e.g. the 1890s and the 1920s). Nonetheless, British employers from the late nineteenth century tended to nurture rather than extirpate the unions. Given the increasing ability of organised labour to disrupt production, particularly in tight labour markets (and indicated in the strike statistics: see Table 8.4), this conciliatory strategy, the employers deduced, was very much in the interests of profit maximisation. This concession of union recognition through collective bargaining significantly stimulated union growth (industrial relations experts agree that such recognition remains a key variable in explaining union implantation across the economy). However, this should be construed as a trade-off that employers increasingly accepted in exchange for the other benefits inherent in this policy – including the constraining of industrial militancy, standardising costs and stabilising industrial relations.

Some recent work on comparative industrial relations history corroborates this interpretation. British employers, on the whole, were far less antagonistic towards trade unions than their North American and continental European counterparts (Mommsen and Husung, 1985; Geary, 1991). Similarly, despite the attempts of Marxists such as Hinton to argue otherwise, recent research suggests that the British state was also less hostile to unionisation. The state proved more willing, by World War One, to treat labour and capital in an even-handed way, at least in principle, if not always in practice. Social stability in a more democratic state, after all, depended upon such a strategy (Davidson, 1982; Wrigley, 1982; Lowe, 1987; Wrigley, 1987).

There remained, however, significant regional variations in experience. Clydeside stands out as something of an exception. Class-consciousness on the Clyde has been the subject of a long-running debate amongst labour historians which we do not have the space here to explore in any depth. Suffice to say perhaps that the revisionism of Harvie and McLean in the 1980s – when the former exhorted us to 'forget the Red Clyde' and the latter dismissed the phenomenon as a 'legend' – has generated a persuasive counterblast from those such as Foster, Melling, McKinlay and Morris, Kenefick and McIvor who still regard Clydeside as a distinctively militant region c. 1910–1920s. Part of the post-revisionist case rests upon the argument that Clydeside employers were more draconian and anti-union than their southern counterparts. This has thus been posited as part of the explanation for the lower levels of trade union implantation in Scotland prior to 1914 *and* the higher levels of strike activity (see Figure 8.1) and of socialist activity.

The expansion of women's history has also made a vital contribution to our understanding of the development of trade unions. Two points stand out. Firstly, such research has demonstrated the sexist, patriarchal strategies of the British labour movement which worked to limit the implantation (and maintenance) of unionisation amongst women workers (Clarke, 1997; Walby, 1986; Braybon and Summerfield, 1987; Gordon, 1988, 1991). By refusing membership, denying access to skills and failing to prioritise issues particularly pertinent to women, British trade unions limited their own representativeness – effectively shooting themselves in the foot. However, saying this is not to deny that despite odds being against them women increasingly organised and resisted capitalist exploitation in the workplace. This is the second point. A plethora of studies of the role of women at work, in unions and in strike activity have demonstrated the active involvement of women (in spite of the patriarchal nature of the male-dominated union movement) and the sterility of the myth of female quiescence in industrial relations (Gordon, 1991; Glucksmann, 1990; Lewenhak, 1980; Boston, 1980; Savage, 1987). Rising rates of unionisation amongst women were the product of improving capacities on the part of female workers to organise as a result of a series of economic, social and political changes. These included more security in labour markets, the wars, rising self-confidence as a result of improved status as citizens, and a gradual erosion in the sexist attitudes of unions. Moreover, as Gordon has pointed out, we need to look beyond institutional membership to other forms of associational and collective activity – such as involvement in strikes – to get a more accurate sense of female 'participation' (Gordon, 1991). Rather than viewing women as subordinate and inactive victims, recent research suggests a much more dynamic scenario, where the capacities of women to engage in collective action were advancing significantly over the long term, despite the chauvinist policies of the male-dominated trade union movement (see Chapter 7).

Recent research on trade unions and industrial relations has tended to corroborate the role of the wars as primary catalysts for trade union growth. Historians such as Wrigley, Clegg, Reid and Lowe have demonstrated how the wartime state encouraged trade unionism and collective bargaining (for example through creating the Joint Industrial Councils and extending the Wages

Boards) in response to labour's enhanced bargaining power during wartime. Expansion was also partly the product of tight labour markets and the labour movement gaining prestige, respectability and status through integration into decision-making. Braybon has identified the increased self-confidence which war work brought to women and charted a disproportionately high increase in female union membership over 1914–20. Other commentators have explored the situation within the workplace, arguing that wartime work intensification and the pressures of dilution radicalised many craft artisans and incubated shop stewards' movements and campaigns for work control (Hinton, 1973; Burgess, 1980; Price, 1986). Some of these gains were eroded in the Depression years of the 1920s but, as Clegg has shown, workers covered by collective bargaining agreements increased threefold between 1910 and 1933 and the shop stewards, whilst widely victimised (Duncan and McIvor, 1992), were never fully extirpated and their numbers grew again from the mid-1930s, notably in the aircraft factories. The catalytic role of the wars, however, must be kept in perspective. Union membership was rising, collective bargaining accelerating and state intervention in industrial relations was intensifying in the periods c. 1910–14 and 1933–9, before the wars broke out, and was sustained thereafter (though in the case of World War One only until the sharp economic recession in 1921).

Labour historians are now less inclined to accept the chronological framework laid down by the Webbs, or to view labour's development as characterised by rather dramatic watersheds, or to see the rise of trade unions as either inevitable, or all-pervasive. Recent work suggests that the whole concept of skilled artisans operating as an intrinsically conservative 'labour aristocracy' holding back the broader diffusion of trade unionism over c. 1850–1914 should be jettisoned once and for all (Harrison and Zeitlin, 1985; Knox, 1990, 1999; Lummis, 1994). The earlier claims for the 'new unionism' of 1888–90 are now widely accepted as exaggerated, including the view that these organisations were markedly more radical and strike-prone pre-World War One. Labour historians now tend to stress longer-term changes in union structure and orientation over the period c. 1880–1920 and to emphasise the fact that existing 'old' unions gained considerable numbers of members, moved to the left over these years and continued to dominate the movement. Such reinterpretations have also addressed the issue of ideology in the rise of trade unionism. Romanticised notions of an extensive socialist and syndicalist presence within the unions has been placed firmly in perspective in the recent work by Laybourn, Clegg, Gordon, Knox, Fraser and others. Pre-First World War syndicalism was relatively ineffective and evidently did not play a major role in union growth, nor, indeed, in the massive surge in strike activity which characterised the so-called 'labour unrest' of the years 1910–14. Recent work has also tended to undermine the idea that the General Strike of 1926 was a pivotal watershed in British industrial relations history. Clegg has demonstrated how union membership and strike activity were clearly on the wane from 1921, with the onset of a sharp and sustained economic recession. Nor was the General Strike an unmitigated disaster. Wages held up relatively well thereafter and the collective bargaining system survived the ravages of the economic crisis of 1929–32 (we shall come back to this). Limited economic recovery and rearmament from the mid-1930s provided the basis for tangible recovery in union membership (see Table 8.1) and a cranking-up of strike activity (albeit largely through very small 'demonstration' strikes, mostly without official union backing). This suggests that the prevailing view of the 1930s as a barren period of contraction and decline in the union movement merits some reconsideration.

Having said that, it remains the case that World War Two had a critical, enervating effect upon British trade unionism. Membership increased by almost 50 per cent between 1939 and 1950, bringing 3 million more workers into the unions. Tight labour markets provided a basis for growth, and, with around half of the labour force drawn off to the armed forces, the bargaining power of those remaining was raised commensurately. Moreover, the demands of war brought radical changes in working conditions and labour processes. The scale and pace of production increased significantly and the injection of inexperienced workers into wartime factories created pressures and changes which drew workers towards collective organisation. This led directly to an enhanced union presence within Westminster as well as on the shop floor, with the growth of shop stewards' and workplace committees. More so than ever before, the state (and especially the wartime Minister of Labour Ernest Bevin) directly encouraged collective organisation and collective bargaining during the war, and the

immediate post-war years. In a markedly changed milieu characterised by notions of social unity and harmony during wartime,
employers' attitudes mellowed and there was a more open willingness to recognise and work with trade unions as the legitimate
representatives of labour. Clearly, the trade unions were deeply
embedded as an integral part of the fabric of British society by
1950.

Democratising Work? The Role and Functions of Trade Unions

How did the trade unions influence the shape and nature of work
in Britain? The role of trade unions in British society has long
been the subject of intense discussion and debate. Some Marxist
historians have shown a tendency to conceptualise the unions as
weak and ineffective in the face of omnipotent monopoly capitalism in the twentieth century, and to denigrate these organisations
for their moderation, 'reformism' and failure to challenge the capitalist mode of production (Braverman, 1974; Hinton, 1973, 1983;
Saville, 1988; Burgess, 1980). Thus unions operated to reform, regulate and manage capitalism, rather than move workers towards
democratic control of industry. At the other end of the spectrum,
and largely (though not exclusively) from rightist perspectives,
there have been trenchant criticisms of the inordinate power and
disruptive capacity of the unions. These organisations, according
to this interpretation, germinated 'restrictive practices' which undermined productivity, created a high wage economy and were
responsible for the strike-proneness of British industry – the
so-called 'British disease' – and, hence, have been held primarily
responsible for the economic retardation of Britain (Correlli
Barnett, 1996; Phelps Brown, 1983).

There have also been more positive evaluations. The approach
of the Webbs and the plethora of individual trade union histories
through to the 1950s tended to equate the experience of workers
with the experience of the trade unions and emphasise the ameliorative impact of these institutions. The standard of wages and
working conditions achieved by the unions tended to be perceived as universal. The 'Oxford school' developed out of this
institutional preoccupation and came to stress a fairly unproblematic and linear movement towards collective organisation and

collective bargaining – from archaic to more mature, institutionalised industrial relations (Clegg *et al.*, 1964; Clegg, 1985, 1994).
Recently, there has been a sharp move away from the institutional
approach to British labour history and a re-emphasis upon the
social experience of workers at the point of production – an
approach facilitated by the opening up of new sources and
methods, including oral history. Interpretations within what has
become a vast literature on the social history of work vary enormously, but one significant strand in this research has reiterated
the importance of workers themselves, acting independently and
through their collective organisations at a number of levels, as an
agency, responsible for regulating working conditions and the
labour process (Price, 1980, 1986; Burawoy, 1985). Thus workers
responded to changes in production and reacted and adapted
to managerial authority. As the latter became more direct and
sophisticated (see Chapter 4), so workers increasingly turned to
trade unions – at both the industry and workplace levels – to protect
and advance their interests. In turn, this prompted revisions of
strategy and organisation on the part of the employers. Thus
capital and labour were both active agencies in the regulation of
work; fleshing out wages, bargaining over working conditions
and forging the labour process.

Over the period 1880–1950 it is undeniably the case that trade
union influence and control in employment matters extended
dramatically, though this was no unilinear process and was subject to attack and reversal depending upon prevailing economic,
social and political circumstances. Notions of capital and labour in
perpetual conflict have been eroded in recent research, and
replaced by more nuanced theories of the coexistence of co-operation
and conflict in employment relations (Joyce, 1990; Burawoy,
1985). This is reflected in much of the 'new' labour history.
Capital–labour relations did involve violence, conflict and confrontation, with the strike weapon really coming of age from *c.*
1870 to the 1920s. Conflict, however, was episodic and capital/
labour relationships were also characterised over long periods by
co-operation and peaceful coexistence. The prevailing nature
of work is thus most appropriately conceptualised as the outcome
of a process of struggle, co-operation and adaptation between
capital and labour (and their collective organisations), rather than
something unilaterally imposed from above. Certainly by the

1940s, the British system of industrial relations was dominated by collective bargaining and work was regulated more often than not through joint consultation between the workplace representatives and management at both the shop floor and the industry-wide levels.

Having said that, labour, and the unions, at least over the period 1880–1950, were invariably the inferior protagonist in this struggle. Whilst the regulatory capacity of the unions and work groups was undoubtedly advancing over time we still need to guard against over-extrapolation from trade union experience when, even in 1950, less than half of all workers were members of unions. Significant 'protective' job controls at the point of production, which ate into managerial prerogative, were unevenly spread across the labour force – with marked differences based upon gender and skill, and across the manual / white-collar divide – and fluctuated with prevailing economic and political conditions. Nonetheless, it will be argued here that unions had an influence beyond their members and that cumulatively, the very nature of capitalism in Britain was transformed by 1950. The rest of this section explores the main ways that unions came to play an important role in shaping the nature of work in Britain.

Around 1880, trade unionism was irrelevant to the vast majority of British workers. It was synonymous only with the skilled crafts, and, to some extent, with the traditional 'leading sectors' of cotton manufacturing and coal mining. As we have seen, it was customary for craftsmen to practise a high degree of autonomous job regulation, the customs of their craft being upheld in their trade society rules defining such areas as the rate for the job, control over apprenticeship, hours of work and overtime rates. Price provides perhaps the most detailed analysis of craft regulation at the mid-late nineteenth century and the ongoing struggle to control work in his case study of the building industry (Price, 1980). This formalised system of craft regulation was highly localised. Because of this, and the lack of collective bargaining elsewhere, there were wide variations in wages, work hours and conditions across the country, as Hunt and Bienefeld have shown. Underlying this was the existence of more informal job controls, built up through custom and practice and protected by the collective solidarity of the work group. Restriction of output, for example, was quite common amongst coal miners and metalworkers. However, the vast majority of workers in the late Victorian period – over 90 per cent – had no access to trade unions and were unable to develop rules and regulations governing their employment. Whilst the norms of a particular locality influenced wage determination, in essence the labour contract was one struck individually between master and worker. Workers took employment on the terms offered by the employer and exercised little or no control over labour markets. Overstocked labour markets in urban areas continued to have a depressing impact upon wages and working conditions, indicated, for example, in the recession years of the mid-1880s (Treble, 1979). Wage reductions on the downswing, were as common as wage rises. Thus immiseration was endemic and intimately linked to volatile product and labour markets, employment insecurity and casualisation, as the Booth and Rowntree poverty surveys demonstrated. Because of the severely restricted franchise labour's political power, moreover, was limited. There existed no legislation providing a floor to prevent wage cutting below poverty levels (by either a minimum wage or unemployment pay) and no effective control of the labour market to curb exploitation. The Factory and Mines Acts provided some regulation, but the coverage was extremely patchy and failed to influence the working conditions of the majority of workers in 1880 (see Chapter 5). Victorian employment legislation was predominantly an expression of patriarchal concerns, not an attempt to reform grim working conditions *per se*, or to interfere in the notion of the individual contract struck between master and the adult male worker.

Between the late 1880s and 1920 the British workplace became warrened with trade union members, represented at the workplace level by shop stewards and higher up by a growing bureaucracy of union officials and executives. By 1920 half of the workforce were in unions and the influence of workers' collective organisations at the point of production had increased massively. The older, established unions worked during this period to protect craft regulation against the encroachments of more aggressive employers' strategies designed to deskill work and extend managerial control and authority deep down into the workplace. The newer unions, spreading across the unskilled and semi-skilled occupations in transport, gas, metalworking, textiles and elsewhere, sought to provide such workers with the necessary bargaining power to raise wage levels, reduce working hours and humanise the labour contract, protecting members in the face of work intensification, technological change and reorganisations of work. By the 1910s, there emerged a strand of trade unionist activists – much influenced by syndicalist ideas – who were campaigning to democratise work and extend workers' control over production. This was most evident on Clydeside, where the shop stewards and the Clyde Workers' Committee pressed deep into areas of managerial prerogative. However, British trade unions, in the main, worked to reform and regulate capitalism, operating within the framework of the existing system, rather than trying to overturn it. These tendencies were to become even more marked over the 1920–50 period.

The unions used a range of methods to protect their interests and extend their influence, including the withdrawal of labour and restrictions on output. James Cronin has identified how workers from around 1870 came to integrate the strike weapon more effectively into their strategies for protecting members' interests, and here the union played a key role, providing leadership, co-ordination, inspiration and support (Cronin, 1982). The growth of membership and accumulation of defensive funds were of critical importance. These enabled the workers to sustain longer and more broadly based strikes, which were more likely to be successful, especially when they were initiated at strategic times when labour was relatively scarce. Hence, government figures indicate a rising incidence of strikes and a rising success rate for labour in strike activity over the period 1890–1920. There were some really spectacular successes for union organisation and collective action, even in the most inauspicious circumstances. Notable, for example, are the inspirational victories of the matchgirls and dockers in London in 1888 and 1889, and the gasworkers, led by Will Thorne, who forced the transition from 12-hour to 8-hour work shifts upon their industry in 1889. Over the subsequent couple of decades, the growing power of the unions was indicated in the eroding capability of the employers to forcibly break strikes and the declining popularity of the lockout weapon (McIvor, 1996, pp. 92–117). This was particularly evident by the 1910s (see Table 8.6).

A key objective of many union-initiated strikes over the period (even those 'new unions' of the unskilled) was to gain recognition from their employers and the right to bargain collectively on

Table 8.6   Strike settlement by labour replacement, 1891–1919

	% of strikes	% of workers involved
1891–99	14.8	3.1
1900–9	12.9	2.4
1910–19	4.8	0.3

Source: Board of Trade, *Annual Reports on Strikes and Lock-Outs*, 1891–1913; *Abstract of Labour Statistics*, 1898–1937.

a permanent basis on wages and conditions of work within formalised disputes procedures and negotiating machinery. The achievement of the latter was frequently perceived as the way in which the gains made during a strike or industrial action could be made irreversible. This cut through the prevailing pattern of the nineteenth century where gains made at the peak of the trade cycle when labour was much in demand were quickly rolled back by concerted employers' counter-attacks in ensuing depressions. This happened, for example, over 1870–5 and again over 1889–95. It was much more difficult to do this, however, by the 1920s and thus the gains made over 1910–20 were eroded only in an incomplete fashion and workers' bargaining power revived quickly from the mid-1930s. Similarly, the gains made by labour in the 1940s were sustained and built upon in subsequent decades.

By 1920, there were three distinct levels at which trade unionism was affecting the shape and organisation of work in Britain; industry-wide, in the workplace and through the political process at Westminster. At the industry-wide level, the collective regulation of matters relating to the labour contract was well established, with national, industry-wide collective bargaining on substantive issues and the creation of formal stage-by-stage disputes procedures spreading rapidly in the 1900s and 1910s. By 1920 most of the major industries had embraced national collective bargaining, including cotton, wool, coal, engineering, building, shipbuilding, iron and steel, printing, chemicals, railways and road transport. At this point probably 6–7 million workers – or around 40 per cent of all employed – had their basic working conditions regulated by joint agreement. Moreover, in periods of tight employment these basic rates became a norm, influencing wage payment across the unorganised sectors.

The state played a key role in all this. From the early 1890s the government directly encouraged workers and employers to regulate work conditions through collective bargaining, seeing this as the best way to stabilise industrial relations in the public interest. With the 'labour unrest' of 1910–14 and the war, the state was drawn into more direct intervention as a mediator in the major industrial disputes (Wrigley, 1982, 1987). Moreover, the model of trade union / employer collective bargaining was directly extended by the state to many of the poorly organised occupations through the Trades Boards legislation of 1909 and the creation of the Whitley Committees from 1917. By 1920, this added around 2 million more workers to the list of those covered by nationally negotiated agreements on wages and work conditions. One consequence of all this was a distinct narrowing of local and regional differences in wages and working hours, though wide differentials continued to exist based on gender and skill. The union campaign for shorter hours also achieved very widespread conversion to the 48-hour working week across manufacturing industry by 1920.

Moreover, with the growing power of the unions and the prestige of the Trades Union Congress (much enhanced by their co-operative stance and participation during wartime), the political muscle of the trade unions was consolidated. This was reflected in tangible improvements in labour conditions through legislation. It was no coincidence that it was in coal mining – where trade union densities were amongst the highest in Britain in the 1910s – that an eight-hour day and a minimum wage (by region) was achieved by legislation before World War One. The extension of factory and mines legislation and workmen's compensation also owed much to trade union pressure, and these reforms, whilst uneven, did play a significant part in reducing the death rate through industrial accidents (see Chapter 5). The trade unions were also involved in the see-sawing guerrilla warfare to curb pro-employer judge-made law and to attain the passage of new employment laws which consolidated and extended the legal rights of the unions. The notable legislation here was the Trades Disputes Act of 1906 (which reversed the Taff Vale decision of 1901), reviving the possibility of effective picketing and facilitating unfettered strike action in defence of work conditions and wages. A further expression of the political muscle of the unions was their success in attaining state assurances that pre-war employment conditions would be protected in the Restoration of Pre-War Practices Act (1918). The virtually unopposed implementation of this legislation over 1919–20 speaks volumes for the power of the trade unions in the tight labour markets of the immediate post-war boom years. Moreover, the emergence of the Labour Party as a credible political force provided the unions with a vehicle through which employment legislation could be channelled. Rowe recognised this in his comprehensive survey of wage determination in Britain in 1928:

> In matters common to all wage earners, such as trade boards and minimum wage legislation, health and safety, social insurance and so on, trade unionism, through its close association with the parliamentary Labour Party is able to make its voice heard, and with considerable effect (Rowe, 1928, p. 185).

In parallel with the increasing role of the unions at the political and industry-wide levels was a marked enhancement of the power of the trade unions at the workplace level. By 1920, shop stewards and workplace committees were well established across a wide range of industries – although most extensive in engineering and metalworking – and were responsible for the day-to-day regulation of many areas of workshop life (Hinton, 1973, 1983). Even before the war, the number of workplace representatives was increasing and their role was widening (Cole, 1923). In cotton manufacture, for example, the shop representatives were reacting with unofficial action to the myriad grievances over poor quality raw material ('bad spinning') and were operating as conduits through which mill-workers' grievances over the work environment, health and safety (such as lighting, temperature, dust and humidity) were channelled through to management. This function as a conductor was vitally important because it removed the fear of victimisation which had operated as a powerful constraint upon workers who were understandably reluctant to face up to their employers themselves, or, as McFeely has shown, to report employers to state officials, such as factory or Trades Boards inspectors. World War One, however, had a critical impact. Over 1917–19 both the trade unions and the employers came to accept the existence of the shop stewards, formally enshrined in engineering in the Shop Stewards' Agreement of 1919 (Cole, 1923, pp. 130–1).

As unions grew and formalised industry-wide collective bargaining developed, there emerged a wider gulf between the trade union leaders and officials on the one hand and the mass of workers on the other. Historians disagree on the extent and the implications of this gap between leaders and 'rank and file' (Zeitlin, 1987; Price, 1986). The schematic postulation of a 'reformist' and 'incorporated' leadership contrasted with a revolutionary and dissenting 'rank and file' embedded in much Marxist writing has now largely been discredited. There existed a perpetual tension between national leaders and local activists, examples of which can be found in the syndicalist traditions of the South Wales miners, the rank and file railwaymen's committees, and the Minority Movement between the wars. However, to equate the views of the mass of inactive and frequently non-organised workers with the local activists and shop stewards (often themselves active socialists, syndicalists and communists) is in itself problematic. Be that as it may, what is evident is that the workplace dimension in industrial relations was becoming more important. By 1920 there is clear evidence of the coexistence of two systems of industrial relations; one informal and located in the workplace, the other formal, involving relationships and agreements between national trade unions and employers' organisations. To some extent workers' disillusionment with formalised procedure sharpened as real wage levels eroded over 1900–12 and they became aware of how the system operated in the employers' interests. The escalating rank-and-file revolt expressed itself in an increased propensity towards unofficial strikes and a crop of abrogations of official agreements during the 'labour unrest' of 1910–14. These tendencies were even more evident by the 1940s.

The unofficial dimension of workplace activity had links back to traditions of 'primitive democracy' within the early craft unions, and was strengthened by the germination of the shop stewards' movement during World War One. Amongst the key mechanisms of work regulation at this level was restriction of output – a type of industrial sabotage designed to prevent the premature draining of workers' energy, to 'spread' work (thus easing unemployment) and, at its extreme (in the syndicalist-inspired concept of an escalating general strike), to undermine the viability of capitalist production (Brown, 1977; Holton, 1976). Whilst this form of action was unpopular amongst trade union leaders, the widespread prevalence of forms of ca'canny, or going slow, shows the potency of unofficial collective activity within the British workplace and emphasises the point that collectively workers could resist and mediate the conditions of labour imposed upon them by capital. Trade union rules against the employment of female labour provide another example of successful regulation of the labour market, in theory at least in the face of employers' desire to utilise the cheapest labour possible. Witness, for example, successful union campaigns to keep women out of cotton mule spinning, to exclude women from the printing industry pre-1914 and to eject women from the jobs they performed during wartime.

Workplace representatives and shop stewards then were in the vanguard of a growing unofficial movement on the shop floor which, especially during the 1910s, was becoming increasingly engaged in the organisation of work (Cole, 1923; Hinton, 1973). The wartime shop stewards' movement, as Hinton has shown, filled a void vacated by the national officials who effectively acquiesced to the wartime exploitation of labour via the Munitions Act of 1915 – what one activist termed 'the workers' slavery bill'. Such legislation facilitated the wartime dilution of labour, severely restricted labour mobility and outlawed strikes, whilst providing some guarantees regarding wages and conditions. With the virtual suspension of the protective factory code and rapid transformations in production methods and wage payments as employers maximised productivity for the war effort, there emerged a great deal of friction on the shop floor. The shop stewards filled this vacuum. During the war, the activities of the stewards and the works committees in towns like Sheffield and Glasgow extended the 'frontier of control' significantly into managerial terrain (on issues like overtime working and the working of payments by results systems).

However, direct encroachment by unions and/or stewards into production matters and labour process issues (such as technological innovation and machine staffing) remained rare outside of engineering. An important distinction to be made here, and it is one noted by the American observer Carter Goodrich in his seminal study in 1920, is that union controls and influence were much more extensive on issues relating to the labour contract – wages, hours, overtime, holidays, etc. – than they were over methods of production. By focusing upon the major heavy sectors of industry in the immediate aftermath of war Goodrich undoubtedly exaggerated the extent to which employers had ceded power and authority to the emerging unions. Clearly, there were limits to which the employers, even with their backs to the wall, were willing to condone direct encroachment into the very kernel of managerial prerogatives (Cole, 1923). The concessions to the unions on production matters that were made pre-1920, moreover, were tactical rather than strategic, and much ground was regained when economic circumstances shifted the balance of power back towards the employers (McIvor, 1996).

The inter-war years were a period of retrenchment for the trade union movement, traditionally viewed as an era of erosion of union power and authority at the point of production (Branson, 1975; Hinton, 1983). Certainly, the capacity of the unions to protect members was severely circumscribed, at all three levels: in the workplace, at the industry-wide level and in relation to the political power of the unions. Despite the centralisation of power in the hands of the TUC and the drift towards more moderate, co-operative and corporatist approaches by the union leaders, the TUC was denied access to the corridors of political power throughout the inter-war years. Pro-labour legislation capable of reforming exploitative working conditions was difficult to attain – as in the case of the new Factory Act, first mooted in 1922 but not made law until 1937 (Lowe, 1987; Rodgers, 1988). Again, anti-labour legislation – notably the 1927 Trade Union and Trade Disputes Act – circumscribed the capacity of the unions to strike and picket. As union densities dropped, so too did the proportion of those employed covered by nationally negotiated collective agreements. There was a discernible tendency to drift back to labour contracts struck between the individual worker and employer. This was aided by some employers breaking away from their employers' organisations to go it alone in the Depression. In two large industries, coal mining and wool manufacture, the system of national collective bargaining broke down and there was a reversion to district bargaining. In the cotton industry, the collective bargaining system collapsed in 1932 and was formally suspended by the employers' associations, leaving mill-owners the discretion to exploit market circumstances to set wages and conditions at whatever level they thought fit (McIvor, 1996). Direct state intervention was required to re-establish collective bargaining in cotton, backed up with legal sanctions. At the same time, workplace bargaining and the power of the shop stewards were seriously diminished by a wave of sackings and victimisation geared towards the elimination of the wartime activists from positions of influence on the shop floor. This process was aided, as we have noted, by the emergence of the Economic League, operating as a centralised political vetting and blacklisting agency from around 1926 (McIvor, 1988). Mass unemployment made it difficult to protest and harder to recruit replacement workplace represen-tatives in a climate of fear and chronic job insecurity. Not surpris-ingly, in the circumstances, workplace representation atrophied and with it the protective matrix provided by the shop stewards.

These developments, however, need to be kept in perspective. Recent research has indicated that it is wrong to view even the 1920s and 1930s as entirely barren years for the unions. Whilst the power of the unions was undermined (and severely so across the basic sectors of the economy), the movement remained capable of protecting members' interests, through largely defensive actions in the 1920s, and, increasingly from 1933 on, by again moving on to the offensive. What is significant about the 1920s is that it took fully six years of mass unemployment to discipline workers and their unions into acceptance of the realities of a changed market place. Thus strike levels, whilst declining from 1921, remained relatively high until the climacteric of the General Strike of 1926. Clegg has argued that the employers' counter-attack during the years of mass unemployment in the 1920s and early 1930s was neutered by the strength of the unions and the solidarity and residual militancy of labour. This was manifest in lower wage cuts over 1929–32 (compared to 1920–2) and the retention, apart from a couple of notable exceptions (including coal), of employers' commitment to union recognition and collective bargaining. At 1933, at the nadir of the Depres-sion, Clegg estimated that some 7 million workers were covered by voluntary collective agreements and a further 2 million or so by state Wages' Boards. This amounted to almost three times the numbers of workers subject to collectively bargained agreements on wages and working conditions in 1910. Rowe's study of wage determination in 1928 stressed the capacity of the trade unions to regulate wages even in the Depression. This he linked to changes in employers' attitudes, with most employers accepting shorter hours and the concept of a minimum wage: 'The general body of employers has swung round from a militant condemnation of trade unionism, to a general recognition of its function in the modern industrial relations system, even though its policies and practices may be the subject of violent denunciation' (Rowe, 1928, pp. 176–7). The result was a radically transformed labour market where the unions played a key role in wage determination:

> The modern developments in trade union organisation are the root cause of the numerous changes which have occurred in the whole structure of wages in this country. Trade unionism has been the yeast which has altered the whole shape and nature of the loaf. In 1886 collective bargaining over wages was unusual. ...For the past seven to ten years...conditions of ordinary competition have ceased to exist in the market for labour, and have been replaced by conditions of almost bi-lateral monopoly (Rowe, 1928, pp. 194–5).

A few years later, in the mid-1930s, John Hilton's wide-ranging survey of restrictive practices illustrated that the ability of work groups to maintain the power to regulate their work survived, in many cases, the worst ravages of the inter-war slump. A whole range of restrictive practices were still effective, including overtime restrictions and bans; opposition to piecework; 'going slow', manning and payment on machines; and apprentice restrictions in engineering, shipbuilding, printing, building and woodworking. Significantly, moreover, Hilton found this to be the case amongst some unskilled groups, for example the dockers, as well as amongst the more skilled in industries such as building, printing and engineering (Hilton *et al.*, 1935).

Evidence of widespread strikes against the Bedaux system between the wars (Littler, 1982; Whitston, 1996) and recent case studies in engineering and shipbuilding confirm the capacity of local work groups and union branches to maintain the power to regulate production and mediate transformations of work in the 1920s and 1930s (see Zeitlin, 1991; Reid, 1991; McKinlay and Zeitlin, 1989). Moreover, the improvements in pay in coal mining in the later 1930s, the passage of a new Factory Act in 1937 and the Holidays with Pay Act in 1939, the revival of strike activity and unofficial organisation and action – in such manifestations as the busmen's unofficial action, the Railway Vigilance Committees and the resurgence of the shop stewards' movement in the aircraft factories – are all signs of an energising of union activities which resulted in tangible gains in the labour contract in the immediate pre-World War Two years. Evidently, the trade unions were still operating, albeit in a more prescribed form, as a protective buffer against overwork and exploitation during the inter-war Depression.

The 1940s, however, witnessed the most radical extension of trade union power and authority, which in turn enhanced the ability of labour to regulate and control work. The power accrued is evident in the three levels of politics, industry and the work-place. This was the consequence of full employment, shifts in public opinion and politics and the growth of union membership (which increased from 6.3 to 9.3 million, or from 32 to 45 per cent of the labour force between 1939 and 1950) and workplace representation (with the proliferation of shop stewards). Of criti-cal importance was the influence of the war and the prevailing political climate. Bevin as wartime Minister of Labour ensured that union recognition was extended and wages and working con-ditions were maintained and improved. This was achieved in a number of ways, including tight price controls and identification of low-paid groups for special treatment (agricultural labourers and, significantly, miners). Moreover, the Labour landslide victory of 1945 led directly to more liberal employment legislation – notably the repeal of the Trade Disputes and Trade Unions Act (1927) in 1946 – which extended unions' legal rights and incu-bated trade union growth and power – and the Industrial Injuries Act (1948). The Welfare State also placed a floor under wages, extending significantly the 'social' wage. The capacity of the unions to regulate working conditions was further enhanced by the access they attained to political power and the close relation-ship they had with the post-war Labour governments. By the late 1940s, as Middlemas has shown, the TUC and the British Employers' Confederation were operating virtually as *equal* part-ners as the major voluntary organisations representing labour and capital in Britain. The war and full employment transformed almost everything. Crosland picked up the essence of this trans-mogrification in *The Future of Socialism* (1956): 'There has been a decisive movement of power within industry itself from management to labour. This is mainly a consequence of the seller's market for labour created by full employment'(pp. 30–1). Crosland identified two pivotal changes which exemplified the altered power relationship: workers lost their fear of the sack, and the 'docility' which went along with it; and employers lost their capacity to 'endure a strike or initiate a lock-out'. The virtual disappearance of the lockout after the 1930s is indicative. As Crosland concluded: 'thus the balance of advantage is reversed, and the result is a transformation of relationships at the shop-floor level' (see Coates, 1982, pp. 160–3).

The recognition of trade unions and joint regulation and bargaining over work conditions proceeded rapidly at both the industry and the workplace levels. The 1940s saw a further considerable extension of collective bargaining, directly encouraged by Bevin, as Minister of Labour, and by wartime demands and planning (Wrigley, 1996, pp. 38–9). Voluntary collective bargaining covered around 9–10 million workers by 1950. On top of that, Bevin created 46 new Joint Industrial Councils and increased the coverage of the Wages Boards (which had replaced the Trades Boards) in 1943 and 1945. The result was that by 1950 virtually all of the lower paid and poorly organised sectors were subject to state-sponsored collective bargaining and wage regulation, whilst in the well-unionised sectors the range and depth of issues covered by such 'joint control' had rapidly extended. One estimate in 1946 placed only 2 million workers – or less than 10 per cent of the total labour force – *outside* of this matrix of collective bargaining (Wrigley, 1996, p. 39). This resulted in a considerable erosion of the local and regional wage differences that Hunt found so prevalent in the late Victorian period. Rowe identified this in his 1928 study of wages in five industries, commenting on the pivotal role of the trade unions in forcing employers to standardise wages and pay what the market would bear (Rowe, 1928, pp. 169–70). However, the unions were less aggressive in attacking gender wage differentials. The Labour government's refusal to act upon the findings of the Royal Commission on Equal Pay (1946) was not challenged by the TUC or the major unions, who failed, before 1950, to actively campaign on this issue.

The encroachment into managerial terrain was also evident in the workplace. At the point of production, the ability of work groups to regulate and control their work was considerably increased

during the 1940s and, significantly, this challenge to management
went beyond the labour contract, deep into production matters
(Hinton, 1994). The war brought a widespread revulsion towards
management (picked up, as noted in the last chapter, in the Mass
Observation surveys) and a considerable extension of workplace
power, exemplified in the joint production committees (see
Chapter 4), which existed in some 4500 factories by 1944 (Price,
1986). Whilst most of the JPCs disappeared in the aftermath of
the war, the number of shop stewards continued to rise (see
Donovan, 1968), prompted in part by the complexities of wage
regulation as full employment encouraged employers to introduce
wage bonuses and other inducements. At least in the larger factories,
the sphere of joint bargaining and regulation had widened to
include productivity issues, discipline, wage systems and the
working of overtime. The regulatory power of the unions
extended both to the national level, further consolidating the
'official', formalised industrial relations system, and, in tandem, to
the workplace level, with the diffusion of shop stewards throughout
manufacturing. One expression of this was the tendency of shop
stewards, by 1950, to be responsible for organising overtime
schedules (Coates, 1982, p. 162). Another was the widespread
disregard for national agreements considered to be outmoded,
including the engineering agreement of 1922, which had famously
enshrined the right of employers to manage.

As Zweig noted in his 1951 study, *Productivity and Trade Unions*,
a measure of the transformation of authority in industry was the
high degree of acquiescence by management to union 'restrictive
practices'. These ranged from the closed shop, through to bans on
piecework (e.g. in printing), going-slow (the 'stint' in mining),
objections to bonuses ('merit money') in building, and seniority
rules – as in iron and steel – which dictated the process of promotion (Zweig, 1951, pp. 15–18). These devices had a very real
impact, enabling labour markets to be regulated, skills to be
protected and workers to be shielded against overstrain and
managerial favouritism. The cumulative impact was the marked
change in workplace relations by 1950. Zweig commented:

Most employers state emphatically that the restrictive spirit
harms more than restrictive rules.... The workers have assumed
such a status that the smooth running of industry depends on

their goodwill and spirit of co-operation....And the main problems turn around the question of how to create and cultivate the spirit of goodwill and cooperation among the workers. Most managers find the answer in the spirit of absolute fairness, the development of welfare services and amenities, and in the cultivation of a human approach to industry; not merely in procedures of conciliation.

We have to realise that every single industry works now under a comprehensive code of rules, controls and regulations, and that freedom of enterprise has gone not only through state interference, but even more so through collective agreements (Zweig, 1951, p. 24).

Employers had little choice but to accept and adapt to this diminution in power.

However, there were trade-offs and there were limits to this process. Whilst employers lost in terms of managerial prerogative they gained in terms of industrial stability. The state curbed union powers through order 1305, which banned strikes. Thus days lost through industrial disputes remained at exceptionally low levels during the 1940s, considering the tight labour markets and strength of the unions. Statutory wage restraint over 1948–50, agreed by the union leaders, also effectively contained wage escalation, much to the frustration of many shop stewards. A reformed and 'humanised' type of capitalism survived the war, the transformation of trade union power and the transition to a mixed economy partly because there existed little will to completely overturn the existing system. Moreover, the extent of workplace control and regulation was still extremely uneven across the economy. To some extent, contemporary commentators such as Zweig and Crosland were as guilty as some historians of over-extrapolating from the experience of the bigger factories and the leading sectors, especially engineering and metalworking. Whilst joint regulation of basic contractual issues such as wages, hours and overtime was common by 1950, workers in the lesser organised sectors, such as office employment, retailing and agriculture, still exerted little effective control over the management of production. This was especially the case in non-manual employment, and female-dominated jobs where unilateral regulation of the labour process by management remained customary.

Moreover, whilst the communist shop stewards in mining, the railways and the postal service continued to campaign for the resurrection of the JPCs and an extension of *real* workers' control in industry through the late 1940s, the reality, as Hinton (1994) has shown, was that opportunities were lost to institutionalise control at this critical juncture. Whilst 'rank and file' activists were calling for equal workers' and employers' representation in the running of the newly nationalised industries, what was achieved was minimal trade union representation, and even less workers' participation in management in the state-owned sector. In 1951, trade union representation on the national and regional boards in the nationalised sector was just 44 out of 350 (Coates, 1982, p. 169). The concept of workers' control, as Currie has argued in his study of factory politics, was 'displaced by managerial control'. Whilst this alienated many of the radical shop stewards, there were few protests from either the trade union leaders, or the mass of workers (at least outside of mining and the railways), who showed no sustained enthusiasm for direct involvement in management decision-making. Hinton has pointed out in his study of the campaign for democracy at work in the 1940s that workers' interest in the JPCs was already declining before the end of the war and that 'the mass of workers remained uninterested in participation' (Hinton, 1994, p. 122). There appears to have existed a great deal of basic contentment over what had been achieved by workers and their organisations since the 1930s. Whiteside has made the point that workers were operating with the Depression years as their benchmark and, despite the war, their expectations may well have been lowered as a result. In 1950, the TGWU secretary (Deakin) recalled:

> I remember, and can never forget those conditions that existed between the wars when our people were out on the stones, unemployed and underemployed, while the Trade Union Movement had no economic strength to take care of them (cited in Whiteside, 1996, p. 109).

The job security of the 1940s, the extension of collective bargaining, combined with more responsible management and what Zweig termed 'civil rights in industry' appear to have satisfied most. It would thus be wrong to equate the views of the shop stewards with those of the mass of workers at this time, as some interpretations tend to. One railwayman perhaps summed up prevailing sentiments when he wrote in the *Railway Review* in 1949:

> One reads nearly every week that what the railway workers want is a share in management. . . . I venture to suggest that the rank and file railwaymen do not desire that so much as they desire an increase in their wage packet (cited in Currie, 1979, p. 163).

That view was probably echoed by most manual workers, and an even higher proportion of non-manual employees, in Britain in the middle of the twentieth century.

Work, Class and Politics

The changing nature of work incubated trade unions and unions came to play a very significant role, by 1950, in the regulation and structuring of work, exerting influence over labour markets and the labour contract, through informal workplace organisation and action, combined with 'official' industry-wide collective bargaining and an increasing presence in the corridors of political power at Westminster. However, some social historians have argued that experience in the workplace had further ramifications, producing a more unified working class, germinating class-consciousness and incubating an oppositional culture that expressed itself in socialist and syndicalist politics, which facilitated the transition to political power of Labour in Britain in the first half of the twentieth century (Holton, 1976; Burgess, 1980; Hinton, 1983; Price, 1986). In 1985, Jay Winter commented: 'What is important to note is the deep conviction of virtually all labour historians that the labour process itself breeds militancy and radicalism in the same way, in a sense, that a nuclear reactor breeds fissionable material' (Winter, 1985, p. 232). Alienation induced by deskilling and degrading changes in work provided fertile ground for politicisation, leading to a surge in class-consciousness and strengthening commitment to radical socialist politics. Thus Price has located the key developments surrounding the formation and early growth of the Independent Labour Party (ILP) and the Labour Representation Committee (renamed the Labour Party) in the 1890s and 1900s in the intensification of work, especially in the railways, docks and gas industries. Similarly, Howell explained the strength of the ILP in Leicester by reference to the displacement of the boot and shoe workers by new technology. The radicalisation of metal and engineering workers and the emergence of syndicalism have been explained by similar reference to the degradation of work (Hinton, 1973, 1983; Foster, 1992; Holton, 1976, 1985), as has 'Red Clydeside' (Hinton, 1973; Foster, 1990; Kenefick and McIvor, 1996).

But is it right to place such primacy upon the labour process in explaining the rise of labour politics and the germination of class-consciousness? Such interpretations have recently become the subject of much discussion and debate (Phillips, 1992; Laybourn, 1988; Reid, 1992; Savage and Miles, 1994), with major disagreements emerging over the political connotations of changes in the workplace. The literature suggests that there is not much argument with the view that changes at work were a catalyst to union growth, and there remains strong support for the idea that the emergence of the Labour Party prior to World War One was intimately connected to the trade unions. In this period the Labour Party operated, in effect, as the political arm of the unions, with the dominant aim of achieving a larger working-class representation in Parliament and applying pressure on the Liberals to legislate on union and employment rights. Where there has been much dissent has been on the assumption that developments in the labour process necessarily or inevitably have radicalising political connotations. This type of crude economic determinism has been rejected by a number of labour historians who provide empirical evidence – usually in-depth local/regional case studies – which shows the tenuous nature of such connections. The labour process, it appears, was just one of a series of variables, and not necessarily the most important, contributing to the rise of Labour.

Scottish labour historians have made a vital contribution here. Recent research has helped to reconstruct the particular configuration of class relations north of the border. Knox has identified major alterations in the labour process in Scottish manufacturing over c. 1880–1914, yet he observed that this remained a period of Liberal hegemony in popular politics in Scotland: 'political consciousness is shaped by a wide range of social experiences . . . the world of work does not exercise an overdeterministic ideological influence' (Knox, 1990, p. 162). McLean argued that the linkages between the industrial and the political movements were very tenuous over the critical years of 1914–22. The landslide victories of the 'Red Clydesiders' in 1922 were not the direct consequence of labour process developments, workplace campaigns, the shop stewards' movement or even trade unions (to any significant extent), but rather the result, McLean argues, of ILP campaigning on broader community-based issues and winning the Irish vote. Such campaigns had particular relevance in Scotland, given the relatively low wages of Scottish workers and the high levels of overcrowding (Melling, 1983). Poverty and housing were key campaigning issues of the ILP on Clydeside, as Morris and McKinlay have shown. Hutchison lays no stress upon changes at work in accounting for the rise of Labour in Scotland, though he does acknowledge the close correlation between areas of trade union strength and a buoyant Labour vote. Nor should fortuitous events and particular political contingencies be ignored. Gallagher has shown how the success of Labour in winning control of the Glasgow municipal council in 1933 (one year before London fell to Labour) was at least partly the indirect result of sectarianism – the Protestant League vote splitting the anti-Labour forces.

Amongst the most outstanding contributions to our understanding of class formation and Labour's rise to political power is the recent work by Savage (1987) and that of Savage and Miles (1994). Savage's 1987 study focused on the changing nature of working-class politics in Preston, Lancashire, over the period 1880–1940. In his analysis Savage argues that labour process changes and industrial relations developments had a radicalising and politicising impact, particularly in the early years of socialist development and independent labour politics. In his later study with Miles (1994), much evidence is gathered to support the view that changes in labour markets and work were of primary importance in explaining the incubation of the Labour Party in Britain in the 1890s and 1900s: 'The early Labour Party developed largely as a defensive reaction by trade unionists to the loss of autonomy and control which were brought about by the changes in the labour market' (Savage and Miles, 1994, p. 78). Pre-1914 the Labour Party was operating effectively as the political wing of the trade union movement, which, in turn, was politicised by the threats which the bureaucratisation of labour markets, employers' cost-cutting, work intensification, deskilling and the loss of traditional authority and control at work entailed (Savage and Miles, 1994, pp. 41–56, 89). However, Savage asserted that political factors, and particularly the 'strategic defects' of the Liberals and Tories provided space for the Labour Party to grow in the northwest of England and that in Preston there was less of a direct correlation between labour process developments, trade union growth, industrial militancy and the drift towards Labour politics *beyond* the 1900s. Indeed, in Lancashire over 1910–14 intense industrial conflict coexisted with widespread support for the Tories. Moreover, support for Labour grew steadily through the 1920s (to 37 per cent in 1929) just as trade unionism collapsed (from over 8 million to less than 5 million members). Nor was trade unionism necessarily synonymous with voting Labour between the wars. From 1927 only 51 per cent of trade unionists bothered to contract in to the political levy – only 24 per cent in the Amalgamated Engineering Union (Savage and Miles, 1994, p. 81). The thrust of Savage and Miles' thesis, therefore, accepts the importance of trade unionism and developments in labour markets in explaining the rising fortunes of the Labour Party before World War One. Emphasis thereafter is laid on a conjunction of factors: changes in labour markets and the pressures of work *combined with* urban working-class formation in discrete districts, state intervention and political contingencies, and the emergence of 'a politics of service provision and consumption' (Savage and Miles, 1994, p. 82) which, they assert, particularly appealed to female voters. Female participation in the Labour Party in the 1920s grew dramatically. Given the persistently sexist attitudes within the unions and the markedly different labour market experience of women, it is unlikely that the labour process was as significant a factor in politicising women, as it was with male manual workers.

A key factor, however, was the growing homogenisation of the working class, as the gap between the skilled and unskilled narrowed, which translated into a strong identification between the working class and the Labour Party by the 1940s (Savage and Miles, 1994; Price, 1986; Cronin, 1984). The Labour Party was also the beneficiary of the extension of state intervention in economic

and social affairs and egalitarian sentiments during the wars
(Pope, 1991) and of the growth of public sector employment.
Such processes, combined with the onset of mass unemployment,
facilitated a marked transition away from trade union influence
and workplace politics towards what Savage calls 'neighbourhood
based politics' in the 1920s and 1930s.

Few would now accept an unqualified and crude inevitability
thesis, linking the rise of Labour solely with changes in the labour
process, labour markets and the milieux of work. On the other
hand, as Savage and Miles have persuasively argued, the evidence
still strongly supports such an argument up to 1914, with the basis
of Labour's appeal widening thereafter as they embraced other
issues and drew in people politicised by their experience within
working-class urban communities. The increasing identification
of working-class people with the Labour Party in the 1920s and
1930s remains a key factor in explaining its eventual electoral success. Moreover, the prevailing view of the British Labour Party as
distinctively moderate – and hence more broadly appealing – has
also, I think, largely survived unscathed. Dick Geary's recent
work, which investigates the rise of Labour across Europe, provides an instructive comparative perspective. Geary emphasises
the similarities in trade union development and strike patterns
across Europe, c. 1900–39, but the marked divergences in Labour
politics, with Britain's development characterised at one end of
the spectrum as 'manifestly reformist'.The British Labour Party
was a very different political animal from its German counterpart
(the SPD). Similar experiences at the point of production, therefore, produced very different political outcomes in different
countries. Adams has also shown that similar occupational experiences, for example amongst the dockers in the 1920s, produced
markedly different political responses in different docks across
Britain (Adams, 1990).

Debate continues to rage on the relative importance of the two
world wars with a majority view favouring the concept of war as
a pivotal accelerator of Labour's political ascendancy, not least
because war physically demonstrated the viability of state control
of the economy. Key elements in the rise of Labour politics
emphasised in the recent work of McKibbin, Laybourn and, in the
Scottish context, by Jim Smyth and Ian Hutchison have been the
extension of the franchise in 1918 (pre-1914 in Glasgow only 52

per cent of adult males were enfranchised) and the reorganisation and internal dynamism of the Labour Party over the period 1918–29. The opening up of more central Labour archives and the proliferation of detailed local and regional case studies have added considerably to knowledge and suggest a rich mosaic of experience, with different factors combining to account for the electoral fortunes of Labour in different areas, depending upon economic, social and cultural circumstances. For example, the weight of local and municipal evidence suggests strongly that Labour fortunes were buoyant and rising over 1910–14 (Laybourn, 1988), though this was more marked in England and Wales than in Scotland, as Hutchison has demonstrated. Class voting, as Cronin has shown, became more marked between the wars, with two-thirds of working-class voters voting Labour in 1929. Nonetheless, Benson, amongst others, has persuasively demonstrated how the Labour Party drew a disproportionate slice of its vote from high-paid, relatively skilled workers and that there remained throughout this period (and indeed beyond) a clear tendency for the poorest workers to either abstain (from poverty-induced apathy?), or to vote either Liberal or Tory (see also Stedman-Jones, 1971). Somewhat paradoxically, perhaps, the decline of absolute poverty over the period 1880–1950, combined with rising levels of literacy and expectations in a more consumerist society, may well have helped consolidate the Labour vote. The experience of work and changes in labour markets could act as significant politicising forces, but they were amongst many social, economic, political and cultural factors which contributed to the rise of Labour to political power in the period 1880–1950.

Conclusions

Labour history remains a contentious discipline, characterised by intense research activity and a rich and invigorating range of different interpretations, not least on the patterns of collective organisation, the function of unions in structuring work and the role of work in Labour's rise to political prominence and power. Exploitation of new sources, closer and more critical engagement with theory, and the adoption of a somewhat more rigorous, detached, quantitative and comparative methodology (much of which has been borrowed from the social sciences) has led to a reappraisal of much of the 'orthodox' agenda laid down during the great expansion of the discipline in the 1960s and 1970s. Pivotal stereotypes have been challenged such as the 'conservatism' of the skilled labour elite, the disjunctures of 'new unionism' and the General Strike of 1926, and the importance of syndicalism. Recent research indicates that national patterns have to be seriously qualified by reference to local and regional perspectives, which in turn suggest a range of different social relations at any point in time across the country. The working class, moreover, was far less cohesive and homogeneous than earlier accounts in the 'magnificent journey' mould (which assumed that the movement and the working class were synonymous) would have us believe. Differences based on occupation, gender, religion and locality clearly made collective organisation difficult to sustain and go part of the way towards explaining the characteristically fragmented and sectional character of British trade unionism. Furthermore, the rise of the labour movement needs to be kept firmly in perspective – it was neither unilinear nor the inevitable outcome of changes in the experience of work. Rather it was contingent upon a series of fortuitous external factors – including tightening labour markets, the wars, the divisions within the Liberals, changes in the franchise and urban development. Moreover, in quantitative terms, the labour movement was a minority activity: more workers were non-unionised than unionised, most did not vote Labour until very late in our period and many were not involved in strikes.

These are important caveats to make. Nevertheless, in contrast to some recent interpretations, what has been emphasised here has been the emergence of a powerful trade union movement, which became firmly entrenched as part of the fabric of British society by 1950 and which made a meaningful difference in workers' lives. Unionisation is a complex process and has been explained as the product of a number of factors. But fundamentally workers formed and sustained collective organisations as a consequence of more exploitative working conditions which threatened skills, customary work customs and notions of a 'fair day's work for a fair day's pay'. Moreover, as company paternalism atrophied and firms became larger, workers increasingly felt the need to organise horizontally, combining with one another to protect their interests

in a harsher competitive climate. Economic and political circumstances were important, in that unions needed a conducive environment in which to thrive. Full employment, in particular,
facilitated growth, whilst mass unemployment signalled contraction
and retrenchment. State encouragement of trade unionism and
collective bargaining, combined with the increasing tendency of
employers to recognise and work with trade unions, also facilitated growth. This was especially evident during the 1910s and
the 1940s. Cause and effect became entwined as success in organisation and/or industrial action stimulated workers to join and
employees elsewhere to organise. Improving communications,
growing literacy, the influence of the socialist press, the bureaucratisation of labour markets, the decline of casualisation and
erosion of absolute poverty, and rising expectations all contributed
to the growth of mass unionisation.

It is difficult to disentangle the impact that trade unionism
had upon work in Britain between 1880 and 1950. The uneven
penetration of collective organisation translated into patchy and
limited influence in labour markets, the labour process and the
labour contract. The work conditions of female workers and non-
manual workers were far less subject to joint regulation through
either workplace or industry-wide collective bargaining than were
those of the male manual workers. Nonetheless, the situation had
been transformed from 1880, when less than 10 per cent of workers
were members of unions and only the skilled elite exercised any
real control and autonomy at work. By 1950, the wages and working conditions of most workers were decided collectively, rather
than individually between master and worker. This transformed
the labour market in Britain. The existence of the unions at the
national level and the warrening of the workplace with shop stewards and committees did much to extend the frontier of control
deep into managerial terrain, and, as a consequence, this curbed
the unilateral authority of employers and their capacity to dictate
wages and conditions. Moreover, unionisation led to a degree of
standardisation of wages and working hours across the country
which impacted positively upon the non-unionised sector. Employment legislation resulting from hard trade union campaigning,
co-ordinated by the TUC, also often benefited all workers, not just
the card-holding members, as Rowe commented in 1928. Trade
unionism markedly strengthened the power of labour over capital,

indicated in the achievement of the annual wage round by the 1950s, and the virtual disappearance of both the lockout and the practice of wage reductions during trade recessions. The reduction in work time was also largely the product of trade union agitation, which had achieved a 44–5-hour working week (with the 'week-end'), official 'retirement'and the principle of at least one week's holiday with pay enshrined in legislation by the late 1940s (see Cross, 1989, pp. 222–8). Bienefeld's study of working hours indicated the significant impact of strong trade unions which had the effect of standardising hours within industries, whilst at the same time increasingly moving towards a national norm through collective bargaining and legislation such as the Factory Acts.

However, whilst the influence of trade unions over the labour contract and labour markets was considerable by 1950, the unions failed to extend their control significantly into the management of production. This was an area of managerial prerogative that employers were reluctant to abdicate, seeing control over the labour process as fundamental if business was to be able to react to the vagaries of more hostile product markets. Opportunities for the unions to take the initiative to further extend 'joint regulation' into more tangible forms of workers' control in the post-war nationalised industries were also not taken. In part this reflects the rather moderate and economistic nature of the British trade union movement, which was characterised from its outset by a desire to regulate and reform the worst excesses of capitalism, rather than challenge the system of capitalist control and authority *per se*. This was as evident in 1950 – perhaps more so – as it was in 1880. In turn the unions reflected the limited aspirations of most ordinary working people who rarely exhibited a desire to run industry, but who became vociferous defenders of social justice and of workers' rights to jointly determine the conditions under which they sold their labour, exercised through a process of voluntary collective bargaining between their trade unions and their employers. In itself, this represented something of a transformation in the conditions under which work was performed in Britain.

Recent historical research suggests that we need to pay more attention to the workplace and the labour process in explaining the rise of trade unions and to issues and developments *outside* the workplace in accounting for the rise of the Labour Party. The intensification of work and emergence of trade unions may well have played a critical role in the formation of the Labour Party and its early development, but by the 1920s the Party had broadened its base and was winning support on the basis of policies designed to extend public service provision, improve housing and extend citizenship. One important recent thrust of historical research has revised and disentangled the connections between work, trade unions and political developments which were such a key component of the earlier generation of labour history. The labour process may well have had a radicalising influence, but was only one of a series of factors, and not necessarily the most important, which explain the rise of Labour between the mid-Victorian period and 1950.

9

CONCLUSION: LABOUR TRANSFORMED?

In many respects work was transformed in Britain between 1880 and 1950. However, work was a multi-faceted phenomenon involving a rich, diversified mosaic of experience differentiated by class, occupation, gender and age. Given the range of activity involved and the variable pace of economic and social developments across the nation, inevitably the process of labour transformation was uneven and incomplete. The continuities in experience should not be forgotten. Class and gender inequalities remained stark at the mid-twentieth century and continued to be incubated and legitimised at the point of production. Work remained an important component in most people's lives, though it did not dominate people's existence in the way that it had in the late Victorian period.

There were many strands to this transformation of labour; a multiplicity of paths, rather than any single trajectory. The thrust of recent research has resulted in an undermining of all-encompassing theoretical frameworks – Marxist or otherwise – which can only be made to fit if swathes of contradictory evidence and countervailing experience are ignored. The labour process is a case in point. Braverman's seminal contribution in 1974 triggered a mass of empirical research, some of which supported the concepts of deskilling, dehumanisation, degradation, subordination and alienation inherent within monopoly capitalism. We noted in Chapters 3 and 4 strong evidence for such tendencies within the capitalist workplace in Britain between 1880 and 1950, including skill fragmentation.

Almost all work was considerably more mechanised and capital-intensive by 1950 compared to 1880. Mechanisation and new structures of managerial control incorporating 'scientific' methods, the stopwatch and the rate-fixer meant that the all-round skills of the artisan in trades such as engineering, building, mining and printing were far less in evidence. This diminished the freedom, autonomy and creativity of the artisanal elite which had dominated Victorian working-class communities. Nonetheless, it is important not to extrapolate too much from the experience of what was a minority of workers in the late Victorian economy. The expansion of semi-skilled jobs represented opportunities for upward mobility for some – for example female labour during the wars – and there was some reskilling as well as the creation of new skills, as More has argued. The labour force was more highly educated in 1950 compared to 1880 and recent research has shown how some groups of craftsmen resisted the full ramifications of deskilling (Zeitlin, 1985, 1991; Reid, 1991, 1992; Penn, 1985). The nature of British product markets, moreover, where bespoke production remained important, continued to place a high premium on skilled labour, as, for example, in shipbuilding and many branches of engineering. Upward mobility can be detected from closer scrutiny of the ten-yearly Census statistics, disaggregated by socio-economic status, in Table 2.11.

Still, in a very real sense there was degenerative transformation. For many workers, their sphere of influence was narrower, their discretion curtailed, they were subject to tighter discipline and control which went along with a desire on the part of those investing in large factories and technology to recoup their capital and extract some profit. Competition in more hostile product markets from the 1870s led employers into experimentation with a range of strategies to subordinate labour and raise productivity. The process of labour *intensification* was widespread and by 1950 a very different work regime prevailed than in the 1870s. The last vestiges of pre-industrial patterns of work – which had proven particularly persistent – disappeared and labour became regularised, intensified, monitored and codified within the context of a shorter work day and year. Work assumed its 'modern' form.

Social relations in the workplace were also transformed. The close, paternalist relationship between master and worker gave way to more depersonalised industrial relations in larger production units in both manual and non-manual employment. Workers found themselves interacting more frequently with functionalised supervisors, line managers, personnel and planning departments, rather than with the foreman, who had been the pivotal figure of managerial authority in the late nineteenth century. This incubated alienation and dissatisfaction and contributed to the politicisation of groups of workers facing the pressures and uncertainties of such degenerative change, including the craft artisans in the late nineteenth and early twentieth centuries. Combined with the destabilising nature of mechanisation, work reorganisation and intensification of work, such changes in business structure and managerial practices germinated collective organisation amongst workers. Strong and more representative trade unions emerged as a counterpoise, to protect and advance the interests of workers in the labour market. Between 1880 and 1920 union membership grew from representing around 5–10 per cent of the labour force, to almost 50 per cent. This represented one of the most profound transformations, with very significant ramifications for the nature of work and political alignments in Britain by the mid-twentieth century.

Much recent research has emphasised the capabilities of British workers to adapt and react to changes at the point of production, stressing the active role of workers and their organisations as an agency in the labour process and labour markets. Hence craftworkers resisted attempts by management unilaterally to control production and succeeded in ameliorating the managerial attack on skill across a wide range of sectors. However, on balance, the evidence suggests that the influence of work groups and trade unions up to 1950 remained minimal in relation to the labour process and the management of production. These were spheres of activity that with few exceptions remained the prerogative of management. Real workers' control or even participation in production management was rare indeed in 1950. Where unofficial workplace action and official trade union influence were extensive, as we argued in Chapter 8, was in the labour market, the work environment and in the negotiation of the labour contract.

Other continuities were also evident over the period 1880–1950. Britain remained a class-ridden, patriarchal capitalist society, permeated with racial and gender apartheid. Class upbringing, residence, the type of school attended and experience of higher education continued to exercise a strong influence on occupational choices. With few exceptions, top jobs in the professions, the universities, medicine, the civil service, commerce, finance and politics went to those of middle- or upper-class background. The outcome was a society still divided by deep inequalities in wealth distribution, despite the redistributive tendencies of policy during the war and reconstruction period in the 1940s. Race and gender also constrained job choice and opportunities. Whilst discrimination against the Catholic Irish was much in evidence in 1880, the same was the case in relation to East European migrants and blacks at the mid-twentieth century. The labour market was characterised by gender discrimination and segmentation and whilst there had been some positive change – not least in family size – the impact of this by 1950 was probably fairly marginal, given the evidence of time spent within households on unpaid domestic labour. Political emancipation did not translate into fundamental change in the socio-economic sphere, whilst the gains made by women in the workplace in wartime proved to be largely short-lived. Gender inequalities transferred over from traditional to 'new' occupations, from manual to non-manual employment, whilst there was little if any change in the distribution of labour within the unpaid sphere of activity within the home and family from 1880 to 1950. Women benefited least from the transformation of labour in this period.

In other respects the world of work in 1950 was profoundly different from 1880. To some extent, the degenerative tendencies of job fragmentation, depersonalisation, bureaucratisation and intensification were offset by compensations, material rewards and a more healthy, less dangerous work environment. It has become unfashionable to emphasise such outcomes, but it is clear that more efficient working practices generated wealth which in turn enabled working conditions to be improved and real wages to rise substantially. Whilst there remained quite wide wage differentials based on gender, class and skill (as Table 9.1 indicates), in real terms (that is, taking into account price inflation) workers in Britain were earning by 1950 in the region of three times the wages they made in 1880 (Routh, 1982). Table 9.1 gives some sense of wage movements and differentials in the first half of the twentieth century.

Table 9.1 Average wages by occupational class, expressed as a percentage of the mean for all occupational classes (male and female), 1913–14 and 1955–6

		1913–14	1955–6
Men			
1. Professions	A. Higher	405	290
	B. Lower	191	115
2. Managers		247	279
3. Clerks		122	98
4. Foremen		152	148
5. Manual	A. Skilled	131	117
	B. Semi-skilled	85	88
	C. Unskilled	78	82
Male average		116	119
Women			
1. Professions	A. Higher		218
	B. Lower	110	82
2. Managers		99	151
3. Clerks		56	60
4. Forewomen		70	90
5. Manual	A. Skilled	54	60
	B. Semi-skilled	62	51
	C. Unskilled	35	43
Female average		62	60

Source: G. Routh, *Occupation and Pay in Great Britain, 1906–1979* (1980, p. 124).

Whilst new hazards and occupational diseases tended to replace older ones, such as lead poisoning, which were subject to regulation and control, nonetheless it remains true that the British workplace was a much safer place in which to toil in 1950 than in the late Victorian period. Indeed, workers were roughly three times less likely to be killed by an injury at work in 1950, compared to 1880. Perhaps the most revolutionary changes occurred, however, in work time. The proportion of a worker's lifetime spent in employment almost halved, on average, between the 1870s and 1950. The working week contracted by about a quarter (from *c*. 60 to *c*. 44–5 hours). On top of that needs to be added the later start and early termination of employment (with the rising school leaving age and retirement), together with the introduction of the paid holiday. Undoubtedly, however, whilst the degree of physical strain and exhaustion declined, levels of mental stress deepened with closer supervision, increased mechanisation and the more regularised and intensified work regimes. Nevertheless, the introduction of the weekend, the paid holiday (albeit only one week for most workers at 1950) and pensionable retirement, combined with falling working hours to tip the balance away from work towards leisure. Zweig noted in his qualitative surveys of working life around 1950 that most workers were working to live, not living to work. That is, family and community life, leisure, pastimes, the pub and football had all assumed greater importance (and become commercialised) and increasingly work was viewed as the means to these ends – what sociologists were later to term an 'instrumental' attitude to employment. The erosion of the work ethic was particularly evident amongst the younger generation of workers. In mining communities, for example, Zweig recorded the lack of sympathy that young miners had for the older generation who talked of little else but their work and the pit.

The achievement of rising real wages and the contraction of work time was neither uniform, nor automatic, however, but the outcome of struggle and confrontation and subject to reversals and setbacks. Hence the context of confrontational industrial relations between the late 1880s and the 1920s. There was a substantial redistribution of power within the workplace, flowing from capital to labour, which mirrored broader shifts in power in local and national politics as the franchise was extended downwards to embrace first the male and later the female proletariat. The extent of workers' power varied considerably across the economy, linked to such factors as skill, labour market scarcity, gender and levels of trade unionism. However, the manifestations of such workplace power were widely evident, especially in contrast to the situation that prevailed $c.$ 1880. For example, the power of the unions to sustain and improve real wage levels extended, indicated in the contrast between the experience of the 1930s and 1940s and the period $c.$ 1900–12 when real wages stagnated.

By 1950, moreover, the attitudes and behaviour of employers and management were radically different. The capability of employers to manage and control their labour unilaterally was severely circumscribed, both by trade union rules and regulations and by state intervention in the labour market and in industrial relations. The days of the individual contract struck between master and man had passed and by 1950 the majority of workers (perhaps as many as 90 per cent) were governed by rules and labour contracts that were the product of joint collective bargaining either between unions and employers (or their organisations), or between the two sides of industries in the government-created Joint Industrial Councils or Wages Boards. Such agreements typically covered the basic issues of wages, working hours and overtime payments. However, some extended into welfare issues such as canteen provision and occupational health and safety rules, and labour process issues, such as rate fixing and discipline. Labour control policies shifted substantially over these years, with employers moving from coercive, authoritarian and confrontational anti-trade union strategies, towards more consensual, co-operative, incorporative policies. Widely condemned and ignored in 1880, the trade unions had become part of the fabric of British society by 1950 and in many sectors of industry were massively influential in regulating work and dictating the shape of employment, especially in relation to the work environment, the labour market and the labour contract. Not all workers, of course, were in well-unionised occupations, and where a union presence was lacking, basic employment rights could still be undermined – as in banks, insurance companies, many shops and offices and in agriculture. Nonetheless, it is still reasonable to emphasise the positive contribution made by the trade unions in transforming work by 1950. Moreover, through Westminster the power of the unions was extended considerably beyond their own membership base in the 1940s.

Just as employers reached down to the shop floor to more directly manage their labour, so too did the state increasingly intervene in the labour market. Here, again, was quite a profound transformation. In 1880 such involvement was minimal and the prevailing attitude was one of *laissez-faire*, allowing the market, with few exceptions (mostly in relation to child and female labour) to dictate wages and conditions. By 1950 the influence of the state in the workplace was widespread. The government operated as an exemplar, as the largest single employer, with a substantial portion of the entire labour force in the public sector by 1950. Extensive employment legislation maintained a floor of minimum wages, working hours and occupational health and safety standards across much of the economy. The state had also played a critical role in forging more consensual social relations, by directly encouraging employers to recognise and work with trade unions, and providing for state arbitration in the eventuality of a breakdown in the voluntary bargaining system between capital and labour. Moreover, the Welfare State and the post-World War Two commitment to the maintenance of full employment removed much of the insecurity and uncertainty from both work and the loss of employment.

The experience of work also had wider social, cultural and political connotations. The labour process and social relationships in employment forged identities, attitudes and mentalities, incubating class-consciousness and political awareness, which contributed to the rise of socialist politics and the Labour Party in Britain. Deskilling, work intensification and the struggle over the control of work could act as powerful radicalising forces, most evident, perhaps, in the period 1890–1920. By the 1910s and 1920s craftsmen constituted the backbone of socialist, Marxist and labourist political parties in Britain. Moreover, the increased clustering of male workers in blue-collar jobs up to the 1940s sharpened their class awareness, contributing to the close identification of the working class with the Labour Party. That is not to suggest, however, that the workplace was the only site of politicisation. This does need to be kept in perspective. Marxist-driven accounts have sometimes tended to overstate the importance of experience at the point of production in the incubation of labourist and socialist politics. Recent research emphasises the limits of Labour's 'forward march', the importance of other factors – political, cultural and social – than the purely economic. Here there were significant differences between the genders, as Savage and Miles have recently shown. Given the very different experience of women at work within Britain's distinctively patriarchal style of capitalism, and the sexist nature of the trade unions, it appears that work was a less significant catalyst than issues such as housing and health in the politicisation of female labour.

Rather than outright degradation, impoverishment and alienation, surveys of work around 1950 suggest a mixed picture. As somebody who interviewed more than a thousand workers for his several books on workers' lives c. 1950, Zweig's views on this issue carry some weight. Attitudes towards employment, Zweig notes, were wide-ranging, with age, skill and gender still quite significant factors influencing levels of satisfaction at work. Nonetheless,

Zweig estimated that two-thirds of manual workers he interviewed had a positive attitude towards their paid employment, identified with their work and gained satisfaction and enjoyment from it. He classified a further 15–20 per cent as having affirmative views, 'with certain reservations' and the remainder had clearly negative attitudes towards their work. Similar contemporary surveys suggest, however, a clear distinction between work done by men and women, with studies of female workers indicating lower levels of job satisfaction (see Cronin, 1984, pp. 67–8). The camaraderie of the workplace was often noted by such participant surveys and this contrasted sharply with the negative attitudes expressed towards the drudgery, physical exhaustion and isolation of unpaid work within the home. The alienation of the mass production assembly-line car plants may well not have been typical of most workplaces in Britain around 1950. Indeed, it has been estimated that only a tiny proportion of British workers (less than 5 per cent) were engaged in such mass production processes at the mid-twentieth century (interestingly, Oakley's investigation of the work of the housewife in the early 1970s drew a direct parallel with car workers). Moreover, by the 1950s the material compensations afforded by regular and secure employment, backed up by an extensive state welfare safety net and a relatively generous social wage in the eventuality of loss of work, helped to assuage any sense of alienation.

By 1950, British labour had attained a degree of control, status and power, from the workplace up to Westminster, that their forebears would have regarded as inconceivable. Power still remained unevenly distributed. There continued to be groups of workers untouched by trade unionism and unprotected by the benevolence of the state, and a wide range of experience prevailed across the economy. Here, it is worth highlighting again the subordinate position of women in the workplace and the centrality accorded to unpaid domestic labour in family and home. This meant that women drew less meaning from paid employment than their male counterparts and as such paid work had less of a politicising impact upon women than men. Nevertheless, the transfer of power to labour over the period 1880–1950 enabled exploitation at work to be mediated and excesses curbed, making post-World War Two monopoly capitalism in a mixed economy in Britain more tolerable for most folk. In the event, capitalism survived by flexible adaptation, accommodation and incorporation of labour. The most intransigent employers – the railway companies and coal-owners – were replaced with public corporations, whose work regimes proved to be substantially more benign, if impervious to the demands of workplace activists for more workers' control and participation in production management. The masters' servants of the Victorian era had become citizens of the workplace, invariably regulating conditions of employment *jointly* with management, through their unions, through workplace action and practices, through their vote, their party and through the apparatus of the state, albeit within a society that was still wracked by deep and enduring inequalities and injustices in income and wealth based on class, race and gender.

BIBLIOGRAPHY

(The place of publication is London unless otherwise stated.)

Accidents Committee (Report of the Departmental Committee) (1911) Cmd 5535

Adams, T. (1990) 'Labour and the First World War', *Journal of Local and Regional Studies*, 10, 1

Alexander, S. (1984) 'Women, Class and Sexual Difference in the 1830s and 1840s', *History Workshop Journal*, 17

Alexander, S., A. Davin and E. Hostettler (1979) 'Labouring Women', *History Workshop Journal*, 8

Anderson, G. (1976) *Victorian Clerks* (Manchester)

Anderson, G. (ed.) (1988) *The White Blouse Revolution* (Manchester)

Arlidge, J. L. (1892) *The Hygiene Diseases and Mortality of Occupations*

Armstrong, A. (1988) *Farmworkers: A Social and Economic History, 1770–1980*

Askwith, Lord (1920) *Industrial Problems and Disputes*

Bagwell, P. (1963) *The Railwaymen*

Bain, G. and R. Price (1980) *Profiles of Union Growth* (Oxford)

Barnett, C. (1996) *The Audit of War*

Baron, A. (1991) 'Gender and Labour History', in A. Baron (ed.), *Work Engendered*

Bartrip, P. (1987) *Workmen's Compensation in Twentieth Century Britain* (Aldershot)

Bartrip, P. (1996) 'Petticoat Pestering': the Women's Trade Union League and Lead Poisoning in the Staffordshire Potteries, 1890–1914', *Historical Studies in Industrial Relations*, 2, Sept.

Bartrip, P. (1998) 'Too Little, too Late? The Home Office and the Asbestos Industry Regulations, 1931', *Medical History*, 42

Bartrip, P. and S. Burman (1983) *Wounded Soldiers of Industry* (Oxford)

Bartrip, P. and P. T. Fenn (1988) 'Factory Fatalities and Regulation in Britain, 1878–1913', *Explorations in Economic History*, 25

Beddoe, D. (1983) *Discovering Women's History*

Beechey, V. (1982) 'The Sexual Division of Labour and the Labour Process: a Critical Assessment of Braverman', in S. Wood (ed.), *The Degradation of Work?*

Behagg, C. (1979) 'Custom, Class and Change: the Trade Societies of Birmingham', *Social History*, 4

251

Bell, Lady (1911) *At the Works*
Benson, J. (1980) *British Coalminers in the Nineteenth Century*
Benson, J. (ed.) (1985) *The Working Class in England, 1875–1914*
Benson, J. (1989) *The Working Class in Britain, 1850–1939*
Berg, M. (1979) *Technology and Toil*
Beynon, H. (1973) *Working for Ford*
Bienefeld, M. A. (1972) *Working Hours in British Industry*
Black, C. (1915) *Married Women's Work* (1983 Virago edn)
Black, J. (1953) 'Pneumoconiosis of Coal Miners in Scotland', *British Journal of Industrial Medicine*, 10
Blackburn, S. (1989) ' "Some of them gets Lead Poisoned": Occupational Lead Exposure in Women, 1880–1914', *Social History of Medicine*, 2
Bolin-Hort, P. (1989) *Work, Family and the State* (Lund, Sweden)
Boston, S. (1980) *Women Workers and the Trade Unions*
Branson, N. (1975) *Britain in the Twenties*
Braverman, H. (1974) *Labor and Monopoly Capital*
Braybon, G. (1981) *Women Workers in the First World War*
Braybon, G. and P. Summerfield (1987) *Out of the Cage*
Brown, G. (1977) *Sabotage* (Nottingham)
Brown, K. (1982) 'Trade Unions and the Law' in C. Wrigley (ed.), *A History of British Industrial Relations, 1875–1914* (Brighton)
Brown, Y. (1998) 'Did the Second World War Have Any Significant, Permanent Impact on the Employment Status of Working Class Women in the West of Scotland?' (History and Politics Honours Dissertation, Caledonian University, Glasgow)
Bryder, L. (1985) 'Tuberculosis, Silicosis and the Slate Industry in North Wales, 1927–1939' in P. Weindling (ed.), *The Social History of Occupational Health*
Bullen, A. (1988) 'Pragmatism vs Principle: Cotton Employers', in J. Jowitt and A. McIvor (eds), *Employers and Labour in the English Textile Industries, 1850–1939*
Bullock, A. (1960) *The Life and Times of Ernest Bevin*
Burawoy, M. (1985) *The Politics of Production*
Burgess, K. (1975) *The Origins of British Industrial Relations*
Burgess, K. (1980) *The Challenge of Labour*
Burgess, K. (1986) 'Authority Relations and the Division of Labour in British Industry, with Special Reference to Clydeside, c. 1860–1930', *Social History*, 11, no. 2
Burke, G. (1985) 'Disease, Labour Migration and Technological Change: the Case of the Cornish Miners', in P. Weindling (ed.), *The Social History of Occupational Health*
Burnett, J. (ed.) (1974) *Useful Toil*
Busfield, D. (1988) 'Skill and the Sexual Division of Labour in the West Riding Textile Industry', in J. Jowitt and A. McIvor (eds), *Employers and Labour in the English Textile Industries, 1850–1939*
Cadbury, E. (1912) *Experiments in Industrial Organisation*
Calder, A. and D. Sheridan (eds) (1984) *Speak For Yourself: a Mass Observation Anthology, 1937–1949*

Cantrell, J. (1985) *James Nasmyth and the Bridgewater Foundry* (Manchester)

Carson, W. G. (1970) 'Enforcement of Factory Legislation', *British Journal of Criminology*, 10

Chandler, A. D. (1990) *Scale and Scope: the Dynamics of Industrial Capitalism*

Chew, D. Nield (1982) *Ada Nield Chew: Life and Writings of a Working Woman*

Chinn, C. (1988) *They Worked All Their Lives: Women of the Urban Poor in England, 1880–1939* (Manchester)

Church, R. (1986) *The History of the British Coal Industry*, vol. 3, *1830–1913*

Clapham, J. H. (1926–38) *An Economic History of Modern Britain*, 3 vols

Clarke, A. (1899) *The Effects of the Factory System*

Clarke, A. (1997) *The Struggle for the Breeches: Gender and the Making of the British Working Class* (Berkeley, California)

Clegg, H. (1985) *A History of British Trade Unions since 1889*, vol. II, *1911–1933* (Oxford)

Clegg, H. (1994) *A History of British Trade Unions since 1889*, vol. III, *1934–1951* (Oxford)

Clegg, H. A., A. Fox and A. F. Thompson (1964) *A History of British Trade Unions since 1889*, vol. I, *1889–1910* (Oxford)

Coates, K. (1982) 'The Vagaries of Participation', in B. Pimlott and C. Cook (eds), *Trade Unions in British Politics*

Cohn, S. (1985) *The Process of Occupational Sex-Typing: the Feminisation of Clerical Labour in Great Britain*

Cole, G. D. H. (1923) *Workshop Organisation* (Oxford)

Cole, G. D. H. (1937) *The Condition of Britain*

Common, J. (1938) *Seven Shifts*

Coombes, B. L. (1939) *These Poor Hands: the Autobiography of a Miner Working in South Wales*

Corr, H. (1983a) 'The Schoolgirls Curriculum and the Ideology of the Home, 1870–1914', in Glasgow Women's Studies Group, *Uncharted Lives*

Corr, H. (1983b) 'The Sexual Division of Labour in the Scottish Teaching Profession, 1872–1914', in W. M. Hume and H. M. Paterson (eds), *Scottish Culture and Scottish Education, 1800–1980* (Edinburgh)

Cowan, R. S. (1989) *More Work for Mother*

Crompton, R. and G. Jones (1984) *White-Collar Proletariat: Deskilling and Gender in Clerical Work*

Cronin, J. E. (1979) *Industrial Conflict in Modern Britain*

Cronin, J. E. (1982) 'Strikes, 1870–1914' in C. J. Wrigley (ed.), *A History of British Industrial Relations, 1875–1914* (Brighton)

Cronin, J. E. (1984) *Labour and Society in Modern Britain, 1918–1979*

Cronin, J. E. and J. Schneer (eds) (1982) *Social Conflict and the Political Order in Modern Britain*

Crosland, C. A. R. (1956) *The Future of Socialism*

Cross, G. (1989) *A Quest for Time: the Reduction of Work in Britain and France, 1840–1940* (Los Angeles, California)

Crossick, G. (1978) *An Artisan Elite in Victorian Society: Kentish London, 1840–1880*

Croucher, R. (1982) *Engineers at War, 1939–1945*

Crouzet, F. (1982) *The Victorian Economy*

Crowther, A. (1988) *British Social Policy, 1914–1939*

Currie, R. (1979) *Industrial Politics* (Oxford)

Daunton, M. (1985) *Royal Mail: the Post Office since 1840*

Davidoff, L. (1976) 'Rationalisation', in D. L. Barker and S. Allen (eds), *Dependence and Exploitation in Work and Marriage*

Davidoff, L. and B. Westover (eds) (1986) *Our Work, Our Lives, Our Words*

Davidson, C. (1982) *A Woman's Work is Never Done*

Davidson, R. (1982) 'Government Administration', in C. J. Wrigley (ed.), *A History of British Industrial Relations, 1875–1914* (Brighton)

Davy, T. (1986) ' "A Cissy Job for Men; a Nice Job for Girls": Women Shorthand Typists in London, 1900–39', in L. Davidoff and B. Westover (eds), *Our Work, Our Lives, Our Words*

Dickson, A. and J. Treble (eds) (1992) *People and Society in Scotland*, vol. III, *1914–1990* (Edinburgh)

Dobash, R. E. and R. Dobash (1979) *Violence against Wives* (New York)

Donovan Report (Royal Commission on Trade Unions and Employers' Associations, 1965–68), HMSO, 1968, Cd 3623

Drummond, D. (1989) ' "Specifically Designed"? Employers' Labour Strategies and Worker Responses in British Railway Workshops', in C. Harvey and J. Turner (eds), *Labour and Business in Modern Britain*

Duncan, R. and A. McIvor (eds) (1992) *Militant Workers: Labour and Class Conflict on the Clyde, 1900–1950* (Edinburgh)

Dutton, H. I. and J. E. King (1982) 'The Limits of Paternalism: the Cotton Tyrants of North Lancashire,1836–54', *Social History*, 7

Edwards, R. (1979) *Contested Terrain*

Exell, A. (1977, 1978, 1980) 'Autobiography of an Oxford Car Worker', *History Workshop Journal*, 6, 7 and 9

Faley, J. (1990) *Up Oor Close: Memories of Domestic Life in Glasgow Tenements, 1910–1945* (Wendlebury)

Fitzgerald, R. (1988) *British Labour Management and Industrial Welfare, 1846–1939*

Flint, J. B. (1910) 'The Dangers of a Miner's Life', *The Socialist*, August

Foster, J. (1974) *Class Struggle in the Industrial Revolution*

Foster, J. (1990) 'Strike Action and Working Class Politics on Clydeside, 1914–1919', *International Review of Social History*, 35

Foster, J. (1992) 'A Proletarian Nation? Occupation and Class since 1914', in A. Dickson and J. Treble (eds), *People and Society in Scotland*, vol. III, *1914–1990* (Edinburgh)

Fowler, A. and T. Wyke (1987) *The Barefoot Aristocrats* (Littleborough)

Fox, A. (1985) *History and Heritage*

Francis, H. and D. Smith (1980) *The Fed: a History of the South Wales Miners in the Twentieth Century*

Fraser, W. H. (1974) *Trade Unions and Society*

Fraser, W. H. (1999) *A History of British Trade Unionism, 1700–1998*

Fraser, W. H. and R. J. Morris (eds) (1990) *People and Society in Scotland*, vol. II, *1830–1914* (Edinburgh)

Friedman, A. L. (1977) *Industry and Labour*

Fyrth, H. J. and H. Collins (1959) *The Foundry Workers* (Manchester)

Gallagher, T. (1987) *Glasgow: the Uneasy Peace* (Manchester)

Galton, F. W. (ed.) (1896) *Workers on their Industries*

Garside, W. R. and H. Gospel (1982) 'Employers and Managers', in C. J. Wrigley (ed.), *A History of British Industrial Relations, 1875–1914* (Brighton)

Geary, D. (1991) *European Labour Politics from 1900 to the Depression*

Gershuny, J. *et al.* (1986) 'Time Budgets', *Quarterly Journal of Social Affairs*, 2

Glasgow Labour History Workshop (1989) *The Singer Strike, 1911* (Clydebank)

Glasgow Women's Studies Group (1983) *Uncharted Lives* (Glasgow)

Glucksmann, M. (1990) *Women Assemble*

Gollan, J. (1937) *Youth in British Industry*

Goodrich, C. (1920) *The Frontier of Control*

Gordon, E. (1988) 'The Scottish Trade Union Movement, Class and Gender, 1850–1914', *Scottish Labour History Society Journal*, 23

Gordon, E. (1990) 'Women's Spheres', in W. H. Fraser and R. J. Morris (eds), *People and Society in Scotland*, vol. II *1830–1914* (Edinburgh)

Gordon, E. (1991) *Women and the Labour Movement in Scotland, 1850–1914* (Oxford)

Gordon, E. and E. Breitenbach (eds) (1990) *The World is Ill-divided: Women Workers in Scotland in the 19th and early Twentieth Centuries*

Gospel, H. (1974) 'Employers' Organisations, 1918–1939' (unpublished PhD thesis, London School of Economics)

Gospel, H. (1987) 'Employers and Managers', in C. J. Wrigley (ed.), *A History of British Industrial Relations*, vol. 2, *1914–1939* (Brighton)

Gospel, H. (1992) *Markets, Firms and the Management of Labour in Modern Britain* (Cambridge)

Gospel, H. (1996) 'The Management of Labour', in C. J. Wrigley (ed.), *A History of British Industrial Relations, 1939–1979* (Brighton)

Gospel, H. and C. R. Littler (eds) (1983) *Managerial Strategies and Industrial Relations*

Graham, W.(1921) *The Wages of Labour*

Gray, R. (1976) *The Labour Aristocracy in Victorian Edinburgh*

Gray, R. (1981) *The Aristocracy of Labour in Nineteenth Century Britain*

Greenwood, W. (1933) *Love on the Dole*

Greenwood, W. (nd, *c.* 1939) *How the Other Man Lives*

Grieves, K. (1988) *The Politics of Manpower, 1914–18* (Manchester)

Hakim, C. (1979) *Occupational Segregation*

Hakim, C. (1994) 'A Century of Change in Occupational Segregation, 1891–1991', *Journal of Historical Sociology*, 7, no. 4

Hannah, L. (1976) *The Rise of the Corporate Economy*

Hardie, K. (1899) *The Overtoun Horror*

Hardyment, C. (1988) *From Mangle to Microwave: the Mechanisation of Housework* (Cambridge)

Harris, J. (1993) *Private Lives, Public Spirit: a Social History of Britain, 1870–1914*

Harrison, B. and H. Mockett (1990) 'Women in the Factory: the State and Factory Legislation in Nineteenth Century Britain', in L. Jamieson and H. Corr (eds), *The State, Private Life and Political Change*

Harrison, M. (1988) 'Domestic Service between the Wars', *Oral History*, 16, Spring

Harrison, R. and J. Zeitlin (eds) (1985) *Divisions of Labour*

Hartley, J. (ed.) (1994) *Hearts Undefeated: Women's Writing of the Second World War*

Harvey, C. and J. Turner (eds) (1989) *Labour and Business in Modern Britain*

Hay, R. (1978) 'Employers' Attitudes to Social Policy and the Concept of Social Control, 1900–1920', in P. Thane (ed.), *The Origins of British Social Policy*

Higgs, E. (1989) *Making Sense of the Census*

Hill, B. (1993) 'Women, Work and the Census: a Problem for Historians of Women', *History Workshop Journal*, 35

Hilton, J. *et al.* (1935) *Are Trade Unions Obstructive?*

Hinton, J. (1973) *The First Shop Stewards Movement*

Hinton, J. (1983) *Labour and Socialism: a History of the British Labour Movement, 1867–1974*

Hinton, J. (1994) *Shop Floor Citizens: Engineering Democracy in 1940s Britain* (Aldershot)

Hobsbawm, E. J. (1964) *Labouring Men*

Hobsbawm, E. J. (1967) 'Custom, Wages and Workload in 19th Century Industry', in A. Briggs and J. Saville (eds), *Essays in Labour History*

Hobsbawm, E. J. (1984) *Worlds of Labour*

Holford, J. (1988) *Reshaping Labour: Organisation, Work and Politics. Edinburgh in the Great War and After*

Holmes, H. (1997) 'Employment and Employment Conditions of Irish Migratory Potato Workers', *Scottish Labour History Journal*, 32

Holton, B. (1976) *British Syndicalism, 1900–1914*

Holton, B. (1985) 'Revolutionary Syndicalism and the British Labour Movement', in W. Mommsen and H.-G. Husung (eds) *The Development of Trade Unionism in Great Britain and Germany, 1880–1914*

Hopkins, E. (1979) *A Social History of the English Working Classes, 1815–1945*

Howarth, O. (ed.) (1989) *Textile Voices: Mill Life This Century* (Bradford)

Howell, D. (1983) *British Workers and the Independent Labour Party, 1888–1906* (Manchester)

Hughes, A. (1996) 'Popular Pastimes and Wife Assault in Interwar Glasgow' (History Honours Dissertation, University of Strathclyde)

Hunt, E. H. (1973) *Regional Wage Variations in Britain, 1850–1914*

Hunt, E. H. (1981) *British Labour History, 1815–1914*

Hutchins, B. (1909) 'Gaps in Our Factory Legislation' in B. Webb *et al.*, *Socialism and the National Minimum*

Hutchins, B. and B. Harrison (1911 edn) *A History of Factory Legislation*

Hutchison, G. and M. O'Neill (1989) *The Springburn Experience: an Oral History of Work in a Railway Community* (Edinburgh)

Hutchison, I. (1986) *A Political History of Scotland, 1832–1924* (Edinburgh)

Ineson, A. and D.Thom (1985) 'TNT Poisoning and the Employment of Women Workers in the First World War' in P. Weindling (ed.) *The Social History of Occupational Health*

Jamieson, L. (1986) 'Limited Resources and Limiting Conventions: Working Class Mothers and Daughters in Urban Scotland, *c.* 1890–1925', in J. Lewis (ed.), *Labour and Love: Women's Experience of Home and Family, 1850–1940*

Jeremy, D. (1995) 'Corporate Responses to the Emergent Recognition of a Health Hazard in the UK Asbestos Industry: the Case of Turner & Newall, 1920–1960, *Business and Economic History*, 24

John, A. (ed.) (1986) *Unequal Opportunities: Women's Employment in England, 1800–1918*

Johnston, P. (ed.) (1994) *Twentieth Century Britain*

Johnston, R. (1997) 'Clydeside Employers: Individualistic or Class Conscious?', *Scottish Labour History Society Journal*, 32

Johnston, R. and A. McIvor (2000) 'Occupational Health and the National Health Service', in C. Nottingham (ed.), *Fifty Years of the NHS in Scotland*

Jones, H. (1985) 'An Inspector Calls', in P. Weindling (ed.), *The Social History of Occupational Health*

Jones, H. (1994) *Health and Society in Twentieth Century Britain*

Jones, S. (1988) 'Cotton Employers and Industrial Welfare between the Wars', in J. A. Jowitt and A. J. McIvor (eds) *Employers and Labour in the English Textile Industries, 1850–1939*

Joseph, G. (1983) *Women at Work: the British Experience*

Joshi, H. (ed.) (1989) *The Changing Population of Britain*

Jowitt, J. A. and A. J. McIvor (eds) (1988) *Employers and Labour in the English Textile Industries, 1850–1939*

Joyce, P. (1980) *Work, Society and Politics*

Joyce, P. (ed.) (1987) *The Historical Meanings of Work* (Cambridge)

Joyce, P. (1990) 'Work' in F. M. L. Thompson (ed.), *The Cambridge Social History of Britain, 1750–1950*, vol. 2 (Cambridge)

Joyce, P. (1991) *Visions of the People*

Kendrick, S. (1986) 'Occupational Change in Modern Scotland', *Scottish Government Yearbook*

Kenefick, W. and A. McIvor (eds) (1996) *Roots of Red Clydeside, 1910–1914?* (Edinburgh)

Kinnersly, P. (1973) *The Hazards of Work*

Kirk, N. (1998) *Change, Continuity and Class: Labour in British Society* (Manchester)

Klingender, F. D. (1935) *The Condition of Clerical Labour in Britain*

Knox, W. W. (1990) 'The Political and Workplace Culture of the Scottish Working Class, 1832–1914', in W. H. Fraser and R. J. Morris (eds), *People and Society in Scotland*, vol. II, *1830–1914* (Edinburgh)

Knox, W. W. (1992) 'Class, Work and Trade Unionism in Scotland', in A. Dickson and J. H. Treble (eds), *People and Society in Scotland*, vol. III, *1914–1990* (Edinburgh)

Knox, W. W. (1995) *Hanging by a Thread* (Preston)

Knox, W. W. (1999) *Industrial Nation: Work, Culture and Society in Scotland, 1800–Present* (Edinburgh)

Knox, W. and A. McKinlay (1995) ' "Pests to Management": Engineering Shop Stewards on Clydeside, 1939–45', *Scottish Labour History Society Journal*, 30

Lawrence, J. (1994) 'The First World War and its Aftermath' in P. Johnston (ed.), *Twentieth Century Britain*

Laybourn, K. (1988) *The Rise of Labour*

Laybourn, K. (1992) *A History of British Trade Unionism, c. 1770–1990*

Lazonick, W. (1979) 'Industrial Relations and Technical Change: the Case of the Self-Acting Mule', *Cambridge Journal of Economics*, 3

Lee, C. H. (1979) *British Regional Employment Statistics, 1841–1971* (Cambridge)

Lewenhak, S. (1980) *Women and Work*

Lewis, J. (1984) *Women in England, 1870–1950*

Lewis, J. (1992) *Women in Britain since 1945*

Liddington, J. and J. Norris (1978) *One Hand Tied behind Us*

Littler, C. R. (1982) *The Development of the Labour Process in Capitalist Societies*

Livingstone, S. (1994) *Bonnie Fechters: Women in Scotland, 1900–1950*

Lockwood, D. (1958) *The Blackcoated Worker* (2nd edition, 1989)

Lovell, J. (1977) *British Trade Unions, 1875–1933*

Lowe, R. (1987) 'The Government and Industrial Relations, 1919–39', in C. J. Wrigley (ed.), *A History of British Industrial Relations*, vol. 2, *1914–1939* (Brighton)

Lummis, T. (1987) *Listening to History*

Lummis, T. (1994) *The Labour Aristocracy, 1851–1914*

Lunn, K. and A. Day (eds) (1999) *History of Work and Labour Relations in the Royal Dockyards*

McBride, T. (1976) *The Domestic Revolution*

MacDougall, I. (1995a) *Hoggies Angels: Tattie Howkers Remember* (Edinburgh)

MacDougall, I. (1995b) *Mungo Mackay and the Green Table: Newtongrange Miners Remember* (Edinburgh)

MacGill, P. (1914) *Children of the Dead End: The Autobiography of a Navvy* (Horsham, 1982 edn)

McFeely, M. (1988) *Lady Inspectors: the Campaign for a Better Workplace*

McGuffie, C. (1985) *Working in Metal*

Macinytre, S. (1980) *Little Moscows*

McIvor, A. J. (1984) 'Employers' Organisations and Strikebreaking in Britain, 1880–1914', *International Review of Social History*, 29

McIvor, A. J. (1987a) 'Employers, the Government and Industrial Fatigue in Britain, 1890–1918', *British Journal of Industrial Medicine*, 44

McIvor, A. J. (1987b) 'Manual Work, Technology and Industrial Health, 1918–1939', *Medical History*, 31

McIvor, A. J. (1988) 'A Crusade for Capitalism: the Economic League, 1919–1939', *Journal of Contemporary History*, 23, October

McIvor, A. J. (1989) 'Work and Health, 1880–1914', *Scottish Labour History Society Journal*, 24

McIvor, A. J. (1992) 'Women and Work in Twentieth Century Scotland', in A. Dickson and J. H. Treble (eds), *People and Society in Scotland*, vol. III, *1914–1990* (Edinburgh)

McIvor, A. J. (1996) *Organised Capital* (Cambridge)

McIvor, A. J. (1997) 'State Intervention and Work Intensification: the Politics of Occupational Health and Safety in the British Cotton Industry, *c*. 1880–1914', in A. Knotter, B. Altena and D. Damsma (eds), *Labour, Social Policy and the Welfare State* (Amsterdam)

McKibben, R. (1990) 'The Franchise Factor in the Rise of the Labour Party', in R. McKibben, *The Ideologies of Class*

McKinlay, A. (1991) *Making Ships, Making Men* (Clydebank)

McKinlay, A. (1996) 'Philosophers in Overalls? Craft and Class on Clydeside, *c*. 1900–1914', in W. Kenefick and A. McIvor (eds), *Roots of Red Clydeside, 1910–1914?*

McKinlay, A. and R. J. Morris (eds) (1991) *The Independent Labour Party on Clydeside, 1893–1932* (Manchester)

McKinlay, A. and J. Zeitlin (1989) 'The Meaning of Managerial Prerogative: Industrial Relations and the Organisation of Work in British Engineering, 1880–1939', in C. Harvey and J. Turner (eds), *Labour and Business in Modern Britain*

McLean, I. (1983) *The Legend of Red Clydeside* (Edinburgh)

McShane, H. and J. Smith (1978) *No Mean Fighter*

Magrath, I. (1988) 'Protecting the Interests of the Trade: Wool Textile Employers' Organisations in the 1920s', in J. Jowitt and A. McIvor (eds) *Employers and Labour in the English Textile Industries, 1850–1939*

Mahood, L. (1992) 'Family Ties: Lady Child Savers and Girls of the Street, 1850–1925', in E. Breitenbach and E. Gordon (eds), *Out of Bounds* (Edinburgh)

Marshall, R. (1983) *Virgins and Viragos*

Marwick, A. (1982) *British Society since 1945*

Marwick, A. (ed.) (1988) *Total War and Social Change*

Marwick, A. (1991) *The Deluge: British Society in the First World War*, 2nd edn (Basingstoke)

Marx, K. (1972) *Capital*, vol. I (J. M. Dent edn)

Mass Observation (1942) *People in Production*

Matthews, D. (1991) '1889 and all That: New Views on the New Unionism', *International Review of Social History*, 36, no. 1

Meacham, S. (1977) *A Life Apart*

Melling, J. (1980) '"Non-commissioned Officers": British Employers and their Supervisory Workers, 1880–1920', *Social History*, 5

Melling, J. (1981) 'Employers, Industrial Housing and the Evolution of Company Welfare Policies in Britain's Heavy Industry: West Scotland 1870–1920', *International Review of Social History*, 26, No. 3

Melling, J. (1982) 'Scottish Industrialists and the Changing Character of Class Relations in the Clyde Region, *c*. 1880–1918', in A. Dickson (ed.), *Capital and Class in Scotland* (Edinburgh)

Melling, J. (1983) *Rent Strikes* (Edinburgh)

Melling, J. (1989) 'The Servile State Revisited', *Scottish Labour History Society Journal*, 24

Merfyn-Jones, R. (1982) *The North Wales Quarrymen, 1874–1922* (Cardiff)

Middlemas, K. (1979) *Politics in Industrial Society*

Miliband, R. (1972) *Parliamentary Socialism*

Mitchell, B. R. and P. Deane (1976) *Abstract of British Historical Statistics* (Cambridge)

Mommsen, W. and H-G. Husung (eds) (1985) *The Development of Trade Unionism in Great Britain and Germany, 1880–1914*

More, C. (1980) *Skill and the English Working Class*

More, C. (1982) 'Skill and the Survival of Apprenticeship', in S. Wood (ed.), *The Degradation of Work?*

More, C. (1996) 'Reskilling and Labour Markets in Britain, *c.* 1890–1940', *Historical Studies in Industrial Relations*, no. 2, Sept.

Morgan, K. (1979) *Consensus and Disunity: the Lloyd George Coalition Government, 1918–22*

Morris, J. N. (1974) 'Coalminers', *Lancet*, 252

Musson, A. E. (1954) *The Typographical Association*

Myrdal, A. and V. Klein (1956) *Women's Two Roles*

Navarro, V. (1978) *Class Struggle, the State and Medicine*

Noble, T. (1981) *Structure and Change in Modern Britain*

Oakley, A. (1974a) *Housewife*

Oakley, A. (1974b) *The Sociology of Housework*

Oliver, T. (1902) *Dangerous Trades*

Oliver, T. (1908) *Diseases of Occupations*

Pahl, R. E. (ed.) (1988) *On Work*

Peden, G. C. (1985) *British Economic and Social Policy*

Pelling, H. (1987) *A History of British Trade Unionism*

Penn, R. (1982) 'Skilled Manual Workers in the Labour Process, 1856–1964', in S. Wood (ed.), *The Degradation of Work?*

Penn, R. (1985) *Skilled Manual Workers in the Class Structure*

Pennington, S. and B. Westover (1989) *A Hidden Workforce*

Pentland and Calton Reminiscence Group (1987) *Friday Night was Brasso Night* (Edinburgh)

Phelps Brown, H. (1983) *The Origins of Trade Union Power*

Phillips, G. (1992) *The Rise of the Labour Party, 1893–1931*

Phillips, G. and N. Whiteside (1985) *Casual Labour*

Pimlott, B. and C. Cook (eds) (1982) *Trade Unions in British Politics*

Pollock, M. (ed.) (1926) *Working Days*

Pope, R. (1991) *War and Society in Britain, 1899–1948*

Price, R. (1980) *Masters, Unions and Men*

Price, R. (1982) 'Rethinking Labour History: the Importance of Work', in J. E. Cronin and J. Schneer *Social Conflict and the Political Order in Modern Britain*

Price, R. (1984) 'Structures of Subordination' in P. Thane *et al.* (eds), *The Power of the Past*

Price, R. (1986) *Labour in British Society*

Proud, E. D. (1920) *Welfare Work*

Ransome, A. (1890) *The Causes and Prevention of Phthisis*

Reid, A. (1985) 'Dilution, Trade Unionism and the State in Britain during the First World War', in S. Tolliday and J. Zeitlin (eds), *Shop Floor Bargaining and the State* (Cambridge)

Reid, A. (1991) 'Employers' Strategies and Craft Production: the British Shipbuilding Industry, 1870–1950', in S. Tolliday and J. Zeitlin (eds), *The Power to Manage?*

Reid, A. (1992) *Social Classes and Social Relations in Britain, 1850–1914*

Reynolds, S. (1989) *Britannica's Typesetters* (Edinburgh)

Roberts, E. (1984) *A Woman's Place*

Roberts, E. (1987) *Women's Work, 1840–1940*

Roberts, E. (1995) *Women and Families: an Oral History, 1940–1970* (Oxford)

Roberts, R. (1973) *The Classic Slum*

Rodgers, T. (1988) 'Employers' Organisations, Unemployment and Social Politics in Britain During the Inter-war Period', *Social History*, 13, no. 3

Roper, T. and J. Tosh (1991) *Manful Assertions: Masculinities in Britain since 1800*

Rose, M. (1975) *Industrial Behaviour*

Rosner, D. and G. Markowitz (eds) (1987) *Dying for Work* (Indiana)

Routh, G. (1982) *Occupations and Pay in Britain, 1900–1981*

Routh, G. (1987) *Occupations of the People of Great Britain, 1801–1981*

Rowbotham, S. (1973) *Hidden from History*

Rowe, J. W. F. (1928) *Wages in Practice and Theory*

Rubin, G. R. (1987) *War, Law and Labour*

Sabel, C. F. and J. Zeitlin (1997) *Worlds of Possibilities* (Cambridge)

Samuel, R. (1977) 'The Workshop of the World: Steam Power and Hand Technology in Mid-Victorian Britain', *History Workshop Journal*, 3

Sanderson, K. (1986) '"A Pension to Look Forward to . . . ?": Women Civil Service Clerks in London, 1925–1939', in L. Davidoff and B. Westover (eds), *Our Work, Our Lives, Our Words*

Savage, M. (1987) *The Dynamics of Working Class Politics* (Cambridge)

Savage, M. and A. Miles (1994) *The Remaking of the British Working Class, 1840–1940*

Saville, J. (1988) *The Labour Movement in Britain*

Schmiechen, J. (1984) *Sweated Industries and Sweated Labour*

Shann, G. (1914) 'Scientific Management', *The Workers Union Record*, June

Sherard, R. S. (1897) *White Slaves of England*

Simonton, D. (1998) *A History of European Women's Work, 1700 to the Present*

Smith, C. (1905) 'Dangerous Trades', *Economic Review*, 15, Oct.

Smith, H. (ed.) (1986) *War and Social Change*

Smout, T. C. (1986) *A Century of the Scottish People 1830–1950*

Smyth, J. (1990) 'Ye Never Got a Spell to Think about it. Young Women and Employment in the Inter-War Period: a Case Study of a Textile Village', in E. Gordon and E. Breitenbach (eds) *The World Ill-divided: Women Workers in Scotland in the 19th and Early 20th Centuries*

Snell, K. D. M. (1985) *Annals of the Labouring Poor* (Cambridge)

Stearns, P. (1975) *Lives of Labour: Work in a Maturing Industrial Society*

Stedman Jones, G. (1971) *Outcast London*

Stephenson, J. (1988) *'Five Bob a Week': Stirling Women's Work, 1900–1950* (Stirling)

Stephenson, J. and C. Brown (1990) 'The View from the Workplace', in E. Gordon and E. Breitenbach (eds), *The World is Ill-divided: Women Workers in Scotland in the 19th and early 20th Centuries*

Stevenson, J. (1984) *British Society, 1914–45*

Stewart, M. H. and L. Hunter (1964) *The Needle is Threaded*

Stirling, J. (1938) 'Steel Works', in J. Common, *Seven Shifts*

Stirling Women's Oral History Transcripts, Scottish Oral History Centre Archive, University of Strathclyde

Sturt, G. (1923) *The Wheelwright's Shop* (Cambridge, 1993 edn)

Summerfield, P. (1993) 'The Patriarchal Discourse of Human Capital: Training Women for War Work, 1939–1945', *Journal of Gender Studies*, 2

Summerfield, P. (1998) *Reconstructing Women's Wartime Lives*

Supple, B. (1987) *The History of the British Coal Industry*, vol. 4, *1913–1946*

Taylor, F. W. (1911) *The Principles of Scientific Management*

Thane, P. (1994) 'Women Since 1945' in P. Johnston (ed.), *Twentieth Century Britain*

Thompson, E. P. (1963) *The Making of the English Working Class*

Thompson, P. (1975) *The Edwardians*

Thompson, P. (1978) *The Voice of the Past*

Thompson, P. (1983) *The Nature of Work*

Thompson, P. (1988) 'Playing at Being Skilled Men: Factory Culture and Pride in Work Skills among Coventry Car Workers', *Social History*, 13

Tolliday, S. and J. Zeitlin (eds) (1985) *Shop Floor Bargaining and the State* (Cambridge)

Tolliday, S. and J. Zeitlin (eds) (1991) *The Power to Manage?*

Tosh, J. (1999) *A Man's Place*

Trades Union Congress (1910) *Report on the Premium Bonus System*

Trainor, R. (1993) *Black Country Elites* (Oxford)

Treble, J. H. (1979) *Urban Poverty in Britain, 1830–1914*

Treble, J. H. (1988) 'Parliamentary Papers: an Analysis of the Urban Labour Market, 1820–1914', *Journal of Regional and Local Studies*, 8, no. 2

Tressell, R. (1955) *The Ragged Trousered Philanthropists*

Tweedale, G. and P. Hansen (1998) 'Protecting the Workers: the Medical Board and the Asbestos Industry, 1930s–1960s', *Medical History*, 42

Tuckwell, G. M. (1902) *The Anomalies of our Factory Laws*

Turner, J. (ed.) (1984) *Businessmen and Politics*

Turner, J. (1989) *Labour and Business in Modern Britain*

Walby, S. (1986) *Patriarchy at Work*

Waldron, H. A. (1997) 'Occupational Health during the Second World War', *Medical History*, 41

Watterson, A. (1990) 'Occupational Health Education in the UK Workplace', *British Journal of Industrial Medicine*, 47

Webb, B. and S. (1920) *Industrial Democracy*

Webb S. and B. (1902) *The History of Trade Unionism*

Webster, C. (1982) 'Healthy or Hungry Thirties', *History Workshop Journal*, 13

Weindling, P. (ed.) (1985) *The Social History of Occupational Health*

Whipp, R. (1987) ' "A Time to Every Purpose": an Essay on Time and Work', in P. Joyce (ed.), *The Historical Meanings of Work* (Cambridge)

Whipp, R. (1990) *Patterns of Labour: Work and Social Change in the Pottery Industry*

Whiteside, N. (1987) 'Social Welfare and Industrial Relations, 1914–39', in C. J. Wrigley (ed.), *A History of British Industrial Relations*, vol. II, *1914–1939*

Whiteside, N. (1996) 'Industrial Relations and Social Welfare, 1945–79', in C. J. Wrigley (ed.), *A History of British Industrial Relations 1939–1979* (Brighton)

Whitson, K. (1996) 'Scientific Management and Production Management Practice in Britain between the Wars', *Historical Studies in Industrial Relations*, no. 1, March

Wigham, E. (1973) *The Power to Manage*

Williams, A. (1915) *Life in a Railway Factory* (New York, 1969 edn)

Williams, J. L. (1960) *Accidents and Ill-Health at Work*

Winter, J. (1985) *The Great War and the British People*

Wohl, A. S. (1983) *Endangered Lives*

Wood, S. (ed.) (1982) *The Degradation of Work?*

Woolfson, C. and M. Beck (1999) 'Fatal and Major Injuries to Employees', Paper to the Scottish Trade Union Research Network Conference, 2 July

Woolfson, C., J. Foster and M. Beck (1996) *Paying for the Piper: Capital and Labour in Britain's Offshore Oil Industry*

Wrigley, C. J. (ed.) (1982) *A History of British Industrial Relations, 1875–1914* (Brighton)

Wrigley, C. J. (ed.) (1987) *A History of British Industrial Relations*, vol. 2, *1914–1939* (Brighton)

Wrigley, C. J. (ed.) (1996) *A History of British Industrial Relations, 1939–1979* (Brighton)

Wyke, T. (1987) 'Spinners' Cancer' in A. Fowler and T. Wyke, *The Barefoot Aristocrats* (Littleborough)

Young, J. D. (1979) *The Rousing of the Scottish Working Class*

Young, J. D. (1985) *Women and Popular Struggles* (Edinburgh)

Zeitlin, J. (1983) 'Social Theory and the History of Work', *Social History*, 8, no. 3

Zeitlin, J. (1985) 'Industrial Structure, Employer Strategy and the Diffusion of Job Control in Britain, 1850–1920', in W. Mommsen and H-G. Husung (eds), *The Development of Trade Unionism in Great Britain and Germany, 1880–1914*

Zeitlin, J. (1987) 'From Labour History to the History of Industrial Relations', *Economic History Review*, 40

Zeitlin, J. (1991) 'The Internal Politics of Employer Organisation: the Engineering Employers' Federation, 1896–1939', in S. Tolliday and J. Zeitlin (eds), *The Power to Manage?*

Zimbalist, A. (ed.) (1979) *Case Studies on the Labor Process* (New York)

Zimmeck, M. (1986) 'Jobs for the Girls: the Expansion of Clerical Work for Women, 1850–1914', in A. John (ed.), *Unequal Opportunities: Women's Employment in England, 1800–1918*

Zweig, F. (1948a) *Labour, Life and Poverty*

Zweig, F. (1948b) *Men in the Pits*

Zweig, F. (1951) *Productivity and Trade Unions*

Zweig, F. (1952a) *The British Worker*

Zweig, F. (1952b) *Women's Life and Labour*

INDEX

accidents at work, 113, 116–20
  World War Two, 143–4
Accidents, Departmental
    Committee on, 119, 126, 127
AEU (Amalgamated Engineering
    Union), 103, 194, 234
age
  old age, 73–4
  and work, 33
  youths, 73
agriculture
  deskilling, 63
  employment, 34–6
  hours, 114
  and National Insurance, 165
  and the state, 156
  trade unionism, 202
  wages, 167
  work, 29–32, 45–6, 230
alienation, 7, 9, 77, 243
  in agriculture, 63
  and class-consciousness, 231–2
  in construction, 68
  and female workers, 197
  in mass production, 249
  in World War Two, 143
  see also deskilling
anklyostomiasis, 123
anthrax, 123–4, 142
Anti-Sweating League, 156
apprenticeship, 48, 50, 156
  erosion of, 55
  gender and, 192

aristocracy of labour, see labour
    aristocracy
Arlidge, J. L., 116, 124
arsenic poisoning, 122, 142
artisans, 6–7, 46–50, 205,
    211–12
  see also craft production; skilled
    work
asbestos, 122, 133, 142
  see also pneumoconiosis
ASE (Amalgamated Society of
    Engineers), see AEU
Askwith, George, 88, 158
assembly line, 65, 96
  see also mass production
authority at work, 6, 81–4, 228
  see also employers; foremen;
    management; subcontractors

Bedaux system, 58–9, 62–3, 93,
    95–6, 225
Besant, Annie, 123
Beveridge Report, 1942, 165
Bevin, Ernest, 105, 144, 167, 168,
    226
boot and shoe industry, see
    footwear
British Employers' Confederation,
    166, 226–7
British Institute of Management,
    97
bronchitis, 125, 146
Bryant and May Co., 123

building industry, 16, 30–1, 53
    deskilling in, 56–7
    intensification of work, 68
    mortality in, 132
    trade unionism, 202–3
byssinosis, 125, 140
    see also pneumoconiosis

cancer (occupational), 142
    see also spinners' cancer
canteens, 131, 167–8
capitalism, 5–6, 13–17, 249–50
    Clydeside, 90
    and the state, 149–51
    see also employers; employers'
        associations
car industry
    work in, 55, 59, 63, 71–2, 77
carters, 114–15
Census
    and deskilling, 65
    occupations, 26–42
    weaknesses, 26–8
certifying surgeons, 152, 157
Chandler, Alfred, 14, 86
chemical workers, 58, 124
    and trade unionism, 202
Chew, Ada Nield, 113, 180
child labour, 151–2
childminding, 178
Clarke, Allen, 68
class
    formation, 7–9, 23, 42, 150,
        231–2, 237
    employers, 17
    and gender, 20–1, 42
    and occupational change, 42
    and occupational health, 147
clerical work, 10, 33, 61–2, 230
    deskilling in, 58, 61–2
    numbers in, 40–1
    and paternalism, 85
    and the state, 156

trade unionism in, 202
    women in, 186, 189–91
clothing, 32, 38, 47, 192
    deskilling in, 57–8
    domestic system, 81
    intensification of work, 71
    inter-war, 188–9
    and trade unionism, 202
Clydeside, 11
    dilution, 160
    domestic violence, 183
    employers, 90
    Fairfields, 159
    health, 136
    injuries, 126
    lead poisoning, 122
    'Red Clydeside', 209–10, 217,
        222, 232, 233
    women workers, 186
    see also Scotland; Singer; Weirs
coal mining, 32, 46, 53, 246
    collective bargaining, 223–4
    deskilling, 53, 56
    employers, 102
    hours of work, 114
    intensification of work, 70–1
    legislation, 156–7, 219
    mechanisation, 56, 76–7
    Mines Inquiry, 1842, 152
    Mines Inspectorate, 118, 134
    nationalisation, 107–8
    occupational health and
        safety in, 118–19,
        138–40, 146
    occupational mortality in, 117,
        132, 138
    supervision, 83, 88
    trade unionism, 203
    wage cuts in, 162
    World War Two, 167
    see also pneumoconiosis
collective bargaining, 50, 211,
    214–15, 218–19, 223–5, 227

employers and, 89–90, 92, 103,
    105, 108–9, 208–9
government and, 219
and state welfare provision, 162
World War Two, 168, 227
Communist Party, 166
communist shop stewards, 221,
    230
conciliation, see collective
    bargaining
Conciliation Act, 1896, 158
consent, 80, 84, 247
    see also co-operation;
        paternalism; welfarism
construction, see building industry
Coombes, B. L., 56, 102, 138
Cooper, Selina, 180
co-operation, 22, 172, 214, 247
    see also collective bargaining;
        consent; paternalism
Co-operative Wholesale Society,
    189
corporate crime, 112
corporatism, 18, 159, 164, 168
cotton, 14–15, 68
    collective bargaining in, 224
    employers, 14, 96, 101–2
    factory work, 46
    intensification of work in, 68, 71,
        104
    management, 81
    more looms system, 104
    mule spinners, 11, 46, 62, 134
    occupational health and safety
        in, 119–20, 124–5, 134,
        140–1, 157
    skill, 62
    supervision in, 83
    trade unionism, 202–3, 220
    wage cuts in, 162
    weaving, 62
    Workmen's Compensation Act
        and, 127

see also byssinosis
craft production, 6, 44, 83, 215–16
    see also artisans; skill
Crawford, Helen, 180
Cripps, Stafford, 108
Crosland, C. A. R., 227, 229
Cunard shipping line, 117
cutlery grinders, 125

Dangerous Trades Committees,
    1890s, 121, 127
degradation of work, 9, 10
    see also deskilling
dermatitis, 124
deskilling, 6, 10–11, 39–40, 52–9,
    146–7, 241–2
    critique of, 10–13, 59–66, 242
    in engineering, 11–12
    and feminisation of work, 20
    in Scotland, 76
    see also alienation
diseases
    occupational, 120–5, 138–40,
        141–2
    see also under individual names
Diseases Inquiry, 1907, 127
distribution, 33–6, 186, 189, 202
    see also shop work
dockers, 67, 70, 77, 201
    hiring, 84
    occupational health and safety,
        117, 120
    and politics, 235
    subcontracting, 82
    trade unionism, 203
doctors
    company, 136, 137, 144
    see also medicine
domestic service, 29, 38, 47, 60
    decline of, 188
    hours of work, 114
    inter-war, 187–8
    occupational health in, 124

domestic service – *continued*
  and the state, 156
domestic system, 81–2, 177
domestic violence, 183
domestic work, 178–9, 181–4
  see also housewifery
Donovan Report, 15
dust at work, *see* asbestos;
    byssinosis; emphysema;
    pneumoconiosis; silicosis

Economic League, 100, 102, 224
education
  gender and, 176, 193
electricity
  in home, 183
  in workplace, 132–3, 135–6
Emergency Powers Act, 1915, 158
emphysema, 125, 142
employers, 13–17, 40–1, 79–110,
    246–7, 249–50
  Clydeside, 209–10
  and labour management, 64–6
  and occupational health and
    safety, 126–7, 144–5
  political power, 18
  small, 74
  and trade unions, 208–9, 225
  see also capitalism
employers' organisations, 14–17,
    86, 89–93, 100–7
  decline of, 106
  and intensification of work, 71,
    75
  and scientific management, 96
  and state welfare, 165
  and trade unionism, 208
  see also under individual names
Employers' Liability Act, 1880,
    121, 152–3
engineering, 11–12, 47–8, 102–3
  1922 agreement, 228
  1922 lockout, 102–3, 104

  deskilling in, 54, 55, 59, 64–5
  employers, 102–3
  intensification of work in, 67,
    72–3
  occupational health and safety
    in, 120
  shop stewards, 220–1
  Terms of Settlement, 1898, 92,
    104
  trade unionism, 203
  wage systems, 69
  see also Amalgamated
    Engineering Union;
    Engineering Employers'
    Federation
Engineering Employers'
    Federation, 55–6, 64, 102–3,
    115
Equal Pay, Royal Commission on,
    170, 193, 196–7, 228
Essential Works Order, 105, 167
excess profit tax, 160
Exell, Arthur, 72–3, 106

Factory Acts, 88, 128–9, 152, 180
  1878, 153
  1937, 133, 134, 135, 141, 142
  World War Two, 143
factory crime, 128–9, 134, 157
factory inspectors
  educative role, 134
  and factory crime, 128–9, 138,
    157
  female, 121, 146
  and intensification of work, 73
  and lead poisoning, 122
  numbers of, 129
  in World War Two, 144
factory production, 46, 52, 81
  occupational health and safety
    in, 119–20
  occupational mortality in, 117, 132
family wage, 179–80

family and work, 181–4
    see also domestic system;
        housewifery
farming, *see* agriculture
fatigue at work, 113–16
    employers' attitudes towards,
        115
    World War One, 131
    World War Two, 143
Federation of British Industries,
    55, 100
Federation of Master Cotton
    Spinners' Associations, 96
femininity, 179
feminism and work, 18–19
fertility, 181–2
food processing, 56, 58, 84
    trade unionism in, 202
footwear, 57, 68
    domestic system, 81
    trade unionism in, 203
Ford, Henry, 9, 59, 93
Ford UK, 55
foremen, 40–1, 82–3, 87, 94
    see also authority at work;
        management;
        subcontractors;
        supervisors
Foremen's Mutual Benefit Society,
    87
Foucault, Michel, 23
full employment, 226–7

gas industry
    trade unionism in, 203
    work in, 57, 217
gender
    discrimination, 176, 179
    in education, 176
    identities, 21, 174, 197–8
    segregation, 34–9, 40–1, 179,
        191–2, 196
    wage differentials, 179

and work, 11, 18–20, 174–99
    in World War One, 185–6
    in World War Two, 195–6
    see also feminism; patriarchy;
        women
General Strike, 1926, 102, 104,
    163, 201, 212, 224
Gollan, John, 73, 136
Goodrich, Carter, 2, 223
government
    as employer, 154–5
    local authorities, 154
    and occupational health and
        safety, 127–9, 133
    and trade unionism, 154, 155,
        223, 247
    and welfare, 87–8
    and the workplace, 17–18,
        148–73, 247–8
    World War One, 158–61
    see also Factory Acts; factory
        inspectors; the state
Gramsci, Antonio, 149

half-time system, 33
handicraft production, 29, 47–8
    see also artisans; craft
        production; skill
health
    occupational, 111–47, 167
Health of Munitions Workers'
    Committee, 70, 131–2
holidays, 115
Holidays with Pay Act, 133, 169
Horner, Sybil, 146
hours of work, 33, 67, 113–15, 239
    48-hour week, 115, 135, 219
    56½ -hour week, 152
    in distribution, 189
    in domestic work, 183–4
    World War One, 131
    World War Two, 143
    see also work time

household work, 178–9
  see also domestic work
housewifery, 114, 176, 178–9, 249
  see also domestic work

ICI (Imperial Chemical
  Industries), 99, 136
IFRB (Industrial Fatigue Research
  Board), 70, 134–5
IHRB (Industrial Health Research
  Board), 70, 96, 134–5,
  138, 141
  see also medicine
ILP (Independent Labour Party),
  232, 233
Industrial Health Education
  Council, 135
Industrial Injuries Act, 1948, 133,
  134, 169
Industrial Welfare Society, 134, 135
  see also welfarism
injuries at work, see accidents
Institute of Labour
  Management, 97
Institute of Production
  Engineers, 97
intensification of work, 51, 66–75,
  104, 137, 242
Interdepartmental
  Committee on Physical
  Deterioration, 115
Iron Trades Employers'
  Association, 115
iron working, see metalworking

Joint Consultative Committee, 168
Joint Industrial Councils, 211, 227
  see also Whitley Committees
JPCs (Joint Production
  Committees), 105–6, 107,
  134, 168, 228, 230

Kirkwood, David, 161

labour aristocracy, 8, 11, 46,
  48–50, 211
  see also artisans; craft
  production; skill
labour exchanges, 18, 87, 171
labour markets, 47, 63–4, 228, 244
  the state and, 151, 155, 156
Labour Party
  and employment legislation,
  220, 226
  and equal pay, 170
  and full employment, 169
  in Scotland, 232–3
  and trade unions, 163,
  220, 231–2
  and work, 148, 162, 231–6
  see also ILP (Independent
  Labour Party); socialism
labour process, 5–8, 43, 241–2
  Braverman and, 9, 43, 241
  domestic, 181–4
  in manufacturing, 188
  Marxist theory of, 5–7, 9–10, 43
  and politics, 131–6
  in Scotland, 232–3
  and trade unionism, 205–6
Labour Representation
  Committee, 232
  see also Labour Party
labour unrest, 1910–14, 70, 158,
  207–8, 212, 221
lead poisoning, 121–2, 142
leaving certificate, 159
Legge, Sir Thomas, 134
lighting in workplaces, 131,
  135–6, 141
limited liability companies, 86
lockouts, 91, 218, 227

MacArthur, Mary, 180
MacGill, Patrick, 45
management, 40–1, 64–6, 79–110,
  authoritarian, 80–1

and occupational health and safety, 144–5
prerogative, 80, 101
and Taylorism, 94–6
Management Research Groups, 135
manufacturing, 30, 31, 32–3
and piecework, 69
and Taylorism, 95–6
women in, 188–9
see also factory production
marriage bar, 37, 179, 190–1
see also women
Marx
and class, 23
and labour management, 79
and labour process theory, 5–7
and the state, 18
masculinity at work, 129, 138, 183, 190
Mass Observation, 105, 106, 143, 147, 168, 195
mass production, 56, 65, 249
see also assembly line
maternity leave, 196
Mather, William, 115
matriarchy, 177
McShane, Harry, 181
mechanisation, 242
in agriculture, 45, 63
in clerical work, 58, 61–2, 189–90
in clothing, 57–8
in coal mining, 46, 53, 56, 139
in docks, 60
in domestic service, 60
in footwear, 57
in gas industry, 57
in home, 183
in printing, 57
in textiles, 140
mediation in disputes
government, 157–8

Medical Boards (Pneumoconiosis), 133, 140
medical inspection, 133, 135, 141, 156, 171
medicine, occupational, 134–6, 167
Merchant Shipping Act, 1876, 152
mercury poisoning, 122, 142
metalworking, 71, 83, 116, 120, 129
occupational health and safety in, 136, 137–8, 228
see also engineering; shipbuilding
Miners' Federation of Great Britain, 157
Mines Inquiry, 1842, 152
Mines Inspectorate, 118, 134
mining, 30–2
see coal mining
mobility, occupational, 65
Mond–Turner talks, 103, 164
Morris Motors, 72
mortality, occupational, 112, 116, 125–6, 131–3, 143, 145
motor cars, *see* car industry
munitions
Royal Ordnance Factories, 67, 68
tribunals, 159
World War One, 130–1, 158–61
World War Two, 143–4
Munitions Act, 1915, 158, 161, 186

National Federation of Women Workers, 129, 186, 194
National Health Service
and occupational health, 111, 147
National Institute of Industrial Psychology, 96, 134

National Insurance, 87, 133, 156
National Joint Advisory
  Council, 168
NCEO (National Confederation of
  Employers' Organisations),
  16, 100, 103
new unionism, 8, 194, 207,
  211–12, 217
nicotine poisoning, 124
nightwork, 152
noise at work, 140, 141
North British Locomotive
  Works, 137–8
nurses, company, 136, 137, 144
  see also doctors; medicine;
    welfare officers
nursing, 190
nystagmus, 116, 124

occupational change, 26–42
occupational diseases, *see* diseases;
  Diseases Inquiry
occupational medicine, *see*
  medicine
occupational mobility, 65
occupational mortality, *see*
  mortality
office work, *see* clerical work
Oliver, Thomas, 68, 116, 120,
  121
oral history
  and home, 182–3, 190–1
  and work, 19, 21, 60, 214
overtime, 135, 228

part-time working, 191
paternalism, 10, 22, 84–5
  decline of, 87–8
patriarchy
  and gender wage differentials,
    38, 179–80
  and the state, 151–2
  in trade unions, 210

at work, 19–21, 175–6, 177,
  184, 243–4
  see also gender; women
pensions, 33, 87
phosphorus poisoning, 121,
  123, 142
pneumoconiosis, 124–5, 133,
  139–40
  see also asbestos; byssinosis;
    bronchitis; emphysema;
    silicosis; tuberculosis
political levy, 234
post-modernism, 23
post office workers, 22, 154, 155
pottery workers, 12–13
  and occupational health and
    safety, 120, 122, 125
  and trade unionism, 202
printing, 57, 62
  and occupational health and
    safety, 120
  and trade unionism, 203
professions, 40–2, 42, 196
putting-out, *see* domestic system

quarries
  and occupational health and
    safety, 120, 137

railways, 22, 67–8, 231
  and nationalisation, 107–8
  occupational health in, 120
  occupational mortality in,
    117, 132
  and paternalism, 84–5
  supervision in, 88
  wages, 167
'Red Clydeside', *see* Clydeside
Rennie, Jean, 187
Restoration of Pre-War Practices
  Act, 220
'restrictive practices', 217, 221–2,
  225, 228–9

retirement, 33
Royal Commission on Equal Pay, see Equal Pay
Royal Commission on Labour, 1891–4, 158
Royal Commission on Trade Unions and Employers' Associations, see Donovan Report
Royal Ordnance Factories, 67, 88 see also munitions
rural labour, see agriculture

scientific management, 60, 93–8, 160, 208
    see Bedaux; Ford; Singer; Taylor
school leaving age, 33
Scotland
    education, 193
    fishing, 177
    paternalism, decline of, 87
    patriarchy in, 177
    socialism in, 210
    strikes, 204, 210
    trade unionism in, 194, 204–5, 210
    wages, 179
    work, 76
    work and politics, 232–3, 236
    see also Clydeside
semi-skilled work, 53, 242
sexual harassment, 192
Shann, George, 60–1
shipbuilding, 12, 54, 59, 63, 104
    occupational health and safety in, 120, 136
    wage cuts in, 162
shipping
    legislation in, 152
    occupational health and safety in, 120, 133, 136
    trade unionism in, 203

Shipping Federation, 89
Shops Act, 1886, 128
shop stewards, 220–3, 231
    communist, 230
    growth of, 106, 173, 220–3, 228
    inter-war decline, 162, 224
    and occupational health and safety, 134, 220
    and syndicalism, 160
    and workers' control, 107
    in World War One, 100–1, 102, 211, 222–3
    in World War Two, 213
shop work, 27, 33, 60, 114, 189
    trade unionism in, 202
    see also distribution
shuttle kissing (weaving), 124
silicosis, 124–5
Singer Sewing Machine Co., 54, 69, 95, 99, 207–8
skilled work, 6, 40–1, 47, 48–50
    definition of, 48
    persistence of, 47
    wages of, 65–6
    women and, 176, 179–80, 192, 195
    see also artisans; craft production; deskilling
Smillie, Robert, 161
social control, 149, 172
socialism and work, 231–2
social wage, 161, 165
speed-up, 71–2
    see also intensification of work
spinners' cancer, 124, 133, 134, 140–1, 142
state, the
    definition of, 148
    interpretations of, 149–50
    welfare and work, 165
    see also government
steaming (weaving), 141

Stirling, James, 137
strikebreaking, 57, 89, 91, 217–18
  and government, 163
  see also lockouts; strikes;
    victimisation
strikes
  activity, 201, 203, 204, 212,
    217, 224
  order 1305, 229
  women and, 197
  World War One, 160
  World War Two, 105, 143
  see also General Strike; labour
    unrest, 1910–14;
    strikebreaking
subcontracting, 82, 87
subordination
  formal, 6
  real, 6–7, 9
supervisors, 82–3, 94
  see also authority; foreman;
    management;
    subcontractors
'sweated' work, 28, 47, 114, 152,
  155, 156
syndicalism
  attack on, 163
  on Clydeside, 11, 217
  in engineering, 11
  and the labour process, 231, 232
  and shop stewards, 11, 160, 217
  in trade unions, 212, 217
  and workers, 221

tailoring, see clothing
Taylorism, 9–10, 54, 58–9,
  64, 93–8
  see also Bedaux; Ford; scientific
    management
teaching, 190, 196
technology
  domestic, 183–4
  see mechanisation

textiles, 32, 38
  in Dundee, 177
  intensification of work in,
    71, 140
  married women in, 177
  occupational health and safety
    in, 120, 136, 140–1
  overlookers in, 82–3
  trade unionism in, 202
  women in, 188–9
  see also clothing; cotton
time and motion study, see
    Bedaux; scientific
    management; Taylorism
time and work, 145, 239, 245–6
  half-time system, 33
  holidays, 115
  nightwork, 152
  retirement, 33
  school leaving age, 33
tin mining, 123, 137
TNT poisoning, 132
Trade Boards, 87, 128–9, 155,
  180, 189
Trade Disputes Act, 1906, 158
Trade Disputes and Trade Union
    Act, 1927, 161, 164, 169, 223
Trades Union Congress
  and Bedaux, 58
  and equal pay, 228
  and government, 128, 168, 223
  and labour law, 50, 223
  power of, 226–7
  and premium bonus system, 69
  and trade unions, 163, 223
  and women workers, 195, 228
trade unions, 20, 75, 200–40, 247
  and collective bargaining,
    91, 211, 214–15, 218–19
  craft, 50, 205
  and deskilling, 62, 207
  and economic decline, 213
  and employers, 208–9, 225

and government, 163, 168
growth of, 206–7, 237–8, 243
and intensification of work,
   207–8
inter-war years, 223–6
and legislation, 153, 219–20
membership, 201–3
and occupational health and
   safety, 112, 133–4,
   142, 147
and politics, 231–6
and rank and file, 22, 221
and state welfare, 165–6
and wages, 225, 227
and war, 211
and women, 176, 180, 193–5,
   210–11, 222
in the workplace, 213–31, 238–9
see also individual entries;
   collective bargaining;
   restrictive practices; shop
   stewards
transport workers, 30, 31, 46
see also carters; dockers; railways
tuberculosis, 125

unemployment, 32, 136, 162,
   165, 187
Unemployment Act, 1920, 164
unskilled, 40–1, 42, 65, 179, 192
and new unionism, 8
and work control, 201
work regimes of, 83

ventilation, 135, 138, 143
victimisation, 80, 91, 102, 133,
   220–1, 224

wages
artisans, 49
eroding differentials, 65–6, 227,
   244–5
'family wage', 179–80

gender differentials, 179, 192–3,
   196, 244–5
incomes policies, 193
inter-war cuts, 162–3
movements in real wages,
   21–2, 244
piecework, 69–70
social wage, 161, 165
in state employment, 154
and trade unions, 225, 227
in World War Two, 167
see also Trade Boards
Wages Boards, 168, 225
see also Trade Boards
Webb, Sidney, 116
Weber, 14
Weir, Sir Cecil, 166
Weirs, 54
welfare officers, 88, 99
Welfare State, 150
welfarism, 84–5, 87–8, 98–9, 135
company housing, 84–5
see also paternalism
Whitley Committees, 101,
   160, 168
see also Joint Industrial Councils
Williams, Alfred, 29–30, 68,
   70, 88–9
Wilson, D. R., 135
women
in clerical work, 61–2
in decennial Census, 28
in engineering, 55–6
married and work, 33, 36–8,
   143, 165, 170, 178–9,
   190–1, 196
in part-time work, 191
in Scotland, 38
and skill, 176
and trade unions, 176, 180,
   193–5, 210
and work, 18–20, 33–8, 40–1,
   174–99

276 Index

women – *continued*
  in World War One, 130–2
  in World War Two, 143
  see also gender; patriarchy;
      wages
Women's Freedom League, 180
Women's Social and Political
    Union, 180
Women's Trade Councils, 156
Women's Trade Union League,
    121, 128, 156
woodworking, 120
wool, 223–4
work
  attitudes to, 76–8,
      246, 248–9
  discipline, 67, 82–3
  enrichment, 77
  ethic, 246
  time, 33, 115, 145, 152,
      239, 245–6
  unpaid, 178–9
workers' control, 107–8, 169–70,
    217, 230
Workmen's Compensation Acts,
    87, 121, 124, 127, 133, 155
World War One, 11, 36–7, 54–5,
    70, 101
  occupational health in, 130–2
  and politics, 235–6
  and shop stewards, 221, 222
  state intervention in the
      workplace, 158–61
  and trade unionism, 211

women in, 185–7
World War Two
  employers and management in,
      104–6
  occupational health in, 143–5
  and scientific management,
      97–8
  and skill, 59
  state intervention in the
      workplace, 166–8
  and trade unionism, 211,
      212–13, 226–7
  women in, 21, 195–6
  see also Joint Production
      Committees

youths, 73

Zweig, Ferdinand
  on attitudes to work, 77, 246,
      248–9
  on deskilling, 56, 248–9
  on employers and management,
      74–5, 108, 109, 229
  on homework, 184
  on mechanisation, 56
  on miners, 56, 77, 146
  on old age, 73–4
  on restrictive practices, 228–9
  on semi-skilled, 53
  on women workers, 194–5, 197
  on workers' power, 74–5, 107,
      108, 229, 231
  on youth, 74